BUSINESS ISSUES, COMPETITION AND ENTREPRENEURSHIP SERIES

ELECTRONIC BREADCRUMBS: ISSUES IN TRACKING CONSUMERS

BUSINESS ISSUES, COMPETITION AND ENTREPRENEURSHIP SERIES

BUSINESS ISSUES, COMPETITION AND ENTREPRENEURSHIP SERIES

ELECTRONIC BREADCRUMBS: ISSUES IN TRACKING CONSUMERS

DMITAR N. KOVAC
EDITOR

Nova Science Publishers, Inc.
New York

Copyright © 2010 by Nova Science Publishers, Inc.

For permission to use material from this book please contact us:
Telephone 631-231-7269; Fax 631-231-8175
Web Site: http://www.novapublishers.com

NOTICE TO THE READER
The Publisher has taken reasonable care in the preparation of this book, but makes no expressed or implied warranty of any kind and assumes no responsibility for any errors or omissions. No liability is assumed for incidental or consequential damages in connection with or arising out of information contained in this book. The Publisher shall not be liable for any special, consequential, or exemplary damages resulting, in whole or in part, from the readers' use of, or reliance upon, this material. Any parts of this book based on government reports are so indicated and copyright is claimed for those parts to the extent applicable to compilations of such works.

Independent verification should be sought for any data, advice or recommendations contained in this book. In addition, no responsibility is assumed by the publisher for any injury and/or damage to persons or property arising from any methods, products, instructions, ideas or otherwise contained in this publication.

This publication is designed to provide accurate and authoritative information with regard to the subject matter covered herein. It is sold with the clear understanding that the Publisher is not engaged in rendering legal or any other professional services. If legal or any other expert assistance is required, the services of a competent person should be sought. FROM A DECLARATION OF PARTICIPANTS JOINTLY ADOPTED BY A COMMITTEE OF THE AMERICAN BAR ASSOCIATION AND A COMMITTEE OF PUBLISHERS.

LIBRARY OF CONGRESS CATALOGING-IN-PUBLICATION DATA
Electronic breadcrumbs : issues in tracking consumers / editor, Dmitar N. Kovac.
    p. cm.
  Includes index.
  ISBN 978-1-60741-600-5 (hardcover)
 1. Data protection--Law and legislation--United States. 2. Web usage mining--United States. 3. Internet advertising--Law and legislation--United States. I. Kovac, Dmitar N.
  KF1263.C65A2 2009
  342.7308'58--dc22
                                                                          2009032472

Published by Nova Science Publishers, Inc. ✦ *New York*

CONTENTS

PREFACE

This book looks at the issue of "behavioral marketing" which involves the tracking of consumers' online activities in order to deliver tailored advertising. The digital information age, against a backdrop of rising globalization, allows anyone to collect and share information on any subject, corporation, government - or in many cases, other individuals. Companies from retailers to search engines to software makers all collect consumer data - enough to fill vast server warehouses. Of-course, websites have long collected and marketed information about visitors. The latest twist is that behavioral marketing firms "watch" our clickstreams to develop profiles or inform categories to better target future advertisements. Unarguably beneficial, the process however stokes privacy concerns. Thus this book also discusses the Federal Trade Commission's examination of online privacy issues.

This is an edited, excerpted and augmented edition of various government publications.

In: Electronic Breadcrumbs: Issues in Tracking Consumers
Editor: Dmitar N. Kovac

ISBN: 978-1-60741-600-5
© 2010 Nova Science Publishers, Inc.

Chapter 1

BROADBAND PROVIDERS & CONSUMER PRIVACY HEARING- ATTWOOD TESTIMONY

Dorothy Attwood

Thank you, Chairman Inouye and Ranking Member Hutchison, for providing AT&T Inc. the opportunity to discuss online advertising and, more specifically, the issue that has received a good deal of recent attention, so-called online behavioral advertising. We trust that this hearing will help the discussion evolve past slogans and rhetoric to a more thoughtful examination of the facts and the development of a holistic consumer privacy policy framework that all participants in the online behavioral advertising sphere can and will adopt.

Your interest in these matters surely is warranted. Online advertising fuels investment and innovation across a wide range of Internet activities, and provides the revenue that enables consumers to enjoy many free and discounted services. Likewise, website publishers make most of their money from advertising, which revenue in turn funds today's vast wealth and diversity of Internet content and information — most of which consumers enjoy, again, for free. On the other hand, online advertising, especially next-generation forms of highly targeted behavioral advertising that involve tracking consumer web browsing and search activities, raise important consumer-privacy concerns that policymakers and industry must carefully weigh. In short, setting proper policy in this area will be crucial to a healthy and growing Internet ecosystem that benefits consumers.

AT&T does not today engage in online behavioral advertising, but we understand the uniquely sensitive nature of this practice. We have listened to our customers and watched the debate unfold, and are responding by advocating for a consumer-focused framework. As described in more detail herein, the pillars of this framework — *transparency, consumer control, privacy protection, and consumer value* — can be the foundation of a consistent regime applicable to all players in the online behavioral advertising sphere — including not just Internet Service Providers ("ISPs"), but also search engines and third party advertising networks — that both ensures that consumers have ultimate control over the use of their personal information and guards against privacy abuses.[1]

In particular, we believe that effective customer control for online behavioral advertising requires meaningful consent and therefore commit that *AT&T will not use consumer information for online behavioral advertising without an affirmative, advance action by the consumer that is based on a clear explanation of how the consumer's action will affect the use of her information.* This concept — often generically referred to as "opt-in" — means that a consumer's failure to act will *not* result in any collection and use by default of that consumer's information for online behavioral advertising purposes. This affirmative consent model differs materially from the default-based privacy policies that advertising networks and search engines — which already are engaged in online behavioral advertising — currently employ. Given the obvious consumer benefits of such a model, we encourage all companies that engage in online behavioral advertising — regardless of the nature of their business models or the technologies they utilize — likewise to adopt this affirmative-advance-consent paradigm.

WHAT IS ONLINE BEHAVIORAL ADVERTISING?

There is no single, settled definition of online behavioral advertising in statute or case law, but the FTC and others have used the term to refer to it as the tracking of a consumer's web search and web browsing activities — by tracking either the person or a particular Internet access device, be it a computer, data-enabled mobile phone, or some other communications vehicle — to create a distinct profile of the consumer's online behavior. In this sense, it can clearly be distinguished from the simple practice of tracking a consumer's use of an individual website or obviously- related websites (such as those operated under a common trademark, trade name or conspicuously disclosed corporate affiliation), which practice does not necessarily raise the same privacy concerns as online behavioral advertising but which nonetheless can and should expressly be disclosed to Internet users. Privacy concerns about online behavioral advertising are not new — indeed, DoubleClick's (now a Google subsidiary) use of tracking cookies to collect and use information about consumer web browsing activity was the subject of an FTC proceeding in 2000.[2] More recently, the FTC and Congress have appropriately asked questions about the privacy implications of emerging online advertising businesses that involve the tracking of consumer web browsing and search activity. Thus, consistent with the focus of recent public discussion, we consider online behavioral advertising to be (1) the tracking of user web browsing and search activity across unrelated websites, (2) when the tracking and association of the websites or their components are largely invisible to the user, and (3) the resulting information is used to create a distinct user profile and deliver targeted advertising content.

Online behavioral advertising can take many forms. It can, for instance, involve the use by an ISP of technologies to capture and analyze a user's Internet browsing activities and experience across unrelated websites. These more ISP-specific methodologies are not, however, the only — and certainly are not nearly the most prevalent — forms of online behavioral advertising. Advertising-network technologies have evolved beyond solely tracking consumer web surfing activity at sites on which they sell advertising. They now also have the ability to observe a user's entire web browsing experience at a granular level. Techniques include the ad network "dropping" third-party tracking "cookies" on a consumer's computer to capture consumer visits to any one of thousands of unrelated websites;

embedding software on PCs; or automatically downloading applications that — unbeknownst to the consumer — log the consumer's full session of browsing activity.

Ad networks and other non-ISPs employ these capabilities at the individual browser or computer level and they are as effective as any technique that an ISP might employ at creating specific customer profiles and enabling highly targeted advertising. Already ad networks and search engines track and store a vast trove of data about consumers' online activities. Google's practices exemplify the already extensive use of online behavior advertising, particularly by nonISPs. Google logs and stores user's search requests, can track the search activity by IP address and a cookie that identifies the user's unique browser, and can even correlate search activities across multiple sessions, leading to the creation of a distinct and detailed user profile. Through DoubleClick, Google can drop tracking cookies on consumers' computers so that whenever the consumer visits web sites that contain a display ad placed by DoubleClick (which can be for virtually any product or service), the consumer's web browsing activity can be tracked across seemingly unrelated sites (e.g., CNN.com or ESPN.com). Google further has access to enormous amounts of personal information from its registered users, which its privacy policy expressly confirms can be combined with information from other Google services or third parties for the "display of customized content and advertising." And it even scans emails from nonGmail subscribers sent to Gmail subscribers for contextual advertising purposes.

Thus, if anything, the largely invisible practices of ad-networks and search engines raise at least the same privacy concerns as do the online behavioral advertising techniques that ISPs could employ, such as deep-packet-inspection, which have application beyond mere targeted advertising, including managing network congestion, detecting viruses and combating child pornography. In short, the privacy and other policy issues surrounding online behavioral advertising are not technology-specific. The relevant touchstones are the manner in which consumer information is tracked and used, and the manner in which consumers are given notice of and are able to consent to or prohibit such practices. Those factors are entirely technology- neutral.

AT&T's Approach to Online Behavioral Advertising

AT&T does not today engage in online behavioral advertising.[3] This is not because AT&T sees no value in this next-generation form of online advertising. Indeed, if done properly, online behavioral advertising could prove quite valuable to consumers and could dramatically improve their online experiences. We do, however, believe it is essential to include strong privacy protections in the design of any online behavioral advertising program, which is why we will initiate such a program only after testing and validating the various technologies and only after establishing clear and consistent methods and procedures to ensure the protection of, and ultimate consumer control over, consumer information. We further intend to work with privacy advocates, consumer privacy coalitions and fellow industry participants in a cooperative, multifaceted effort that we trust can and will lead to a predictable consumer driven framework in this area. In any event, if AT&T deploys these technologies and processes, it will do so the right way.

Against this backdrop, AT&T has already listened closely to its customers and will adopt meaningful and flexible privacy principles that will guide any effort to engage in online behavioral advertising. We summarize this framework as follows:

- **_Transparency:_** Consumers must have full and complete notice of what information will be collected, how it will be used, and how it will be protected.
- **_Consumer Control:_** Consumers must have easily understood tools that will allow them to exercise meaningful consent, which should be a sacrosanct precondition to tracking online activities to be used for online behavioral advertising.
- **_Privacy protection:_** The privacy of consumers/users and their personal information will be vigorously protected, and we will deploy technology to guard against unauthorized access to personally identifiable information
- **_Consumer Value:_** The consumer benefits of an online behavioral advertising program include the ability to receive a differentiated, secure Internet experience that provides consumers with customized Internet advertisements that are relevant to their interests. But we think the future is about much more than just customized advertising. Consumers have shown that in a world of almost limitless choices in the content and services available on the Internet, they see great value in being able to customize their unique online experience. That is the ultimate promise of the technological advances that are emerging in the market today.

CALL TO ACTION

We believe these principles offer a rational approach to protecting consumer privacy while allowing the market for Internet advertising and its related products and services to grow. But, in order for consumers truly to be in control of their information, _all_ entities involved in Internet advertising, including ad networks, search engines and ISPs, will need to adhere to a consistent set of principles. A policy regime that applies only to one set of actors will arbitrarily favor one business model or technology over another and, more importantly, represent only a partial and entirely unpredictable solution for consumers. After all, consumers do not want information and control with respect to just a subset of potential online advertising or the tracking and targeting that might underlie those ads. Thus, we urge all entities that engage in online behavioral advertising — including especially those who already engage in the practice — to join AT&T in committing to a policy of advance, affirmative consumer consent.

END NOTES

[1] The policy framework that AT&T proposes here is informed by and should complement the Online Behavioral Advertising Self-Regulatory Principles issued by staff of the Federal Trade Commission in December of last year. Online Behavioral Advertising: Moving the Discussion Forward to Possible Self-Regulatory Principles, available at http://www.ftc.gov/05/2007/12/P85900stmt.pdf.

[2] Letter from Joel Winston, Acting Associate Director, Division of Financial Practices, Bureau of Consumer Protection, Federal Trade Commission, to ChristineVarney, Hogan & Hartson, Re: DoubleClick Inc. (Jan 22, 2001)(memorializing closure of FTC staff investigation).

[3] AT&T does engage in some of the more ordinary and established aspects of online advertising. Like virtually every entity with a retail Internet presence, AT&T tracks usage on its own websites, such as att.com, in order to improve the online experience, optimize a particular site's capabilities and ease-of-use, and provide the most useful information to consumers about AT&T's products and services. In addition, like thousands of other businesses that operate websites, AT&T does business with advertising networks and has partnered with providers of online search. For example, on the AT&T broadband Internet access portal, AT&T makes space available for advertising provided by the Yahoo! advertising network, and users of the portal may be shown advertising that is based on their activity across sites signed up to the Yahoo! advertising network. Also by way of example, we have arranged for the Google search box to appear on our my.att.net site. In this regard, then, we are no different than any other website publisher.

In: Electronic Breadcrumbs: Issues in Tracking Consumers
Editor: Dmitar N. Kovac

ISBN: 978-1-60741-600-5
© 2010 Nova Science Publishers, Inc.

Chapter 2

BROADBAND PROVIDERS & CONSUMER PRIVACY HEARING- SOHN TESTIMONY

Gigi B. Sohn

Chairman Inouye, Ranking Member Hutchison and Members of the Committee, thank you for giving me the opportunity to testify about broadband providers and consumer privacy. I'd like to focus today on the growing use of the collection of technologies known as "Deep Packet Inspection," or DPI, which has immense implications for the privacy rights of the American public. Over the past several months, Public Knowledge, in partnership with Free Press, has been analyzing these technologies and their impact on privacy and an open Internet. In June, our organizations published a white paper entitled *NebuAd and Partner ISPs: Wiretapping, Forgery and Browser Hijacking*, which examined the technical and policy aspects of DPI. I applaud the Committee for its continued scrutiny of the use of these technologies.[1]

I. INTRODUCTION

Today's hearing on consumer privacy comes in the wake of two high-profile online consumer privacy violations, both of which involved the use of Deep Packet Inspection (DPI) technology on an Internet Service Provider's (ISP) network.

The first instance came to light in October 2007, when an Associated Press report revealed that Comcast was interfering with its customers' BitTorrent traffic.[2] The report confirmed earlier tests conducted by independent network researcher Robb Topolski, who found that Comcast was analyzing its user's web traffic in order to determine the types of applications and protocols being used. The company then used a technique called "packet spoofing" to delay, degrade and in some cases, block traffic that was identified as being used for BitTorrent, a popular peer-to-peer file sharing protocol. Public Knowledge and Free Press filed a formal complaint with the FCC in November 2007, calling for the Commission to open a formal investigation into the ISP's practices.[3]

In January 2008, the FCC announced that it had opened a formal investigation into Comcast's blocking of BitTorrent traffic. This investigation concluded in August 2008 with the FCC upholding the Public Knowledge and Free Press complaint and reprimanding Comcast for its degradation of its user's traffic. In its ruling against Comcast,[4] the FCC ordered the company to stop blocking BitTorrent traffic and to develop a new set of network management practices that did not violate the FCC's Broadband Policy Statement.[5] In its letter of response to the FCC, Comcast confirmed that it had used DPI equipment from the Sandvine Corporation in order to identify and block BitTorrent traffic.[6]

The second instance surfaced in May 2008, when it was revealed that various regional ISPs had contracted with NebuAd, a company that provided highly targeted behavioral advertising solutions using DPI equipment. In test deployments of this technology, all of the traffic traveling over an ISP's network was routed through a DPI appliance which collected data on specific users, including web sites visited, terms searched for and services and applications used. This data was then sent to NebuAd, which in turn, used the data to create detailed user profiles. These profiles were used to display highly targeted advertisements, which were dynamically displayed to the user as he or she surfed the Web.

In May 2008, Representatives Edward Markey (Chairman, Subcommittee on Telecommunications and the Internet) and Joe Barton (Ranking Member, Senate Committee on Energy and Commerce) sent a letter to NebuAd[7],asking the company to put its pilot tests on hold, pending an investigation into the company's practices. A coalition of 15 consumer advocacy and privacy groups publicly voiced their support for this letter and urged the Congressmen to continue their investigation of NebuAd and other behavioral advertising companies.[8] In June 2008, Public Knowledge and Free Press released a technical analysis of NebuAd's behavioral advertising system, authored by networking researcher Robb Topolski.[9] The report revealed that NebuAd and its partner ISPs repeatedly violated the privacy of users, with little or no notification that DPI equipment was being used. Following the release of the report, the House Committee on Energy and Commerce convened a hearing on the topic of DPI, wherein NebuAd CEO Bob Dykes was asked to testify.

On August 1, 2008, the House Committee on Energy and Commerce followed up with a letter to 33 ISPs and software companies asking for details regarding how they were using DPI and whether and how they were disclosing those uses to their customers.[10] As a result of the Congressional scrutiny, all of NebuAd's ISP partners, including WOW! (Wide Open West), CenturyTel, Charter, Bresnan and Embarq, have decided to put a hold on their test deployments with NebuAd. In September 2008, Bob Dykes announced that he was leaving NebuAd and following his departure, the company announced that it was abandoning its behavioral advertising initiatives, in favor or more traditional advertising technologies.

II. DEEP PACKET INSPECTION

To put it simply, Deep Packet Inspection is the Internet equivalent of the postal service reading your mail. They might be reading your mail for any number of reasons, but the fact remains that your mail is being read by the people whose job it is to deliver it.

When you use the Internet for Web browsing, email or any other purpose, the data you send and receive is broken up into small chunks called "packets." These packets are wrapped in envelopes, which, much like paper envelopes, contain addresses for both the sender and the receiver–though they contain little information about what's inside. Until recently, when you handed that envelope to your ISP, the ISP simply read the address, figured out where to send the envelope in order to get it to its destination, and handed it off to the proper mail carrier.

Now, we understand that more and more ISPs are opening these envelopes, reading their contents, and keeping or using varying amounts of information about the communications inside for their own purposes. In some cases, ISPs are actually passing copies of the envelopes on to third parties who do the actual reading and use. In others, ISPs are using the contents to change the normal ways that the Internet works. And for the most part, customers are not aware that their ISPs are engaging in this behavior–much like if the postal service were to open your letter, photocopy it, hand that copy to a third party and then re-seal the letter, so that you would never know it had even been opened in the first place.

III. THE PRIVACY IMPLICATIONS OF DPI

It should be clear that the very nature of DPI technology raises grave privacy concerns. An ISP, by necessity, sees every piece of data a user sends or receives on the Internet. In the past, ISPs had little incentive to look at this information and the related privacy concerns provided a strong deterrent against doing so. However, now that technology is widely available to make use of and monetize this information, companies are exploring the limits of what they can do permissibly.

When evaluating an implementation of DPI technology, there are three basic questions that must be answered in order to assess both the impact on a user's privacy and acceptability of use of the technology in question:

Purpose: What purpose is the collected data being used for?
Collection: How is the data collected and utilized?
Consent: How was affirmative informed consent obtained?

An understanding of these questions can inform legislators and policymakers in the formation of policies, which will adequately protect users of Internet connections and services. The uses for DPI are myriad, and most raise serious privacy concerns, but each use should be measured individually against a comprehensive privacy policy.

It is also important to note that there are two parties to any Internet communication. In almost all cases, the party on the other end of a user's line will have no meaningful ability at all to know what kind of monitoring is being employed by that user's ISP or what is being done with the collected data, and will have no opportunity at all to give or to deny consent. For example, if I send you an email and my ISP is using DPI to read the contents of my emails, your privacy has just been violated without your knowledge or consent. Any comprehensive privacy policy that addresses technologies like DPI must take into account not only the privacy rights of an ISP's customers, but also those of anyone who communicates with these customers.

A. Purpose

Given DPI's potential to be used as an intrusive tool, we must first ask why the user's traffic is being collected or analyzed at all. Is the use of DPI integral to the functioning of the network or is the technology simply being used to provide the ISP with an additional revenue stream? Does the technology in question primarily benefit the ISP's bottom line, or does it give direct benefits to the customer's use of the Internet? Is it used to protect users or the integrity of the network, or simply to offer new or improved additional services?

Not all uses of DPI are inherently problematic. The first widespread uses of DPI were for security purposes: to stop malicious programs like viruses and worms from passing from one infected computer to another over the Internet. However, as seen in the recent complaint and decision against Comcast at the Federal Communications Commission (FCC), DPI can also be used to engage in impermissible, discriminatory network management practices. Taken to an extreme, we can even imagine a future where DPI is used to record and disseminate every single move a user makes on the Internet–from Web browsing, email and instant messaging to VoIP phone calls and video chats–to the ISP's own business advantage.

Understanding the purpose of DPI use is the first step to understanding whether that use will violate a user's expectations of privacy.

B. Collection

After we understand the purpose of a particular use of DPI, we can analyze how the data is collected and used toward that purpose. Is the user's data being collected by the ISP for its own use, or is it being passed to a third party with no connection to the user? Is all of the user's data collected, or a smaller subset of the data? Is the amount collected narrowly tailored to achieve the stated purpose, or broader than necessary, or is the amount of data actually used smaller than that collected?

It is important to note here that we should evaluate both the amount of data which reaches the party using it, and the amount of that data which is used. This is because additional data that is sent to a third party provides more opportunity for abuse of user privacy – even if that third party later chose to discard some of the more personal information. For instance, even though companies like NebuAd may choose to ignore the personal medical records or emails of its partner's customers, they were provided the data to do exactly that. This problem is compounded by the fact that an ISP or partner must engage in DPI to even discover what type of data is being transmitted, thereby possibly violating the user's privacy before any decision is made regarding what is to be done with the data.

It is also necessary to identify the ways in which the collected data might be tied to the user's actual identity. Is the data obtained using DPI explicitly tied to data obtained through other means–for example, the ISP's billing information, demographic information, or personal information stored on a third-party website? Can the collected data be later aggregated with this type of information? Will the data itself contain personally identifying information (PII), such as names, addresses, and credit card information submitted to web sites? These questions are important because if the data in question contains PII or if it is later connected with other user data, the privacy implications are multiplied.

Implicit in the data collection question are also questions about data storage. Is the collected data kept by the party using it? If so, for how long? Is it kept in its original, complete form, or in some type of summary? Is any PII kept with the stored data?

Understanding what and how data is collected and how well that comports with the stated purpose of the collection is necessary to evaluating whether the collection will violate users' privacy expectations.

C. Consent

No inspection of a user's data will be acceptable without that user's affirmative, informed consent or law enforcement obligations. To ensure this is obtained, we must evaluate both how users are notified of the ways in which their ISP and its partners intend to use DPI, and the method by which those users affirmatively consent (or decline to consent) to those uses. To do this, we must ensure that before a user's data is inspected, the user actually receives complete, useful information, and that the user knowingly and affirmatively assents to the stated uses.

Are the answers to the above questions about purpose and collection accessible for users, and complete in the information they divulge? If any third parties are involved in the monitoring, are their identities provided for the user? Are the answers written so that the average user can make sense of them? Are the policies in question detailed in a place and manner that ensures that the user is likely to read them? Is the user actively notified of the presence of and changes to policies and monitoring activities, or are changes made to Web pages and written into the Terms of Service–without any notification to the user? Without accurate and easily understandable information that a user is actually aware of, that user cannot make informed choices about how best to manage his or her privacy online.

Finally, what is the process by which users agree (or decline to agree) to the use of these technologies? Are they subject to DPI *before* they receive meaningful notice of its use, or is the user required to take an affirmative action before his or her data is recorded or analyzed? Is the information and the action specific to the monitoring activities, or is it hidden in a larger "Acceptable Use Policy," "End User License Agreement," or other document? Does the user have the meaningful ability to change his or her choice later? Is the user actively offered a periodic chance to withdraw consent, or is he or she only asked once? And is the option not to consent a real one, without crippling or disabling of the user's service as the only alternative?

Without meaningful, informed, affirmative consent on the part of the user, personal data should not be used for any purpose that is not necessary to providing basic Internet service.

IV. ISP DISCLOSURES

In response to Chairman Dingell and Ranking Member Barton's letter, 33 ISPs and software companies described whether and how they were using DPI and whether and how they were disclosing those uses to their customers.[11] These responses are helpful in understanding how, to date, the above three questions have been answered unsatisfactorily.

Carriers that responded to the letter fell into two basic camps. The first group of ISPs did not employ NebuAd's services and did not use any similar DPI equipment. These ISPs generally had not deployed any technologies that could track individual users' browsing habits or correlate advertising information with personal information possessed by the I SP.[12]

The second camp contained those ISPs who performed trials of or deployed third-party DPI- based behavioral advertising systems.[13] Importantly, these ISPs generally did not inspect user data themselves, but passed it off to their partners for analysis. According to these ISPs, they were assured that measures were in place to ensure that those partners did not retain medical information, personal data, emails, or other types of especially sensitive data.[14] Also, all of these ISPs stated that they and NebuAd did not tie the tracked Internet data to personal customer data already known to the ISP (billing information, etc.).[15]

However, as a technical matter, the personal data embedded in a user's Internet communications *was* handed off to the ISP's partners, when the ISP itself is actually responsible for safeguarding its users data. In some cases, the identity of the partner was not divulged to the user. These partners had no direct interactions with the user, meaning that final control of what data was used and how rested not with the user or even the ISP, but with this third party. To return to the postal service analogy, it is as if the ISPs photocopied users' letters and handed these copies to third parties, who agreed to only write down which commercial products were mentioned in the letters, and not anything else that someone might consider sensitive. However, the decision as to what, exactly, should be considered 'sensitive,' is not made by the user but rather, by this third- party company.

Customer notification and consent varied from ISP to ISP, but there were significant trends. ISPs generally posted modified terms of service and often updated the 'Frequently Asked Questions' section on their web sites, but usually declined to directly contact users or call attention to the significance of the new service. Knology, for instance, updated their Customer Service Agreement on their web site, which is presented to new users, but apparently made no other attempt to draw attention to the change.[16]

The level of detail in the disclosures also fell far short of the minimum that is necessary for customers to make an informed decision. For example, CenturyTel sent an email informing users only that it had "updated its Privacy Policy concerning Internet Access Services" and provided a web link to the updated policy.[17] The policy in question stated only:

> ONLINE ADVERTISING AND THIRD-PARTY AD SERVERS.
> CenturyTel partners with a third party to deliver or facilitate delivery of advertisements to our users while they are surfing the Web. This delivery of advertisements may be facilitated by the serving of ad tags outside the publisher's existing HTML code. *These advertisements will be based on those users' anonymous surfing behavior while they are online.* This anonymous information will not include those users' names, email addresses, telephone number, or any other personally identifiable information. By opting out, you will continue to receive advertisements as normal; except these advertisements will be less relevant and less useful to you. If you would like to opt out, click here or visit
> http://www.nebuad.com/privacy/servicesPrivacy.php.[18]

A later letter sent out by CenturyTel stated the following:

> CenturyTel continually looks for ways to improve your overall online experience. In that regard, we have enhanced our High-Speed Internet service by working with partners to

provide targeted, online advertising for your convenience and benefit. Targeted, online advertising minimizes irrelevant or unwanted ads that clutter your Web pages. If you do not wish to receive targeted, online advertisements, or if you would simply like more information about CenturyTel's use of online advertising, third-party ad servers and the measures you can take to protect your privacy, please review our Privacy Policy by visiting http://www.centurytel.com/Pages/PrivacyPolicy/#adv.[19]

No mention is made at all of providing actual user data (let alone *all* of a user's packets) to third parties. Only a single mention of ads being "based on those users' anonymous surfing behavior" is offered in the first notice, and the second presents the service only as enhanced, "targeted advertising for your convenience and benefit" without mention of the methods involved to deliver said advertisements. It's worth noting that these examples are not unique to CenturyTel or even unusual; rather, they are indicative of the level of detail provided in many ISP notices. Such notices do not make clear to the user what is actually being done with the data they send and receive over the Internet. *None* of the ISPs appears to have required that a user take any affirmative action at all before having their data handed wholesale to a third party. Inaction or failure to read the notice was simply treated as an 'opt –in'.

It is important to note that nearly every ISPs that responded mentioned that they run their own web sites, and use traditional tracking methods such as cookies to observe and record the behavior of their customers on their sites, much like Google, Yahoo, Microsoft, and many other web service providers do. Likewise, many ISPs also use what is called a "DNS redirect," which, rather than returning an error to a user's web browser when he or she types in an incorrect web address, redirects the user to another web page which may have related suggestions, advertisements, or other information.

These non-DPI practices have privacy implications that overlap with the ones being discussed today, but which are different in kind and scope. It is the difference between you writing down what I tell you on the phone and my phone company recording my conversation with you because unlike my phone company, you cannot record what I've said on my phone calls to other people. Nonetheless, the privacy practices of and personal information available to application providers raise their own serious questions of legal policy, and any regulatory regime we consider must be comprehensive and attempt to ensure the protection of Internet users against privacy invasions from all such sources.

V. CURRENT LAW

Independent analysis by the Center for Democracy and Technology suggests that although it is far from clear, despite ISP claims,[20] past experiments with DPI and behavioral advertising of the type engaged in by NebuAd may run afoul of existing law. Critically, however, some of the laws in question might not apply if the ISP engaged in this behavior internally, instead of delegating responsibility to a third party.[21] Thus, an ISP might legally be able to read and analyze all of its customers' communications as long as it does so itself– hardly an improvement in privacy.

It is extremely important to note that without apparent exception, every ISP that responded to Chairman Markey's letter concluded that both the tracking and opt-out mechanism were legal, or at the very least, were "not unlawful or impermissible."[22] One ISP even went so far as to claim that it "offered customers easy-to-use opt-out mechanisms *as recommended by the FTC*."[23] However, even the "opt-out" method was questionable, as the act of opting out did not stop the delivery to and monitoring by the third-party partner but only the presentation of targeted ads and stored profiles.[24]

Yet to date, no enforcement actions have been taken against a practice that is of significant concern to citizens and lawmakers alike. Regardless of whether or not the actions taken by ISPs are technically legal, the existing legal regime is clearly not effective at preventing such privacy violations. And if ISPs believe they can legally and profitably engage in this behavior with only a minimal effort made to notify and protect users, they will continue to do so.

To the credit of the ISPs here today, several providers have made commitments to ensuring that there is transparency, affirmative consent, and ongoing control by customers. For example, Time-Warner's testimony suggests control, transparency, disclosure, and safeguarding personal information as principles on which to base a privacy framework. AT&T states that the company will not engage in behavioral advertising without a ffirmative, advance action by the consumer that is based on a clear explanation of how that information will be used. But while these are laudable principles and we applaud the carriers here today for their stated commitment to customer privacy, promises by individual ISPs are not enough and do not obviate the need for a comprehensive governmental policy.

Part of the reason for the current lack of enforcement can be traced to ambiguity in the FCC's authority to protect the privacy of Internet users, despite the FCC's time-honored role in protecting the privacy of communications as a whole. Congress has long recognized that providers of communications services occupy an especially sensitive position in society. As data conduits, communications services are uniquely positioned to track customers and collect information about their daily lives. The Communications Act, which created the FCC, contains provisions designed to protect the privacy of telephone and cable customers. But those same protections have yet to be unambiguously extended to Internet customers. As a result, customers cannot be confident that their sensitive information is protected from unwanted intrusion. In a society where Internet services are increasingly used to transmit personal and sensitive information, this is clearly problematic.

Section 222 of the Communications Act applies to the privacy of customer information collected by common carriers.[25] The statute recognizes that "individually identifiable consumer proprietary network information" is created by, and critical to the functioning of, telecommunications services.[26] However, the statute strictly limits the use of that information to applications that handle tasks like billing and the maintenance of network integrity.[27] Carriers are allowed to provide aggregate consumer information to third parties, but this information must have both "individual customer identities and characteristics" removed.[28] Viewed holistically, this section manifests a Congressional understanding that common carriers have access to sensitive personal information, and that common carriers have legitimate reasons to use that data. However, this understanding is balanced by strict prohibitions against any non-essential use or the disclosure of sensitive data.

Although many common carriers provide Internet services to consumers,[29] such Internet services are not covered under Section 222.[30] As a result, plain old telephone customers can be confident that sensitive information contained in their phone records will be kept confidential, but they cannot enjoy the same level of confidence when it comes to sensitive information that Verizon might compile using their DSL Internet activity.

Section 631 of the Communications Act also marks an attempt by Congress to protect the privacy of consumers, this time from cable system operators. Again, the statute recognizes the fact that operators will need to collect and use some personally identifiable information in order to operate their systems. However, these operators are required to obtain written permission from consumers in order to collect any personally identifiable information that is not crucial to the operation of the system.[31] Additionally, operators are required to obtain prior written or electronic consent before disclosing any personally identifiable information.[32] The statute does not impose these same protections on aggregate data that does not identify a particular customer,[33] and allows an operator to disclose names and addresses of subscribers as long as that information is not tied to use or transactional information.[34]

As with Section 222, Section 631 specifically protects sensitive information that network operators are uniquely positioned to collect. However, unlike Section 222, which applies to phone customers but not Internet service customers, Section 631 is written to apply to both cable television subscribers and cable Internet subscribers.[35]

Unfortunately, not all customers access the Internet by way of a cable system. In addition to unprotected DSL service, customers can access the Internet via a fiber optic network, a satellite based service, or by using one of many wireless Internet standards. Instead of relying on old categories that may protect some (but certainly not all) consumers, Congress must recognize that all Internet service providers share the same privileged position of access to their users' personal data. As a result, Congress should collectively protect customers with legislation that specifically addresses all Internet service providers, rather than legislation that effectively forces customers to access the Internet via a single, protected pathway.

The time has come for a comprehensive regulatory structure that will ensure that the privacy rights of all Internet users are protected, and one that, like the Telecommunications Act of 1996, "expands very important privacy protections to individuals in their relationships with these very large companies."[36]

VI. FIXING THE LAW

Given the power of the technology and the scope of possible uses, it is critical that we establish industry guidelines and legal protections for users. And while the use of personal data by application providers is not the focus of our discussion today, as discussed above, any solution should strive to be comprehensive in scope and ensure that the basic principles of privacy protection are applied across the entire Internet ecosystem. These protections should meet three major goals that parallel the privacy inquiries described above:

- They must ensure that the purpose of the use of customer data is one which can be consistent with consumers' privacy expectations.
- They must ensure that the amount and type of data collected is narrowly tailored to the proposed use, and that the data is not kept or disseminated to third parties past what is necessary to that use.
- They must ensure that customers have access to and actually receive adequate information about the proposed use, and have affirmatively and actively consented to any practices which could violate customers' expectations of privacy.[37]

In order to achieve these goals, the Committee should seek to pass legislation to encapsulate these requirements and to make it clear that the FCC has the power to enforce them. As the Commission observed in 1998, "The [Communications Act] recognizes that customers must be able to control information they view as sensitive and personal from use, disclosure, and access by carriers."[38] The Committee and Congress need only make it clear that Internet user privacy is another area of communications where the Commission is empowered to protect consumer privacy.

VII. CONCLUSION

I would like to thank the Committee again for giving me the opportunity to testify today. Public Knowledge is eager to work with the Committee to craft comprehensive privacy legislation that will protect Internet users. I look forward to your questions.

END NOTES

[1] I would like to thank Public Knowledge's Equal Justice Works Fellow JefPearlman, Policy Analyst Mehan Jayasuriya, and Law Clerk Michael Weinberg for assisting me with this testimony.

[2] *See* Associated Press article, "Comcast blocks some Internet traffic", (October 19, 2007), *available at* http://www.msnbc.msn.com/id/21376597.

[3] See Free Press and Public Knowledge, *Formal Complaint ofFree Press and Public Knowledge Against Comcast Corporation for Secretly Degrading Peer to Peer Applications*, (November 1, 2007), *available at* http://www.publicknowledge.org/pdf/fp_pk_comcast_complaint.pdf [hereinafter Comcast Complaint].

[4] See Federal Communications Commission, *Memorandum Opinion and Order* (August 1, 2008), *available at* http://hraunfoss.fcc.gov/edocs_public/attachmatch/FCC-08-1 83A1 .pdf.

[5] *See* FCC, *Policy Statement*, (August 5, 2005), *available at* http://www.publicknowledge.org/pdf/FCC -05 - 1 5 1 A 1 .pdf.

[6] *See* Comcast Corporation, *Attachment A: Comcast Corporation Description of Current Network Management Practices,* (September 19, 2008), *available at* http://downloads.comcast.net/docs/Attachment_A_Current_Practices.pdf.

[7] Representative Edward J. Markey and Representative Joe Barton, *Letter to Neil Smit, President and CEO, Charter Communications* (May 16, 2008), *available at* http://markey.house.gov/docs/telecomm/letter_charter_comm_privacy.pdf.

[8] Center for Democracy and Technology et al., *Letter to Representatives Markey and Barton* (June 6, 2008), *available at* http://www.cdt.org/privacy/20080606markeybarton.pdf.

[9] *See* Public Knowledge and Free Press, *NebuAd and Partner ISPs: Wiretapping, Forgery and Browser Hijacking* (June 18, 2008) *available at* http://www.publicknowledge.org/pdf/nebuad-report-2008061 8.pdf.

[10] See John D. Dingell (Chairman, Senate Committee on Energy and Commerce), Joe Barton (Ranking Member, Senate Committee on Energy and Commerce), Edward J. Markey (Chairman, Subcommittee on Telecommunications and the Internet), Cliff Stearns (Ranking Member, Subcommittee on Telecommunications and the Internet), *Letter to ISPs* (Aug. 1, 2008), *available at* http://markey.house.gov/docs/telecomm/letter_dpi_33_companies.pdf.

[11] All 33 response letters are available at the House Energy and Commerce Committee's Subcommittee on Telecommunications and the Internet web site at http://energycommerce.house.gov/Press_110/080108.ResponsesDataCollectionLetter.shtml.

[12] *See, e.g.*, Response Letters of AT&T, Verizon, and Time-Warner.

[13] *See, e.g.*, Response Letters of WOW!, Charter Communications, Knology, and CenturyTel.

[14] *See* Response Letter of Charter Communications 2.

[15] *See* Response Letter of Knology 1.

[16] *See* Response Letter of Knology 2.

[17] Response Letter of CenturyTel 3.

[18] *Id.* 3 (emphasis added).

[19] *Id.* 3-4.

[20] *See* Center for Democracy and Technology, *An Overview of the Federal Wiretap Act, Electronic Communications Privacy Act, and State Two-Party Consent Laws of Relevance to the NebuAd System and Other Uses of Internet Traffic Content from ISPs for Behavioral Advertising*, (July 8, 2008), *available at* http://www.cdt.org/privacy/20080708ISPtraffic.pdf [hereinafter *CDT Behavioral Advertising Overview*].

[21] *See id.* at 6-9.

[22] Response Letter of CenturyTel 2-3 (Aug. 7, 2008). Cable One does describe their disclosures in their Acceptable Use Policies as "opt-in" because the user must check and acceptance box, but this does not qualify as either an affirmative step specific to monitoring or a meaningful opportunity to deny consent, because the alternative is no Internet service at all. *See* Respo nse Letter of Cable One 3 (Aug. 8, 2008).

[23] Response Letter of Charter Communications 2 (Aug. 8, 2008) (emphasis added).

[24] Ryan Singel, *Congressmen Ask Charter to Freeze Web Profiling Plan*, Threat Level from Wired.com (May 16, 2008). *See also* Ryan Singel, *Can Charter Broadband Customers Really Opt-Out of Spying? Maybe Not*, Wired (May 16, 2008).

[25] 47 U.S.C. § 222

[26] *See* 47 U.S.C. § 222(c)(1).

[27] *See* 47 U.S.C. § 222(d).

[28] *See* 47 U.S.C. § 222(c)(3), (h)(2).

[29] *See , e.g.*, Verizon, http://www.verizon.com/.

[30] *See National Cable & Telecommunications Assn. v. Brand X Internet Services*, 545 U.S. 967 (2005).

[31] *See* 47 U.S.C. § 55 1(b).

[32] *See* 47 U.S.C. § 551(c)(1).

[33] *See* 47 U.S.C. § 551(a)(2)(A).

[34] *See* 47 U.S.C. § 551(c)(2).

[35] *See* 47 U.S.C. § 551(a)(2)(C)(ii).

[36] Statement of Congressman Edward Markey, 142 Cong. Rec. H1 145-06 (Feb. 1, 1996).

[37] The FCC has already presented us with an example of how Commission action and ISP disclosures can be used to help protect Internet users from privacy invasions and impermissible network management practices. In its order finding that Comcast's interference with customer traffic was not reasonable network management, the Commission ordered Comcast to fully disclose the details of its past and planned practices, including use of DPI. *See* Federal Communications Commission, *Memorandum Opinion and Order* ¶ 54-56 (August 1, 2008), *available at* http://hraunfoss.fcc.gov/edocs_public/attachmatch/FCC-08-1 83A1.pdf. Given the authority, the Commission could make this type of disclosure an industry-wide baseline to ensure that customer's decisions about granting consent are based on good, complete information backed the force of law.

[38] Federal Communications Commission, *Common Carrier News Release* (Feb. 19, 1998), *available at* http://www.fcc.gov/Bureaus/Common_Carrier/News_Releases/1 998/nrcc801 9.html (clarifying permissible uses of Customer Proprietary Network Information).

In: Electronic Breadcrumbs: Issues in Tracking Consumers
Editor: Dmitar N. Kovac

ISBN: 978-1-60741-600-5
© 2010 Nova Science Publishers, Inc.

Chapter 3

BROADBAND PROVIDERS & CONSUMER PRIVACY HEARING- STERN TESTIMONY

Peter Stern

Good morning, Mr. Chairman, Members of the Committee, my name is Peter Stern. I am Executive Vice President and Chief Strategy Officer at Time Warner Cable, where I am responsible for strategy and planning, including for our Road Runner high-speed online service.

I am pleased to testify before you today and appreciate this Committee's diligent effort to grapple with the complex and still-evolving Internet advertising marketplace and to assess its impact on consumer privacy.

Presently, Time Warner Cable does not engage in targeted Internet advertising as an ISP or as a website operator.

Should Time Warner Cable decide to engage in such activities, our customers' privacy will be a fundamental consideration. The protection of subscriber privacy is not only important as a matter of public policy, but it is also central to the success of our business. The bedrock foundation of our business is our relationship with our subscribers. We operate in a highly competitive marketplace, and our ability to succeed depends on winning and retaining the trust of those customers. Accordingly, we support a framework that would provide consumers with the opportunity to affirmatively consent to receive online targeted advertising.

In the context of targeted online advertising, we believe that achieving and sustaining our subscribers' trust requires adherence to a privacy framework that addresses four principles: first, giving customers *control;* second, providing *transparency* and *disclosure;* third, *safeguarding personal information;* and fourth, providing customers with *value*.

Let me also add, however, that we strongly believe that any such framework can only truly protect the privacy interests of consumers if it is universally adopted by all providers of targeted online advertising, including ad networks, application providers and ISPs. Quite simply, it makes no difference to a consumer whether a targeted online ad is based on data collected by an ISP, an ad network or an applications provider. A framework that leaves any provider uncovered would leave all users unprotected. In addition, a common set of rules protecting consumer privacy is the only way to ensure that all businesses that provide online advertising can compete and innovate on a level playing field.

Before I go any further, allow me to clarify our definition of targeted online advertising for the purposes of applying the framework I described. At Time Warner Cable, we define it as displaying different online ads to a consumer based on that consumer's behavior on unrelated websites. So, if ads are delivered to a consumer based on that consumer's particular history of visits to multiple unrelated websites, that's targeted online advertising.

On the other hand, delivering relevant ads to a consumer based on their behavior on an *individual* website (or group of related websites) is *not* targeted online advertising. For example, if you go to Apple's website and search for an iPod, and Apple delivers ads and promotions for iPods while you are still on the Apple website, that's not targeted online advertising. That's being responsive to what you asked for, when and where you wanted it. It becomes targeted online advertising, however, if this information is retained in order to deliver ads for iPods and other portable music players while you are visiting unrelated websites.

Let me elaborate briefly on the four principles I've mentioned.

First, *customer control* means consumers will be able to exercise *affirmative* consent to having their activities collected and used for targeted online advertising. Internet subscribers that decline to consent or fail to act should not have their online activities tracked or used for targeted online advertising. Control also means that the consent mechanisms should be easy to use, to ensure that customers are free to change their election at any time, and that their election will remain in effect unless they change it.

Second, *transparency and disclosure* means ensuring that a customer's consent to targeted online advertising is informed. This means giving Internet users clear and timely notice regarding what type of online usage information is tracked and collected, how that information is used to provide targeted online advertising, and what steps consumers can take should they decline to participate. And by this, we don't mean fine print. We mean prominent and plain English.

Third, *safeguarding personal information* means preventing unauthorized access to customers' personal information. It also should mean preventing disclosure or sale of such information to third parties absent consent of the customer. We also believe that policy makers and the public should continue to discuss whether there are categories of particularly sensitive information, such as personal medical information, that should be entirely off limits to targeted online advertising or subject to special controls.

Last, *providing value* means offering targeted online advertising in a manner that enhances the Internet experience for consumers. Time Warner Cable firmly believes that targeted online advertising can benefit consumers. Instead of a barrage of irrelevant ads, subscribers can receive information about services and offerings tailored to reflect their interests. Targeted online advertising can also be used to protect consumers from seeing ads they don't want. Advertising can be a public good, when it educates consumers about relevant choices. Properly implemented, technology can help advertising achieve this potential, possibly even increasing the number of ads consumers want to see.

In addition, targeted online advertising provides important benefits for advertisers and providers of Internet applications and services. Revenues from such advertising can offset the costs of providing services to consumers, and can allow businesses to offer services at discounts or even without direct payment from end users. In this manner, targeted online advertising can deliver value to consumers while helping to preserve and promote access to and enjoyment of the rich diversity of the Internet.

Most companies that provide services on the Internet are presently under no obligation to disclose, or obtain consent for, the collection and use of consumers' online usage information. And in the case of some of the largest ad networks and applications providers, the amount of information such companies possess about consumers dwarfs that obtained by ISPs.

It is certainly true that many providers of targeted online advertising already voluntarily disclose the extent to which they collect and use data about consumers. And some may also provide consumers the ability to "opt out" of participating in such an arrangement. But the extent of such disclosure varies greatly and is often opaque; and the process for opting out can be complicated, and in any case falls short of the principle of consumer control I have articulated.

Therefore, Time Warner Cable believes that the four principles I have outlined — customer control, transparency and disclosure, safeguarding personal information, and providing value — should serve as the cornerstone of a uniform policy framework that would apply to *all* companies involved in targeted online advertising. Time Warner Cable stands ready to work with this Committee and other stakeholders to help foster the development and implementation of such a framework.

I thank the Members of this Committee for the opportunity to appear before you today on this important issue, and I would be happy to answer any questions you might have.

In: Electronic Breadcrumbs: Issues in Tracking Consumers   ISBN: 978-1-60741-600-5
Editor: Dmitar N. Kovac   © 2010 Nova Science Publishers, Inc.

Chapter 4

BROADBAND PROVIDERS & CONSUMER PRIVACY HEARING- TAUKE TESTIMONY

Thomas J. Tauke

Chairman Inouye, Ranking Member Hutchison and Members of the Committee: thank you for the opportunity to discuss the important concerns and perspectives surrounding consumer privacy in the area of online advertising.

Today, more than 60 million American homes are connected to the Internet via broadband, and the wide range of content, services, and applications online – most offered for free – draws more people online every day.

While Verizon does not rely on online advertising as a significant source of revenue, we recognize that it has been a key business model that has helped make the Internet a growth engine for the U.S. economy.

Yet, using consumers' web-surfing data to foster targeted online advertising raises complex and important issues surrounding online privacy. Consumers and policy makers want to understand what personal information is being collected and used for advertising purposes. They want to know what privacy and consumer protections are in place, and what choices are available to participate – or not – in behavioral advertising models.

In a rapidly changing and innovative environment like the Internet, maintaining consumer trust is essential. It is critical that consumers understand what forms of targeted online advertising their service providers and favorite websites employ. If certain practices cause consumers to believe that their privacy will not be protected, or their preferences won't be respected, they will be less likely to trust their online services, and the tremendous power of the Internet to benefit consumers will be diminished. So, maintaining consumer trust in the online experience is critical to the future success of the Internet.

With that in mind, let me begin by describing the online advertising techniques Verizon uses today over its wireline networks.

Verizon's online advertising involves the practices commonly accepted throughout the Internet, such as the use of cookies or ad delivery servers to provide advertising that is limited to users of Verizon's own services or websites. We also provide ad-supported search results to help consumers find the websites they are looking for when they mistype an address. These practices, which are neither new nor unique, improve consumers' interaction with our websites and services, and increase the relevance of the advertising displayed to our customers or to visitors of our sites.

One technology that has received attention of late is "packet inspection." To be clear, Verizon has not used – and does not use – packet inspection technology to target advertising to customers, and we have not deployed the technology in our wireline network for such purposes.

Packet inspection can be a helpful engineering tool to manage network traffic and enable online services and applications consumers may wish to use. The perceived problem with "packet inspection" is not the technology. Many useful technologies can be used for nefarious purposes. The problem arises if packet inspection is used to inappropriately track customers' online activity without their knowledge and consent and invade their personal privacy.

In fact, any technology that is used to track and collect consumer online behavior for the purposes of targeted advertising – regardless of which company is doing the collecting – should only be used with the customer's knowledge and consent in accordance with the law, a company's specific privacy policies, and the privacy principles outlined below.

Protecting our customers' privacy has long been, and will continue to be, a priority at Verizon. We are committed to maintaining strong and meaningful privacy protections for consumers in this era of rapidly changing technological advances. We are strong proponents of transparency and believe that consumers are entitled to know what kinds of information we collect and use, and should have ready access to effective tools that allow them to control the use of that information.

At Verizon we have worked to craft – and communicate to our customers – responsible policies aimed at protecting online privacy.

We can commit – and believe that all companies should commit – to a set of best practices in the area of online behavioral advertising. The principles and best practices should apply to all online companies regardless of their technology or the platform used. The principles underlying the consumer protection practices we support are these:

FIRST, MEANINGFUL CONSENT

Verizon believes that before a company captures certain Internetusage data for targeted or customized advertising purposes, it should obtain meaningful, affirmative consent from consumers. Meaningful consent requires: 1) transparency, 2) affirmative choice, and 3) consumer control.

Transparency involves conspicuous, clearly explained disclosure to consumers as to what types of data are collected and for what purpose that data is being used, how that data is retained and for how long, and who is permitted access to the data.

Consumers would then be able to use these clear explanations to make an *affirmative choice* that their information can be collected and used for online behavioral advertising. Importantly, a consumer's failure to consent should mean that there is no collection and use of that consumer's information for online behaviorally targeted advertising based on tracking of the consumer's Internet usage.

Finally, *consumer control* means that consumers have an ongoing opportunity to make a different choice about behavioral advertising. In other words, should consumers at some later time choose not to participate in the behavioral advertising, there are equally clear and easyto-use instructions to make that change. That preference should remain in effect unless and until the consumer changes it.

SECOND, SECURITY PRACTICES

Any company engaged in tracking and collecting consumer online behavioral information must have appropriate access, security, and technological controls to guard against unauthorized access to any personal information.

THIRD, SAFEGUARDS FOR SENSITIVE INFORMATION

Special attention must be given to the protection of information of a sensitive nature (e.g., accessing medical web sites). This information should not be collected and used for online behavioral advertising unless specific, affirmative consent, and customer controls are in place to limit such use. Specific policies may be necessary to deal with this type of information.

Consistent with our long-standing policies and practices, Verizon also believes that the content of communications, such as e-mail, instant messages, or VoIP calls, should not be used, analyzed, or disclosed for purposes of Internet-based targeted advertising.

FOURTH, CERTIFICATION

It is critical that all participants in online advertising – ad networks, publishers, search engines, Internet service providers, browser developers and other application providers – commit to these common sense principles and best practices through a broad-based, third party coalition. To achieve this, we plan to work with stakeholders in the Internet and advertising arenas, including other companies, industry groups and policy organizations.

The focus of this coalition and the principles should be the protection of consumers, not the technology or applications that happen to enable the data collection. Widespread and uniform adoption of principles will greatly enhance the public trust, address expressed privacy concerns regarding web tracking practices, and serve as a foundation for further discussion with policy makers and consumer groups.

We believe that companies engaged in online behavioral advertising should agree to participate in a credible, third-party certification process to demonstrate to consumers that they are doing what they say with regard to the collection and use of information for online behavioral advertising. This process would confirm that companies are complying with and respecting consumers' expressed choices regarding such data collection.

We believe a framework such as this is a rational approach that protects consumer privacy, while allowing the market for Internet advertising and its related products and services to grow.

Should a company fail to comply with these principles, we believe the Federal Trade Commission has authority over abuses in the privacy area and can take appropriate measures against companies that intentionally violate applicable consumer protection laws.

We hope to use the next few months to work with all players in the Internet space to create and agree to live by industry best practices for online advertising.

Thank you.

In: Electronic Breadcrumbs: Issues in Tracking Consumers   ISBN: 978-1-60741-600-5
Editor: Dmitar N. Kovac   © 2010 Nova Science Publishers, Inc.

Chapter 5

HARBOUR ON SELF-REGULATORY PRINCIPLES FOR ONLINE BEHAVIORAL ADVERTISING

Pamela Jones Harbour

I have voted to authorize staff to issue today's report on behavioral advertising. The report reflects tremendous efforts by staff to explore the complex issues surrounding behavioral advertising, and I thank staff for their diligence in tackling this important topic. The release of this report is yet another positive step in an ongoing dialogue between the Commission and relevant stakeholders, including industry representatives, consumer groups, and legislators.

I write separately to explain where I depart from the Commission's present approach to the study of behavioral advertising. Simply stated, today's staff report, while commendable, focuses too narrowly. Threats to consumer privacy abound, both online and offline,[1] and behavioral advertising represents just one aspect of a multifaceted privacy conundrum surrounding data collection and use. I would prefer that the Commission take a more comprehensive approach to privacy, and evaluate behavioral advertising within that broader context.

In recent years we have witnessed an explosion of "free" online content and services that collect, integrate, and disseminate data. Examples include web mail, blogs, mapping and location- based services, photo sharing, desktop organization, social networking, instant messaging, and mobile applications. These technologies offer valuable benefits, but not all consumers understand how the business model works. Consumers repeatedly pay for "free" content and services by disclosing their personal information, which is used to generate targeted advertising or for other commercial purposes. Once data is shared, it cannot simply be recalled or deleted – which magnifies the cumulative consequences for consumers, whether they realize it or not. This potential disconnect between consumer perception and business reality is troubling, and it merits increased Commission attention.

The current economic climate adds another layer of concern. Consumer data is a valuable asset under any circumstances, and most companies act in good faith to safeguard it. But in difficult economic times, when pressure mounts to extract the greatest possible value from every asset, some firms may be tempted to stray further into the zone of uncertainty between acceptable and unacceptable uses of consumer data.

Individuals ultimately must select the online tools they prefer, as well as the extent and scope of information they disclose. Consumers cannot make informed choices, however, unless they have complete and accurate information about how their data may be collected and used. Informed consent should not be assumed based on consumers' willingness to click through cryptic disclosures and licenses. Furthermore, once consumers exercise their choices, companies must be held accountable for the promises they make to consumers regarding collection and use of personal data.

A legislative approach to behavioral advertising is not prudent at this time, for two reasons. First, there are still more questions than answers. Second, and more importantly, any legislation should be part of a comprehensive privacy agenda, rather than fostering the current piecemeal approach to privacy. But nor can I fully support a self-regulatory approach to behavioral advertising, which the staff report appears to advocate. Industry consistently argues that self- regulatory programs are the best way to address privacy concerns, but the evidence is mixed at best. Self-regulation has not yet been proven sufficient to fully protect the interests of consumers with respect to behavioral advertising specifically, or privacy generally. For this reason, the Commission has played, and must continue to play, an integral role in facilitating the ongoing privacy discussion.

I. IS THE CURRENT SELF-REGULATORY APPROACH ADEQUATE TO PROTECT CONSUMERS?

My reluctance to fully embrace a self-regulatory approach has two bases. The first basis is philosophical: what are the appropriate parameters for the use of self-regulation? The second basis reflects more practical concerns: given the current state of technology, are consumers able to exercise meaningful privacy choices?

A. The Circumstances Supporting Appropriate and Effective Self-Regulation Are Not Present Here

Many consumer advocates question why the Commission continues to steadfastly support self-regulation in the privacy realm. The staff report offers one possible justification, at least in the context of behavioral advertising: self-regulation provides flexibility to adapt to rapidly-changing technology. In theory, flexibility is a valid and worthy goal. But taken alone, it is insufficient to justify a self-regulatory approach. Other conditions must be met if consumers' interests are to be adequately protected. The Commission should not endorse self-regulation under circumstances where industry still has not articulated meaningful standards or agreed to be held accountable.

In practice, industry-driven self-regulation in the privacy arena has been characterized by inactivity. For many years, industry and its primary self-regulatory body took their collective eyes off the ball.[2] A 2006 consumer complaint[3] resuscitated interest by the Commission and, consequently, by the industry. I supported staff's issuance of proposed self-regulatory principles for behavioral advertising in December 2007 because I hoped that staff's carefully-crafted guidance would spark greater industry action. The proposed principles were intended as a floor, not a ceiling.

But now, even after years of discussion, no metric exists to evaluate the effectiveness of self- regulatory efforts. Nor has a workable enforcement mechanism been developed. The recent 2008 Network Advertising Initiative ("NAI") principles, while offering notable improvements over the original 2000 NAI principles, do not approach the level of protections outlined in staff's proposed principles. While the Interactive Advertising Board ("IAB") and affiliated organizations are developing alternative guidelines, they come more than a year after the Commission's Ehavioral Advertising Town Hall and the subsequent issuance of staff's proposed principles.[4]

I would prefer to see all of industry, in consultation with consumer groups and the Commission, working toward a single set of guidelines. Multiple sets of conflicting principles do nothing to move past the *status quo*, and provide an inadequate basis for the Commission to condone a self-regulatory approach.

B. Consumers Lack the Information and Ability to Exercise Privacy Choices

Turning to more practical matters, most consumers do not fully understand the types and amount of information collected by businesses, or why the information may be commercially valuable. Small, discrete disclosures of information may not trouble an individual consumer. But large aggregations of data, based on a lifetime of Internet use, might evoke a different response.

Already, it is possible to assemble a "digital dossier" that captures an individual's interests and habits, runs them through a predictive model, and determines what that person likely will do in the future. Car registrations are data-mined to target potential voters.[5] In the credit industry, behavioral scoring is used to justify lowering the credit limits of "at risk" card users.[6] At the mall, cameras embedded in advertising kiosks identify viewers' faces to deliver target ads.[7] It requires little stretching of the imagination to envision how firms may use data to make decisions that will have tangible effects on consumers' lives. There may be a "tipping point" – a point where consumers become sufficiently concerned about the collection and use of their personal information that they want to exercise greater control over it, but where any such attempt to exercise control becomes futile because so much of their digital life already has been exposed.

Many companies have represented to the Commission that consumers are aware of the "bargain" they have struck: they overwhelmingly choose to disclose information online, in exchange for free content, goods, and services. I am not yet convinced that the average consumer understands and embraces this arrangement. To the extent that industry currently attempts to provide notice and choice to consumers, such efforts are insufficient. Disclosures about information collection, use, and control are not meaningful if they are buried deep within an opaque privacy policy that only a lawyer can understand.

Nor is it meaningful to offer the illusion of consumer choice via inadequate technology. The primary mechanism by which consumers currently can exercise choice online – the opt-out cookie – is fundamentally flawed.[8] Cookies are imperfect tools that serve multiple functions, including some never originally intended.[9] It is a counterintuitive concept to put a cookie on a user's computer to inform websites and servers not to place subsequent cookies on the same computer. It is unrealistic to rely on an assumption that the opt-out cookie will remain on a user's computer indefinitely. Cookies can be and are deleted (intentionally or unintentionally) by individual users, automated software (e.g., anti-virus and anti-spyware tools), or chance. Even assuming that opt-out cookies could be placed permanently on a computer, it is difficult for consumers to find opt-out cookies at all. They are typically buried in the depths of a privacy notice or, worse, on an unrelated third-party website. And when a user successfully locates an opt-out cookie, the cookie frequently does not download properly.[10]

Rather than continuing to embrace this confusing and unreliable tool, industry should accept the reality that opt-out cookies are inadequate to protect consumer privacy. I encourage the technology community, including companies that develop browsers and software utilities, to focus their efforts on developing viable and transparent alternatives.[11]

II. NEXT STEPS

Today's staff report is the culmination of extensive conversations with relevant parties, the Ehavioral Advertising Town Hall, and comments received in response to issuance of the staff's proposed behavioral advertising principles. While I may disagree with some of the conclusions and the overall focus of the report, its release is an extremely positive step.

In an effort to continue this important dialogue, I ask my fellow Commissioners to consider directing staff to complete, by Summer 2010, a report that evaluates the efficacy of self-regulation in the realm of behavioral advertising. This timeline would enable industry to review today's report, seriously re-evaluate existing self-regulatory efforts, and revise them as needed. Meanwhile, Commission staff could continue its discussions with stakeholders, expand inquiry into new areas, conduct further study, and report back in a comprehensive manner. Where necessary, the use of compulsory process (for example, 6(b) orders)[12] is warranted to obtain the information necessary to complete this evaluation.

In the interim, I encourage the Bureau of Consumer Protection to enlist the resources of the Bureau of Economics and the Office of Policy Planning to develop a series of roundtable discussions or workshops on effective privacy notices,[13] and also to conduct a study of consumer attitudes and expectations regarding data collection and use (offline as well as online). Particularly with respect to online activities, a productive discussion of privacy policy is hampered by a lack of reliable empirical data about what consumers want from their online experience, as well as what they understand about the data controls they may exercise while online. Recent surveys of consumer attitudes have begun to scratch the surface of these essential questions. Preliminary findings suggest that consumers are concerned about their online privacy, and are willing to take steps to protect it.[14]

Additionally, it would be helpful if Town Hall participants developed additional scholarship to supplement the Commission's efforts. As the Town Hall demonstrated, expert research from diverse disciplines provides valuable insights and enhances everyone's ability to think through these issues. Expanded scholarship not only will guide completion of the Commission's workshops and follow-up report, but also will help the Commission better react to evolving technology, and will inform Congress as legislative action is considered.

The new Administration should actively engage in the debate surrounding behavioral advertising, as well as privacy more generally. I restate[15] my recommendation for the development of comprehensive federal privacy legislation, which would unify and supplement the current piecemeal approach to privacy in the United States, while also acknowledging the global nature of information flows and the international diversity of approaches to these critical issues.

III. COMPETITION ASPECTS OF PRIVACY

When the Commission approved the Google/DoubleClick merger in December 2007, I wrote a dissenting statement that, among other things, highlighted the nexus between privacy and competition.[16] That nexus only became stronger in 2008, and I continue to believe that the Commission is uniquely positioned to explore it further in 2009 and beyond.

Increasingly, the market is exhibiting competition on non-price dimensions such as privacy,[17] and this trend is likely to continue as consumer awareness grows. In particular, the issues raised by data collection and use will provide ripe opportunities for companies to develop pro-consumer privacy tools, and to market these features to distinguish themselves from competitors. Firms that offer such controls may be vulnerable to criticisms from advertisers, who depend on a constant influx of consumer data for their own products and services to work as intended. In the long run, however, I believe that innovative responses will be embraced by consumers and developers[18] and should be encouraged. Of course, some firms still may choose to condition the use of their products and services on disclosure of information, and each firm is free to strike whatever balance it deems appropriate.[19]

My dissent in Google/DoubleClick also suggested the concept of a market for data itself, separate from markets for the services fueled by the data.[20] The dissent discussed John Battelle's "database of intentions" concept, which he describes as the "aggregate results of every search ever entered, every result list ever tendered, and every path taken as a result."[21] Battelle asserts that no single company controls this collection of information, but posits that a few select companies share control. One of my key concerns in Google/DoubleClick was that the merged entity might move closer to dominating the database of intentions, and that the network effects generated by combining the two firms might have long-term negative consequences for consumers. Over the past two years, a series of mergers has further concentrated the competitive landscape in a putative market for consumer data,[22] and merger analysis should take this trend into account. Today's economic climate likely will accelerate such concentration, potentially on a scale similar to the previous dot-com collapse.

IV. COMMENTS ON STAFF REPORT

As a necessary predicate for condoning a self-regulatory approach, the Commission should more completely identify and explore the increasing range of "free" online services that operate by collecting consumer information. I would like to highlight a few specific areas mentioned in the report.

A. First-Party and Contextual Advertising

Staff concluded, after analysis of comments, that under certain circumstances first-party and contextual advertising should be exempted from the principles. I would prefer that staff solicit additional feedback before recommending that the Commission adopt such a policy. As a general matter, sweeping exemptions are never advisable until empirical due diligence has been performed.[23] My concerns are heightened in this particular instance because the original proposed behavioral advertising principles did not directly address this issue. Meanwhile, the technologies underlying online advertising have been, and still are, changing rapidly. The Web 2.0 and emerging Web 3.0 environments – characterized by embedded applications, new delivery mechanisms (e.g., video), and migration to new platforms (e.g., mobile devices) – complicate existing definitions and demand increased understanding.

B. PII versus Non-PII

Staff distinguished between personally identifiable information and non-personally identifiable information, and appropriately indicated that the line separating the two has blurred. Information can no longer be classified as anonymous or not; at best, it may be placed somewhere along a continuum. Depending on context, information that at first glance appears non-identifiable may, in fact, reveal significant information about an individual.[24] As analytical tools improve, the line between PII and non-PII will continue to waver.[25] I applaud staff for thinking about this distinction and its potential effects.

C. Secondary Use

Secondary use encompasses the combination of online and offline data from multiple public and private sources and from families of online services (e.g., email, search history, mapping software, social networking, mobile, etc.). The Commission knows very little about secondary uses of data. Staff sought comment on this topic and, unfortunately, received minimal response. More information is needed before we can fully understand and analyze the complex linkages among data collectors and users.[26]

D. Emerging Technologies

New technologies signal a need to be more circumspect in developing broadly applicable principles. As processing capacity improves and storage prices decline, companies can and will more easily process and store vast quantities of data. As constraints on timing and space are alleviated, privacy concerns likely will become more germane on new platforms and devices. The emerging areas of deep packet inspection,[27] mobile advertising,[28] electronic personal health records, and cloud computing are a few examples where further inquiry will be needed.

V. CONCLUSION

The issues surrounding online advertising and behavioral targeting are layered and complex, and must be considered in the context of difficult economic, technology, and social issues. They also must be encompassed within a broader privacy framework that prioritizes the interests of consumers. Almost ten years ago, representatives from companies involved in all aspects of the online experience sought to create a self-regulatory scheme. A decade later, we are, in many respects, back at the beginning of this process.

I hope that today's staff report will re-invigorate a serious dialogue between industry and all other stakeholders regarding the future of self-regulation in the realm of behavioral advertising and privacy. Large portions of the industry are joining the discussion for the first time, which is refreshing. Many new participants bring differing opinions on how, if at all, to self-regulate. Consumers, and organizations that advocate on their behalf, are still struggling to be full partners in the conversation; their voices must be heard as well. Self-regulation cannot exist in a vacuum.

As technology develops, industry needs to reconsider old strategies and listen to new perspectives, including international ones.[29] The Commission will play a pivotal role in focusing these efforts.

Last fall, the Commission expressed "cautious optimism" for a self-regulatory approach to online advertising.[30] Today's staff report reflects more optimism, but less caution – even though nothing has happened to justify a change in tone. Much like the "Man Restraining Trade" in the beautiful sculpture outside my office window, I owe it to consumers to encourage the Commission to rein in unbridled optimism and ensure continued caution. For this reason, I share my thoughts today.

END NOTES

[1] Offline sources of data, including public records (e.g., property records) as well as private databases (e.g., credit reporting agency files), also may pose potential risks to maintaining privacy.

[2] See, e.g., Pam Dixon, World Privacy Forum, *THE NETWORK ADVERTISING INITIATIVE: Failing at Consumer Protection and at Self-Regulation* (Nov. 2, 2007), *available at* http://www.worldprivacyforum.org/pdf/WPFNAIreportNov22007fs.pdf; Chris Jay Hoofnagle, *Privacy Self Regulation: A Decade of Disappointment*, EPIC.ORG (Jan. 19, 2005), *available at* http://papers.ssrn.com/sol3/papers.cfm?abstract id=650804.

[3] *See* Complaint and Request for Inquiry and Injunctive Relief Concerning Unfair and Deceptive Online Marketing Practices from Jeffrey Chester, Executive Director, Center for Digital Democracy, and Ed Mierzwinski, Consumer Program Director, U.S. Public Interest Research Group (Nov. 1, 2006), *available at* http://www.democraticmedia.org/news room/press release/FTC online adv2006.

[4] In February 2008 the Interactive Advertising Board released some high-level privacy principles, a*vailable at* http://www.iab.net/iab products and industry services/1421/1443/1464. In January of this year, the American Association of Advertising Agencies, the Association of National Advertisers, the Direct Marketing Association, and the IAB announced efforts to develop self- regulatory guidelines. See Press Release, Interactive Advertising Bureau, *Key Advertising Groups to Develop Privacy Guidelines for Online Behavioral Advertising Data Use and Collection* (Jan. 13, 2009), *available at* http://www.iab.net/insights research/530468/iab news/iab news article/634777.

[5] *See* Todd Wasserman & Wendy Melillo, *Why the Candidates Watch What You Buy*, ADWEEK, Oct. 30, 2006, *available at* http://www.adweek.com/aw/images/pdfs/polifeature.pdf.

[6] The Commission might wish to devote some of its resources to explore these uses of data. *See, e.g.*, Ron Lieber, *A Very Watchful Eye on Credit Card Spending*, NEW YORK TIMES, Jan. 31, 2009, *available at* http://www.nytimes.com/2009/01/31/your-money/credit-and-debit-cards/31money.html;

Chris Cuomo *et al.*, *"GMA" Gets Answers: Some Credit Card Companies Financially Profiling Customers*, ABC NEWS, Jan. 28, 2009, *available at*
   http://abcnews.go.com/GMA/GetsAnswers/story?id=6747461&page=1.

[7] Software manufacturers claim to accurately determine the gender of a viewer 85 to 90 percent of the time. *See* Dinesh Ramde, *When You Watch These Ads, the Ads Check You Out,* FORBES, Jan. 31, 2009, *available at* http://www.forbes.com/feeds/ap/2009/01/31/ap5991271.html.

[8] *See* Peter Swire & Annie I. Antón, *Online Behavioral Advertising: Technical Steps Needed to Ensure Consumer Control,* (Apr. 10, 2008), *available at* http://www.americanprogress.org/issues/2008/04/swire anton testimony.html; Dixon, *supra* note 2, at 14.

[9] For a nice discussion of the history of cookies, *see* David M. Kristol, *HTTP Cookies: Standards, Privacy and Politics,* ACM TRANSACTIONS ON INTERNET TECH., Vol. 1, Issue 2, Nov. 2001, *available at* http://arxiv.org/abs/cs/0105018.

[10] Many consumers have complained of their inability to locate privacy policies and exercise opt-out on their favorite websites. The NAI website maintains an opt-out mechanism for its members, but consumers have had mixed results. *See* http://www.networkadvertising.org/managing/opt out.asp.

[11] Several consumer groups offered the idea of a "Do Not Track" list that would allow consumers to decide whether they want to be tracked on the Internet. I do not endorse the details of the specific proposal submitted to the Commission. I do, however, support a solution that addresses universality, accessibility, persistence and technological neutrality – unifying concepts that one consumer organization used to describe the Do Not Track proposal. *See* Comment to Federal Trade Commission from Ari Schwartz, Deputy Director, Center for Democracy and Technology; Linda Sherry, Director, National Priorities Consumer Action; Mark Cooper, Director of Research, Consumer Federation of America; Lee Tien, Senior Staff Attorney, Electronic Frontier Foundation; Deborah Pierce, Executive Director, Privacy Activism; Daniel Brandt, President, Public Information Research; Robert Ellis Smith, Publisher, Privacy Journal; Beth Givens, Director, Privacy Rights Clearinghouse; Pam Dixon, Executive Director, World Privacy Forum, to FTC, submitted in advance of the FTC Town Hall, *Ehavioral Advertising: Tracking, Targeting, and Technology* (Oct. 31, 2007), *available at* http://www.cdt.org/privacy/20071031consumerprotectionsbehavioral.pdf.

[12] The Commission has issued 6(b) orders in other contexts. *See, e.g., News Release, Federal Trade Commission, FTC Orders Nine Insurers to Submit Information for Study of the Effect of Credit-Based Insurance Scores on Consumers of Homeowners Insurance* (May 19, 2008), *available at* http://www.ftc.gov/opa/2008/12/facta.shtm; FTC For Your Information: *Federal Register Notice Issued on Authorized Generic Drug Study* (April 30, 2007), *available at* http://www.ftc.gov/opa/2007/04/fyi07238.shtm (includes link to Federal Register notice). "Based on a preliminary analysis, approximately 80 brand-name drug manufacturers, several authorized generic drug companies, and 100 generic companies will receive Special Orders." 72 Fed. Reg. 25306 (May 4, 2007).

[13] The staff report praised and encouraged the development of innovative mechanisms for providing notice to consumers. This correctly reflects a common theme at the Town Hall: frustration over the inability of privacy policies to offer consumers meaningful notice of data collection and use. The Commission, industry, and all other stakeholders should continue to investigate the creation of simplified notices to consumers (for example, a short-form chart or standardized layered approach). The Commission has led efforts to develop more effective notices in the financial sector, and these lessons are applicable in the privacy realm as well. See, e.g., Financial Privacy Rule: Interagency Notice Research Project, available at http://www.ftc.gov/privacy/privacyinitiatives/financialruleinrp.html; Interagency Public Workshop: Get Noticed: Effective Financial Privacy Notices (Dec. 4, 2001), available at http://www.ftc.gov/bcp/workshops/glb/index.shtml.

[14] *See, e.g.*, Press Release, Consumers Union, *Consumer Reports Poll: Americans Extremely Concerned About Internet Privacy* (Sept. 25, 2008), *available at* http://www.consumersunion.org/pub/core telecom and utilities/0061 89.html; Press Release, Harris Interactive Inc., *Majority Uncomfortable with Websites Customizing Content Based Visitors Personal Profiles* (Apr. 10, 2008), *available at* http://www.harrisinteractive.com/harris poll/index.asp?PID=894; Press Release, TRUSTe, TRUSTe Report Reveals Consumer Awareness and Attitudes About Behavioral Targeting (Mar. 26, 2008), *available at* http://www.truste.org/about/press release/03 26 08.php.

[15] *See, e.g.*, Dissenting Statement of Commissioner Pamela Jones Harbour, *In the Matter of Google/DoubleClick*, F.T.C. File No. 071-0170 at 11-12 (Dec. 20, 2007), *available at* http://www.ftc.gov/os/caselist/0710170/071220harbour.pdf; Pamela Jones Harbour, Commissioner, Federal Trade Commission, Remarks Before the International Association of Privacy Professionals National Summit entitled, "Respecting the Individual: Privacy Frameworks for the 21st Century," at 15 (Mar. 10, 2006), *available at* http://www.ftc.gov/speeches/harbour/06309iapp.pdf.

[16] *See* Dissenting Statement Of Commissioner Pamela Jones Harbour, *In the Matter of Google/DoubleClick*, supra note 15.

[17] For example, search companies have continually changed their data retention policies, primarily by modifying the amount of time data is retained and applying improved techniques to de-identify such data. While debate exists

over the relative merits of each individual company's technique, such actions are driven by demands from regulators, consumer advocates, and users themselves. *See, e.g.,* Press Release, Yahoo!, *Yahoo! Sets New Industry Privacy Standard with Data Retention Policy* (Dec. 17, 2008), *available at* http://yhoo.client.shareholder.com/press/releasedetail.cfm?ReleaseID=354703; Posting of Peter Fleischer, Global Privacy Counsel; Jane Horvath, Senior Privacy Counsel; and Alma Whitten, Software Engineer to google.blogspot.com (Sept, 8, 2008), *available at* http://googleblog.blogspot.com/2008/09/another-step-to-protect-user-privacy.html; Press Release, Microsoft Corporation, *Microsoft Supports Strong Industry Search Data Anonymisation* Standards (Dec. 8, 2008), available *at* http://www.microsoft.com/emea/presscentre/pressreleases/TrustworthyComputingPR081208.m spx#text.

[18] Open-source solutions most efficiently leverage the creativity and expertise of developers and users. If industry does not create such tools, alternatives will develop that bypass traditional channels.

[19] Some commentators have argued that the online advertising business model cannot function adequately if it is subject to dramatic limitations, including the ability to opt-out. *See, e.g.,* Randall Rothenberg, *War Against the Web,* THE HUFFINGTON POST, April 21, 2008, *available at* http://www.huffingtonpost.com/randy-rothenberg/war-against-the-web b 97811 .html?show co mment id=12691561.

[20] *See* Dissenting Statement Of Commissioner Pamela Jones Harbour, *In the Matter of Google/DoubleClick* at 9, supra note 15. "In the future, the Commission likely will issue Second Requests in other merger investigations that implicate combinations of data as well as potentially overlapping products and services. When those deals arise, the Commission should ensure that the combinations of data are included squarely within the scope of Second Requests. In this case, for example, it might have been possible to define a putative relevant product market comprising data that may be useful to advertisers and publishers who wish to engage in behavioral targeting."

[21] JOHN BATTELLE, THE SEARCH: HOW GOOGLE AND ITS RIVALS REWROTE THE RULES OF BUSINESS AND TRANSFORMED OUR CULTURE, 1-17 (Portfolio, Penguin Group [USA] 2005); Posting of John Battelle to battellemedia.com (Nov. 13, 2003), *available at* http://battellemedia.com/archives/000063.php.

[22] During 2007, Microsoft bought aQuantive, Google acquired DoubleClick, Yahoo obtained complete control over Right Media, and WPP purchased 24/7 Real Media.

[23] *See, e.g.,* Concurring Statement Of Commissioner Pamela Jones Harbour, *Regarding Federal Register Notice Rescinding the FTC's 1966 Guidance Concerning the Cambridge Filter Method* (Nov. 24, 2008) *available at* http://www.ftc.gov/speeches/harbour/081124tobaccopjh.pdf; Pamela Jones Harbour, Commissioner, Federal Trade Commission, *An Open Letter to the Supreme Court of the United States from Commissioner Pamela Jones Harbour* at 18-19 (Feb. 27, 2007), *available at* http://www.ftc.gov/speeches/harbour/070226verticalminimumpricefixing.pdf.

[24] See, e.g., Michael Barbaro & Tom Zeller, Jr., *A Face Is Exposed for AOL Searcher No. 4417749,* N.Y. TIMES, Aug. 9, 2006, *available at* http://www.nytimes.com/2006/08/09/technology/09aol.html?r=1&scp=1&sq=aol%20queries& st=cse&oref=slogin.

[25] The line between sensitive and non-sensitive data may also vacillate, affecting the collection and use of financial and health information and targeting of segments including children.

[26] This inquiry may demand compulsory process.

[27] A series of Congressional hearings last year inquired into the practice and identified a series of potentially significant concerns to personal privacy. *See Broadband Providers and Consumer Privacy: Hearing Before the S. Comm. on Commerce, Sci. & Transp.,* 110th Cong. (2008), *available at* http://commerce.senate.gov/public/index.cfm?FuseAction=Hearings.Hearing&Hearing ID=778 594fe-a1 71 - 4906-a5 85-1 5f1 9e2d602a.

[28] The Commission in January 2009 received a complaint to investigate deceptive and unfair practices in the mobile marketplace. *See* Complaint and Request for Inquiry and Injunctive Relief Concerning Unfair and Deceptive Mobile Marketing Practices from Jeffrey Chester, Executive Director, Center for Digital Democracy, and Ed Mierzwinski, Consumer Program Director, U.S. Public Interest Research Group (Jan. 13, 2009), *available at* http://www.democraticmedia.org/files/FTCmobilecomplaint0109.pdf.

[29] *See, e.g.,* Peter Cullen, Microsoft Corporation, Remarks before the 30th International Conference of Data Protection and Privacy Commissioners, "Moving Information Across Borders: The Need for a Global Accountability Framework" (Oct. 16, 2008), *available at* http://blogs.technet.com/privacyimperative/archive/2008/10/16/moving-information-across-bord ers-the-need-for-a-global-accountability-framework.aspx.

[30] *See Privacy Implications of Online Advertising: Hearing Before the S. Comm. on Commerce, Sci. & Transp.,* 110th Cong. (2008), *available at* http://commerce.senate.gov/public/index.cfm?FuseAction=Hearings.Hearing&Hearing ID=e46b 0d9f-562e-41 a6-b460-a7 14bf3701 71.

In: Electronic Breadcrumbs: Issues in Tracking Consumers   ISBN: 978-1-60741-600-5
Editor: Dmitar N. Kovac   © 2010 Nova Science Publishers, Inc.

Chapter 6

LEIBOWITZ ON SELF-REGULATORY PRINCIPLES FOR ONLINE BEHAVIORAL ADVERTISING

Jon Leibowitz

Behavioral marketing is complicated, and determining its appropriate regulatory framework is complicated, too. The FTC staff's commendable Report continues to examine emerging practices, consider public comments and consumer expectations, and fashion an appropriate and flexible approach for industry self-regulation. As the Report points out, targeted advertising can benefit consumers, subsidize free content, and promote a robust online market. But the concomitant online tracking and data collection, coupled with inadequate notice to consumers about what information is collected and how it is used, raise critical privacy concerns. How companies collect, combine, disclose and dispose of this data has serious ramifications for consumers.

I write separately to ensure that the Report's endorsement of self-regulation is viewed neither as a regulatory retreat by the Agency nor an imprimatur for current business practice. Indeed, despite a spotlight on e-commerce and online behavioral marketing for more than a decade, to date data security has been too lax,[1] privacy policies too incomprehensible,[2] and consumer tools for opting out of targeted advertising too confounding.[3]

Industry needs to do a better job of meaningful, rigorous self-regulation or it will certainly invite legislation by Congress and a more regulatory approach by our Commission.[4] Put simply, this could be the last clear chance to show that self-regulation can – and will – effectively protect consumers' privacy in a dynamic online marketplace. Commissioner Harbour's thoughtful statement underscores this point.

To their credit, many companies and organizations recently have reinvigorated efforts to address privacy issues and have made noteworthy attempts to empower consumers. For example, leading search engines such as Yahoo! are reducing the amount of time they retain consumers' personal data.[5] Microsoft and other developers of Internet browsers are designing better tools for consumers to control the amount of information they share online.[6] Such "competition" to protect consumer privacy is a welcome development. Other industry groups are coming together and attempting to formulate (and reformulate) better practices.[7] In addition to these industry efforts, a coalition of consumer and privacy groups proposed a national "Do Not Track List," which deserves serious consideration.[8] But it is uncertain whether these fledgling efforts will fulfill their promise. More work needs to be done.

The Report's revised principles provide a sound baseline for further self-regulatory efforts. Notably, the Report clarifies that the self-regulatory principles should stretch beyond traditional concepts of personally identifiable information to cover practices involving information that "could reasonably be associated with a particular consumer or computer or other device" (e.g., IP addresses, cookie data). The Report further clarifies that the principles should apply to information collected outside the traditional website context, such as through mobile devices and Internet Service Providers' "deep packet inspection" to mine data from consumers' Internet traffic streams for targeted advertising.[9] These are significant and necessary steps for enhancing consumer privacy.

Beyond the principles, I offer a few observations regarding privacy, transparency, and consumer control both within and outside the behavioral advertising context:

To begin, as the Report should make clear, there is no free pass for those who engage in "first-party" or "contextual" online advertising outside the scope of the principles. That is, *all* companies must implement reasonable security for and limit their retention of sensitive consumer data. *All* companies must keep their promises about how they will use consumers' information. If they fail to do so – whether first party or third party, online or offline – we will go after them.

Moreover, I continue to be troubled about some companies' unfettered collection and use of consumers' "sensitive data" – especially information about children and adolescents. Some data is so sensitive and some populations so vulnerable that extra protection may be warranted.[10] Perhaps more companies (even those outside the scope of the behavioral advertising principles) should allow consumers to "opt in" when it comes to collecting their personal information – particularly when the information is "sensitive," or disclosed to third parties, or collected or shared across various web-based or offline services. Perhaps more companies should simply say "hands off" when it comes to targeting ads to children based on their online activities, as even the Network Advertising Initiative proposed (although it has not mustered the industry support to adopt this principle).[11]

Finally, we need to better understand if and how companies combine online and offline data to build detailed consumer profiles and uses of online tracking data for purposes unrelated to behavioral advertising. The possibility that companies could be selling personally identifiable behavioral data, linking click stream data to personally identifiable information from other sources, or using behavioral data to engage in price discrimination or make credit or insurance decisions are not only unanticipated by most consumers, but also potentially illegal under the FTC Act. Industry's silence in response to FTC staff's request for information about the secondary uses of tracking data is deafening. As a result, the Commission may have to consider using its subpoena authority under Section 6(b) of the FTC Act to compel companies to produce it.

In sum, almost all of us want to see self-regulation succeed in the online arena, but the jury is still out about whether it alone will effectively balance companies' marketing and data collection practices with consumers' privacy interests. A day of reckoning may be fast approaching.

END NOTES

[1] *See* Report at n.8 and accompanying text (citing numerous FTC enforcement actions challenging online and offline companies' failure to provide reasonable security for consumers' sensitive information); *see also* Michael Barbaro & Tom Zeller Jr., *A Face is Exposed for AOL Searcher No. 4417749,* N.Y. Times (Aug. 9, 2006), *available at*
http://query.nytimes.com/gst/fullpage.html?res=9E0CE3DD1F3FF93AA3575BC0A9609C8B63 (describing incident in which AOL released purportedly "anonymous" user search data, but some users were identified based on their queries).

[2] A study of the privacy policies of Fortune 500 companies found that they were essentially incomprehensible for the majority of Internet users. Only one percent of the privacy policies were understandable for those with a high school education or less (like most teens and many consumers). Thirty percent of the privacy policies required a post-graduate education to be fully understood. Felicia Williams, *Internet Privacy Policies: A Composite Index for Measuring Compliance to the Fair Information Principles* at 17 & Table 2 (Sept. 2006), *available at*
http://www.ftc.gov/os/comments/behavioraladvertising/071010feliciawilliams.pdf.

[3] For example, the NAI opt-out tool can be difficult for consumers to find and use and the cookie-based methodology is problematic. Privacy conscious consumers who routinely delete all their cookies or use anti-spyware programs may unintentionally delete the opt-out cookies. *E.g.,* Prof. Peter P. Swire & Prof. Annie I. Anton, *Comments on the FTC Staff Statement, "Online Behavioral Advertising: Moving the Discussion Forward to Possible Self-Regulatory Principles"* (Apr. 10, 2008), *available at*
http://www.ftc.gov/os/comments/behavioraladprinciples/080410swireandanton.pdf.

[4] *See, e.g.,* Saul Hansell, *Senators Weigh Possible Rules for Advertising and Online Privacy,*
http://bits.blogs.nytimes.com/2008/07/09/senators-weigh-possible-rules-for-advertising-andonline-privacy/ (July 9, 2008, 4:15 PM); John Eggerton, *Senate Commerce Committee holds hearing on 'Privacy Implications of Online Advertising,'* Broad. & Cable (July 9, 2008), *available at* http://www.broadcasting cable.com/article/114482-Senate_Commerce_Committee_Examines_Online_ Privacy.php; John Eggerton, *Markey Pushes for Online-Privacy Legislation,* Broad. & Cable (July 9,2008), *available at* http://www.broadcastingcable.com/article/114606-Markey_Pushes_for_Online_Privacy_Legislation.php.

[5] Miguel Helft, *Yahoo Limits Retention of Search Data,* N.Y. Times, Dec. 18, 2008, at B3, *available at*
http://www.nytimes.com/2008/12/18/technology/internet/18yahoo.html?_r=1&fta=y&pagewanted=print.

[6] *See, e.g.,* Ctr. for Democracy & Tech., *Browser Privacy Features: A Work in Progress,* CDT Report 6. (Oct. 2008), *available at* http://www.cdt.org/privacy/20081022_browser_priv.pdf (comparing the privacy features of Mozilla Firefox 3, Microsoft Internet Explorer 8 Beta 2, Google Chrome, and Apple Safari 3).

[7] For example, in January, 2009, the American Association of Advertising Agencies, the Association of National Advertisers, the Direct Marketing Association, the Interactive Advertising Bureau, and the Council of Better Business Bureaus announced that they formed a coalition to develop self-re gulatoryguidelines for behavioral targeting. Mike Shields, *Online to Obama: We Can Police Ourselves; Concern about new regulation prods speedy digital ad industry reaction,* Adweek (Jan.19, 2009),
http://www.adweek.com/aw/content_display/news/digital/e3iecbc44179b8d6b3130e3a2b509fa0f52.

[8] Ctr. for Democracy & Tech., Consumer Action, Consumer Fed'n of Am., The CryptoRights Found., Elec. Frontier Found., Privacy Activism, Public Info. Research, Privacy Journal, Privacy Rights Clearinghouse & World Privacy Forum, *Consumer Rights and Protections in the Behavioral Advertising Sector* at 4 (Oct. 31, 2007), *available at*
http://www.ftc.gov/os/comments/behavioraladvertising/071115jointconsensus.pdf.

[9] Even if deep packet inspection might conceivably be used for pro-consumer network management, protection for consumers in this area is essential. ISPs can in principle use deep packet inspection ("DPI") to scrutinize everything that consumers do on the Internet using the ISP's network. In addition, consumers typically only use one ISP for their broadband access (i.e., the broadband provider has a "terminating access" monopoly to that consumer in telecom terms), and would only be able to avoid deep packet inspection by that ISP by switching to another ISP entirely. Under some frameworks, DPI was conducted so that information from consumers who had opted out was still sent to third parties who were engaged in behavioral targeting. Consumers concerned about this sharing could not avoid it except by switching ISPs.

[10] *See, e.g.,* Am. Acad. of Child & Adolescent Psychiatry, Am. Acad. of Pediatrics, Am. Psychological Ass'n, Benton Found., Campaign for a Commercial Free Childhood, Ctr. for Digital Democracy, Children Now, and Office of Commc'n, United Church of Christ, Comment at 13 (Apr. 11, 2008), *available at*
http://www.ftc.gov/os/comments/behavioraladprinciples/080411childadvocacy.pdf (recommending voluntary industry guidelines that define "sensitive data" to include the online activities of all persons under the age of eighteen and prohibit the collection of sensitive information for behavioral advertising purposes); Consumer Fed'n of Am. & Consumers Union, Comment at 4 (Apr. 11, 2008), *available at*
http://www.ftc.gov/os/comments/behavioraladprinciples/080411cfacu.pdf.

[11] *Compare* NAI, *2008 NAI Principles, Draft: For Public Comment* at 8 (Apr. 10, 2008), *available at* http://www.networkadvertising.org/networks/NAI_Principles_2008_Draft_for_Public.pdf (prohibiting use of information about children under 13 for behavioral advertising) *with* NAI, *2008 NAI Principles, The Network Advertising Initiative's Self-Regulatory Code of Conduct* at 9 (Dec. 16, 2008), *available at* http://www.networkadvertising.org/networks/2008%20NAI%20Principles_final%20for%20Website.pdf (permitting use of information about children under 13 for behavioral targeting with parental consent).

In: Electronic Breadcrumbs: Issues in Tracking Consumers   ISBN: 978-1-60741-600-5
Editor: Dmitar N. Kovac   © 2010 Nova Science Publishers, Inc.

Chapter 7

LEIBOWITZ REMARKS ON BEHAVIORAL ADVERTISING

Jon Leibowitz

Good Morning. I'm Jon Leibowitz, one of the FTC Commissioners.[1]

Let me start by thanking the first panel for setting out some of the issues that this workshop will grapple with. As you can tell, reasonable people approach behavioral marketing from very disparate perspectives. Let me also thank *all* the participants in this Town Hall meeting – you are an impressive group and your presence is a testament to the "white heat" of these issues. And finally, a big thank you to the Commission staff for its hard work in organizing this event.

We all bring different privacy expectations to the table:

- It doesn't especially bother me that Amazon keeps track of the books I've ordered and recommends new ones – that's targeted advertising. And it doesn't bother me that search engines deliver sponsored links based on my queries – that's targeted advertising, too.
- Somewhat more disturbing is the new Internet telephone service that uses voice recognition technology to monitor phone conversations and send targeted ads to the subscriber's computer screen during the call.[2] But this service is **opt in,** the product is new, and there are plenty of competitors offering telephone service with different privacy practices.
- I *am* concerned, though, when my personal information is sold to or shared with third parties – or when my online conduct is monitored across several websites or across different web-based services – especially when there is no effective notice or consent to these practices.
- And it should *really trouble all of us* that seemingly anonymous searching and surfing can be traced back to specific individuals – and that not all information that companies have collected about us is secure from data breaches or release.[3]

Don't take my word for it; just ask AOL customers.

Last year AOL released a cache of supposedly anonymized search records, but some people were identified based on their queries. The results were somewhat embarrassing, and it could have been much worse.

In my view, all this is a real paradox: you can go online from the privacy of your home and enter searches or surf websites that involve your sensitive medical conditions or reveal your deepest secret desires – or even your most trivial curiosities. You can create a personal profile on a social networking site and reserve access only for your close friends and family. It all *seems* so private – but because online marketers are tracking our Internet searching, surfing and socializing, it may be more public than we would like to think.

If you have teenagers, you probably know the texting acronym "pos" – parent over shoulder. Well, when you are surfing the Internet, you never know who is peering over your shoulder. Or how many are watching.

To be fair, most of our web searching and browsing and social networking is free – thanks in large part to advertising – and most consumers seem to like it this way. As the Internet has evolved, the ad targeting has become more sophisticated, arguably bringing greater benefits and a richer Internet experience to consumers.

But the question is: at what cost? Are we paying too high a price in privacy?

In his seminal 1983 book, *The Rise of the Computer State*, David Burnham worried that detailed data bases and the expanding network of computerized record systems were enabling large organizations to track the daily lives of individual citizens.

And that was *then* – the Jurassic Age of big mainframes – when personal computers were just entering the market, the Internet was still an academic/military experiment, and AT&T was *the* commercial telecommunications behemoth.

Of course, some things never change.

And some things never stop changing. Today, the Internet, computerized data collection, and targeted advertising are creeping into nearly every aspect of our social and commercial transactions. Seventy-one percent of U.S. adults use the Internet.[4] Nearly half of all Americans have broadband at home.[5] Internet advertising revenues for the first half of 2007 were nearly $10 billion – a 26 percent increase over the first half of 2006.[6] Make no mistake: the business of online behavioral marketing is big business.

In *An Ideal Husband*, Oscar Wilde wrote, "Private information is practically the source of every large modern fortune."

That's especially true today with online behavioral marketing. Just last week, Microsoft announced a $240 million agreement that gives it exclusive rights to sell worldwide ads targeting Facebook's 50 million members. Google already invested $900 million in MySpace, which announced that it can tailor ads based on what users write on their profile pages.[7] Meanwhile, Google is trying to buy online ad server Double Click, Microsoft acquired aQuantive, and Yahoo purchased Right Media. With all these big- money deals comes big-time pressure to push more – and more effective – ads on the Internet.

Collectively, all this tracking of our online conduct – our searching, web browsing, social networking, emailing, and telephone chatting – all this *massive collection of our private information,* purportedly to serve precision-guided ads, can be disconcerting.

Perhaps it is because we don't quite understand what websites and online advertisers are doing or how they are doing it. Perhaps it is because we feel like we don't really have any meaningful choice or control in the matter – other than to stay offline. Perhaps it is because we don't really know what information websites and others have collected about us. Perhaps it is because we have no assurance that they will protect the security and confidentiality of our sensitive personal or financial information.

When the Commission first confronted these issues nearly a decade ago, there was general acceptance of four core "fair information practice principles": notice, choice, access, and security.[8] Industry efforts to implement these principles resulted in many websites developing and posting so-called privacy policies.

Initially, privacy policies seemed like a good idea. But in practice, they often leave a lot to be desired. In many cases, consumers don't notice, read, or understand the privacy policies. They are often posted inconspicuously via a link at the very bottom of the site's homepage – and filled with fine-print legalese and technotalk.

A recent study submitted as a comment for this Town Hall examined privacy policies of Fortune 500 companies and found that they were essentially incomprehensible for the majority of Internet users.[9] Only one percent of the privacy policies were understandable for those with a high school education or less (like most teens and many consumers). Thirty percent of the privacy policies required a post-graduate education to be fully understood.[10]

The study also found that fewer than 27 percent of the privacy policies allowed consumers to opt-out of collection of data. *None of the privacy policies surveyed allowed consumers to opt in. Not one.*[11] The vast majority of the privacy policies simply state that consumers signify their acceptance to the collection of data by using the website.[12]

Your only choice: take it or leave it.

Even the title "privacy policy" is arguably a misnomer in some cases because many consumers believe that the term "privacy policy" means that the website will protect their privacy and will not share their information.[13]

All the online tracking and targeting is especially worrisome when it involves our children. A whopping 93 percent of American teens age 12 to 17 use the Internet – and 55 percent of these online teens use social networking sites.[14] Internet use by children even younger is growing as well. When Congress passed the Children's Online Privacy Protection Act, it clearly recognized that young children deserve special protections in cyberspace. To that end, COPPA imposes certain requirements before websites may collect personal information from children under the age of 13.

But today, is that really enough?

Based on the focus group I convened over the weekend – that is, my 12-year-old daughter and four of her friends – the online ads that target children aren't always appropriate for their age. They see ads with titles like, "How Long Is Your Next Kiss," and "Touch Me Harder." The FTC's most recent Report on marketing violent entertainment products to children seems to confirm some disturbing practices in this area. For example, sites like MySpace ran banner ads for R-rated movies, even though the site reaches a large number of children under 17.[15]

We enacted COPPA to place a parental buffer between advertisers and our children – but the rise of sophisticated behavioral marketing techniques is eroding this parental control.

So what should the Commission do?

Well, sometimes the answer to problems in cyberspace is clear, like in the case of unfair and deceptive nuisance adware. Put the malefactors under order. Disgorge their profits. Pass a law giving the FTC the authority to impose fines.

For behavioral marketing, the solution is not so certain. Behavioral marketing is complicated. In some cases the privacy tradeoff may make sense. But one thing is clear: the current "don't ask/don't tell" mentality in online tracking and profiling needs to end.

And while I don't presume to have all of the answers, I do have a few thoughts: let's start with providing better information and more meaningful choices for consumers.

- *Standardized Privacy Policies & Shorter Notices.* First, some have called for standardized privacy policies – including former Commissioner Sheila Anthony.[16] And some have called for shorter notices.[17] The take-away from the Commission's recent workshop on "negative option" marketing was that short, conspicuous online notices work better for consumers. All these ideas are worth exploring in the behavioral marketing context.

- *Opt In Rather Than Opt Out.* Another improvement would be for more firms to allow consumers to "opt in" when it comes to collecting information – especially when it comes to sharing consumer information with third parties and sharing it across various web-based services. Consider changing the widespread opt-out default for ad-serving cookies – ***why not make it opt in?*** At this point, I'm not sure that government should mandate an opt-in model but, in my view, it is a far more preferable result.

- *More Competition to Protect Privacy.* There is some good news here too. With all the attention on online data collection these past few months, the leading search engineshave been tripping over each other to have the strongest privacy protections. For example, Google announced in March that it would anonymize its server logs after 1 8 to 24 months — so that search histories can no longer be identified with individual users.[18] A few months later, Microsoft announced it would make search queries anonymous after 18 months. Within days, Yahoo announced its plans to make users' search history anonymous within 13 months. Ask.com announced that it will offer a new feature – AskEraser – that will allow users to erase their search histories at will.

  Let's hope we see more competition to give consumers more understandable information, more choice, and more control. Indeed, today's Town Hall already inspired a number of creative new approaches, including a "Do Not Track" list. We do need to take a closer look at this, of course, but it's the kind of idea we were hoping our Town Hall would spur.

- *Enforcement When Necessary.* It's always great when the competitive marketplace can solve these types of problems, although my sense here is that the market alone may not be able to resolve all the issues inherent in behavioral marketing. So at the Commission, we will listen closely to what online marketers are doing, how they are doing it, and who they are doing it to – and we will think about how to ensure all the wonders of the Internet while respecting consumers' sense of privacy.

We will also continue to monitor industry behavior – and if we see problematic practices, the Commission won't hesitate to take action to protect consumers.

Thank you.

END NOTES

[1] The views expressed here are my own and do not necessarily represent the views of the Federal Trade Commission or of any other Commissioner.

[2] Louise Story, *Company Will Monitor Phone Calls to Tailor Ads*, N.Y. Times, Sept. 24, 2007 (Business Section). Pudding Media, a Silicon Valley start-up, asks users for their sex, age range, native language and ZIP code when they sign up for the service so it can better target the ads. Pudding Media is also working on a way to email the ad to the person on the other end of the line or display it on that person's cellphone screen. *Id.*

[3] Over the past few years, the FTC has initiated more than a dozen enforcement actions against online and brick-and-mortar companies for failure to provide adequate security for sensitive consumer data.

[4] Pew Internet & American Life Project, *Demographics of Internet Users* (last updated June 15, 2007), available at http://www.pewinternet.org/trends/User_Demo_6.15.07.htm.

[5] John B. Horrigan & Aaron Smith, Pew Internet & American Life Project, *Home Broadband Adoption 2007* (June 2007) (Data Memo), available at http://www.pewinternet.org/pdfs/PIP_Broadband%202007.pdf

[6] Interactive Advertising Bureau, Inc., press release, *Internet Advertising Revenues Continue to Soar, Reach Nearly $10 Billion in First Half of '07; Historic Second Quarter Revenues Exceed $5 Billion for First Time* (Oct. 4, 2007).

[7] Brad Stone, *MySpace Mining Members' Data to Tailor Ads Expressly for Them,* N.Y. Times, Sept. 18, 2007, at C1.

[8] FTC, *Privacy Online: A Report to Congress* (1998). The Commission also identified **enforcement** – the use of a reliable mechanism to identify and impose sanctions for noncompliance with these fair information practices – as a critical ingredient in any governmental or self-regulatory program to ensure privacy online. *Id.*

[9] Felicia Williams, *Internet Privacy Policies: A Composite Index for Measuring Compliance to the Fair Information Principles* at 17 & Table 2 (Sept. 2006) (submitted as a public comment to the FTC on Oct. 10, 2007).

[10] *Id.*

[11] *Id.* at 26. Fifteen percent of the privacy policies stated the firm would obtain permission before sharing or selling collected data.

[12] *Id.* at 27.

[13] In fact, some privacy experts have argued that the "privacy policy" label is deceptive unless the website obtains affirmative consent from consumers before sharing their personal information. Joseph Turow, Chris Jay Hoofnagle, Deirdre K. Mulligan, Nathaniel Good & Jens Grossklags, *The FTC and Consumer Privacy In the Coming Decade,* at 18-19 (Nov. 8, 2006), available at http://www.ftc.gov/bcp/workshops/techade/pdfs/Turow-and-Hoofnagle1.pdf.

[14] Amanda Lenhart, Pew Internet & American Life Project, *A Timeline of Teens and Technology,* presented at APA Policy and Advocacy in the Schools Meeting at 4, 21 (Aug. 16, 2007), available at http://www.pewinternet.org/ppt/APA%20School%20Psychologists_Teens%20and%20Tech_08_1_607revsflnn.ppt.

[15] FTC, *Marketing Violent Entertainment to Children: A Fifth Follow-up Review of Industry Practices in the Motion Picture, Music Recording & Electronic Game Industries* at 6, 11 (Apr. 2007), available at http://www.ftc.gov/reports/violence/070412MarketingViolentEChildren.pdf.

[16] Sheila F. Anthony, *The Case for Standardization of Privacy Policy Formats*, available at www.ftc.gov/speeches/anthony/standardppf.shtm; *see also* Williams, *supra* note 9, at 56.

[17] E.g., Turow et al., *supra* note 13, at 12-13.

[18] The Official Google Blog, *Taking Steps to Further Improve Our Privacy Practices* (Mar. 14, 2007), available at http://googleblog.blogspot.com/2007/03/taking-steps-to-further-improve-our.html.

In: Electronic Breadcrumbs: Issues in Tracking Consumers   ISBN: 978-1-60741-600-5
Editor: Dmitar N. Kovac   © 2010 Nova Science Publishers, Inc.

Chapter 8

POSSIBLE SELF-REGULATORY PRINCIPLES REPORT

Federal Trade Commission

BACKGROUND

Since the 1990's, the Federal Trade Commission and its staff have engaged in investigations, law enforcement, studies, and other policy developments to protect consumer privacy in the online environment. The FTC's work in this area is part of its broader, longstanding program to address privacy concerns in both the online and offline markets. In the online environment, innovation in consumer services and products – photo-sharing, blogging, the creation of virtual communities, and robust search, to name but a few – has significantly enhanced consumers' use of the Web. The FTC's privacy program seeks to balance support for such innovation with the need to protect against harms to consumers' privacy.

In November 2006, the FTC held three days of public hearings, "Protecting Consumers in the Next Tech-ade," to examine anticipated technological developments that could raise consumer protection policy issues over the next decade.[1] Online behavioral advertising – the practice of tracking consumers' activities online to target advertising – received considerable attention at the hearings. In the year since Tech-ade, the FTC staff has continued to examine online behavioral advertising. Among other things, to explore issues raised by consumer advocates and others,[2] the staff has held many dozens of meetings with consumer representatives, industry members, academics, technologists, and others to gain a better understanding of current and anticipated online advertising models.[3]

Most recently, on November 1 and 2, 2007, building on the Tech-ade hearings, the FTC hosted a Town Hall entitled "Ehavioral Advertising: Tracking, Targeting, and Technology." The event brought together interested parties to discuss the privacy issues raised by online behavioral advertising. The FTC selected the Town Hall format to convey the importance of launching a continuing dialogue and debate about the key issues. To prepare for the event and supplement the record, the FTC sought public comment on the issues.[4]

In examining the practices, the FTC has applied a broad definition of online "behavioral advertising," one meant to encompass the various tracking activities engaged in by diverse companies across the Web. Thus, for purposes of this discussion, online "behavioral advertising" means the tracking of a consumer's activities online – including the searches the consumer has conducted, the web pages visited, and the content viewed – in order to deliver advertising targeted to the individual consumer's interests.

In advance of the Town Hall, the FTC identified certain key questions related to behavioral advertising for discussion by participants. These questions included what consumers know about the practice, whether consumer disclosures in this area are necessary and effective, how data collected for behavioral advertising is used and protected, and what standards do or should govern the practice as we move into the future. In addition, a number of industry groups, consumer advocates, and individual companies developed proposals and recommendations regarding the privacy issues raised by behavioral advertising. These include a Do Not Track proposal, submitted by a coalition of consumer groups; several reports discussing and critiquing the current practices and self-regulatory initiatives in this area; and a variety of industry initiatives to address the privacy issues raised.[5] From all of these discussions and activities, certain core issues and concerns have emerged.

First, while behavioral advertising provides benefits to consumers in the form of free web content and personalized ads that many consumers value, the practice itself is largely invisible and unknown to consumers. The benefits include, for example, access to newspapers and information from around the world, provided free because it is subsidized by online advertising; tailored ads that facilitate comparison shopping for the specific products that consumers want; and, potentially, a reduction in ads that are irrelevant to consumers' interests and that may therefore be unwelcome. Although many consumers value these benefits, few appear to understand the role that data collection plays in providing them. Second, business and consumer groups alike cherish the values of transparency and consumer autonomy, and view them as critical to the development and maintenance of consumer trust in the online marketplace. Third, regardless of whether one views behavioral advertising as beneficial, benign, or harmful, there are reasonable concerns about the possibility of consumer data collected for this purpose falling into the wrong hands or being used for unanticipated purposes.

Given the importance of these issues, FTC staff has proposed some governing principles for behavioral advertising and now seeks comment on the principles from interested parties. The principles are intended to address the unique concerns expressed about behavioral advertising and thus are limited to these practices. The purpose of this proposal is to encourage more meaningful and enforceable self-regulation to address the privacy concerns raised with respect to behavioral advertising. In developing the principles, FTC staff was mindful of the need to maintain vigorous competition in online advertising as well as the importance of accommodating the wide variety of business models that exist in this area. The staff intentionally drafted the principles in general terms to encourage comment and discussion by all interested parties and further development of the principles based on the comments.

PROPOSED PRINCIPLES

1. Transparency and Consumer Control

Issue

- Interested parties cite the need for greater transparency and consumer control to address the privacy issues raised by behavioral advertising. Many criticize existing disclosures as difficult to understand, inaccessible, and overly technical and long. They also stated that, with clearer disclosures, consumers can make more informed decisions about whether or not they want personalized advertising or, alternatively, whether they would prefer not to do business at particular websites. At the same time, panelists recognized that many consumers do not read privacy policies and raised a genuine question about consumers' willingness and ability to read and understand long disclosures about privacy.

Proposed Principle

- Every website where data is collected for behavioral advertising should provide a clear, concise, consumer-friendly, and prominent statement that (1) data about consumers' activities online is being collected at the site for use in providing advertising about products and services tailored to individual consumers' interests, and (2) consumers can choose whether or not to have their information collected for such purpose.[6] The website should also provide consumers with a clear, easy-to-use, and accessible method for exercising this option.

2. Reasonable Security, and Limited Data Retention, for Consumer Data

Issue

- Stakeholders express concern that data collected for behavioral advertising may not be adequately secured and could find its way into the hands of criminals or other wrongdoers. They stated that appropriate security measures therefore are needed to minimize the risk of unauthorized access. On the other hand, some of the data that is collected may not be traceable to any individual consumer or computer, and therefore may do little harm if obtained by a wrongdoer.

Proposed Principle

- Any company that collects and/or stores consumer data for behavioral advertising should provide reasonable security for that data. Consistent with the data security laws and the FTC's data security enforcement actions, such protections should be based on the sensitivity of the data, the nature of a company's business operations, the types of risks a company faces, and the reasonable protections available to a company.[7]

Issue

- Stakeholders express concern about the length of time that companies are retaining consumer data collected for behavioral advertising. The longer that data is stored in company databases, the greater the risks to the data. On the other hand, there may be good reasons for retaining data, such as maintaining and improving customer service or tracking criminal activities on the website.

Proposed Principle

- Companies should retain data only as long as is necessary to fulfill a legitimate business or law enforcement need.[8] FTC staff commends recent efforts by some industry members to reduce the time period for which they are retaining data. However, FTC staff seeks comment on whether companies can and should reduce their retention periods further.

3. Affirmative Express Consent for Material Changes to Existing Privacy Promises

Issue

- Industry and consumer representatives alike state that the privacy policy – a set of commitments about how information is handled – not only is an important tool for providing information to consumers, but also serves to promote accountability among businesses. It is widely recognized, however, that businesses may have a legitimate need to change their privacy policies from time to time.

Proposed Principle

- As the FTC has made clear in its enforcement and outreach efforts, a company must keep any promises that it makes with respect to how it will handle or protect consumer data, even if it decides to change its policies at a later date.[9] Therefore, before a company can use data in a manner materially different from promises the company made when it collected the data, it should obtain affirmative express consent from affected consumers. This principle would apply in a corporate merger situation to the extent that the merger creates material changes in the way the companies collect, use, and share data.

4. Affirmative Express Consent to (or Prohibition Against) Using Sensitive Data for Behavioral Advertising

Issue

- Stakeholders express concern about the use of sensitive data (for example, information about health conditions, sexual orientation, or children's activities online) to target advertising, particularly when the data can be traced back to a particular individual. They state that consumers may not welcome such advertising even if the information is not personally identifiable; they may view it as invasive or, in a household where multiple users access one computer, it may reveal confidential information about an individual to other members.[10] At the same time, panelists recognized that some consumers may view personalized advertising and content as a desirable source of education about their medical conditions or personal concerns.

Proposed Principle

- Companies should only collect sensitive data for behavioral advertising if they obtain affirmative express consent from the consumer to receive such advertising. FTC staff seeks specific input on (1) what classes of information should be considered sensitive, and (2) whether using sensitive data for behavioral targeting should not be permitted, rather than subject to consumer choice.

5. Call for Additional Information: Using Tracking Data for Purposes Other Than Behavioral Advertising

Issue

- Interested parties express concern that consumer tracking data collected and stored for behavioral advertising could be used for other potentially harmful purposes. To the extent that the collection of data for behavioral advertising is invisible to consumers, such secondary uses of the data may be especially so. Further, such uses may be contrary to consumers' reasonable expectations as they navigate the web. On the other hand, there may be secondary uses of data that provide benefits to consumers. For example, companies may use data to develop new products that appeal to their customer base or to enhance existing products and services that they offer.

Additional Information Needed

- FTC staff seeks additional information about the potential uses of tracking data beyond behavioral advertising and, in particular: (1) which secondary uses raise concerns, (2) whether companies are in fact using data for these secondary purposes, (3) whether the concerns about secondary uses are limited to the use of personally identifiable data or also extend to non-personally identifiable data, and (4) whether secondary uses, if they occur, merit some form of heightened protection.

NEXT STEPS: REQUEST FOR COMMENT

- FTC staff seeks comment and discussion on the appropriateness and feasibility of these principles for both consumers and businesses, including the costs and benefits of offering choice for behavioral advertising. FTC staff recognizes that, to the extent that behavioral advertising supports free web content and other benefits, the choice by consumers not to participate could reduce the availability of such benefits. FTC staff welcomes comment on these and other issues raised by the proposed principles.
- Comments should be sent by Friday, February 22, 2008, to: Secretary, Federal Trade Commission, Room H-135 (Annex N), 600 Pennsylvania Avenue, N.W., Washington, D.C. 20580, or BehavioralMarketingPrinciples@ftc.gov. The comments will be posted on the FTC's behavioral advertising web page for possible use in the development of self- regulatory programs.[11]

These principles represent FTC staff's efforts to identify common themes and possible norms to govern behavioral advertising. They draw upon the issues and concerns raised at the Town Hall, the complaints and proposals submitted beforehand and afterwards, and the research and many dozens of interviews that FTC staff conducted in preparation for the event. In proposing these principles, FTC staff notes that it in no way intends to foreclose (1) other ideas suggested and being considered to address behavioral advertising, or (2) use of the FTC's enforcement or regulatory authority, including its authority to challenge unfair or deceptive practices under Section 5 of the FTC Act.

END NOTES

[1] *See* http://www.ftc.gov/bcp/workshops/techade/index.html.
[2] *See,* e.g., Center for Digital Democracy and U.S. Public Interest Research Group Complaint and Request for Inquiry and Injunctive Relief Concerning Unfair and Deceptive Online Marketing Practices (Nov. 1, 2006), http://www.democraticmedia.org/files/pdf/FTCadprivacy.pdf.
[3] The FTC examined similar issues in 2000, when it held a workshop (jointly with the Department of Commerce) to examine online profiling, an early form of behavioral advertising that has evolved considerably since that time. *See* http://www.ftc.gov/opa/1999/09/profiling.shtm.
[4] *See* http://www.ftc.gov/os/comments/behavioraladvertising/index.shtm.
[5] *See, e.g.,* Center for Democracy and Technology et al., *Consumer Rights and Protections in the Behavioral Advertising Sector* (Do Not Track proposal) (Oct. 31, 2007), http://www.cdt.org/press/20071031press.php; World Privacy Forum, *The Network Advertising Initiative: Failing at Consumer Protection and at Self-Regulation* (Nov. 2, 2007), http://www.worldprivacyforum.org; Press Release, AOL, *AOL Launches Innovative Privacy Education Program for Behaviorally Targeted Advertising* (Oct. 31, 2007), http://press.aol.com/article display.cfm?article id= 1327.
[6] Many FTC laws, rules, and policies require clear and conspicuous disclosures to prevent deception and possible consumer harm. For more information and guidance on the use of such disclosures in online advertising, see *Dot Com Disclosures, Information About Online Advertising,* http://www.ftc.gov/bcp/conline/pubs/buspubs /dotcom/index.shtml (May 2000).
[7] For more information on the FTC's data security program and data security enforcement actions, *see* http://www.ftc.gov/privacy/privacyinitiatives/promises enf.html.

[8] FTC enforcement actions and educational materials have highlighted the risk of storing consumer data longer than it is reasonably needed. *See, e.g.,* DSW Inc., Docket No. C-4157 (Dec. 1, 2005), http://www.ftc.gov/opa/2005/12/dsw.shtm; *Protecting Personal Information: A Guide for Business,* http://www.ftc.gov/infosecurity.

[9] *See, e.g, Gateway Learning Corp.,* Docket No. C-4120 (Sept. 10, 2004),http://www.ftc.gov/opa/2004/07/gateway.shtm (company made material changes to its privacy policy and allegedly applied such changes to data collected under the old policy; opt-in required for future such changes).

[10] At least one self-regulatory program currently prohibits the use of sensitive personally identifiable data and has stated its intention to expand its guidance on the issue. *See* NAI Principles, http://www.networkadvertising.org/networks/principles.asp.

[11] *See* http://www.ftc.gov/bcp/workshops/ehavioral/index.shtml.

In: Electronic Breadcrumbs: Issues in Tracking Consumers   ISBN: 978-1-60741-600-5
Editor: Dmitar N. Kovac   © 2010 Nova Science Publishers, Inc.

Chapter 9

PRIVACY & ONLINE ADVERTISING HEARING- CREWS TESTIMONY

Wayne Crews

The Competitive Enterprise Institute (CEI) is a non-profit public policy research foundation dedicated to individual liberty, limited government, and markets. We appreciate the opportunity to discuss policy issues surrounding online advertising.

Privacy dilemmas are inevitable on the frontiers of an evolving information era, but CEI maintains that competitive approaches to online privacy and security will be more nimble and effective than rigid political mandates at safeguarding and enhancing consumer well¬being, facilitating commerce and wealth creation, and even contributing to the rise of the anonymous approaches to commerce we'd like to see.

THE RISE OF PRIVACY AND CYBERSECURITY AS PUBLIC POLICY ISSUES

The marvelous thing about the Internet is that one can contact and learn about anyone and anything. The downside is that the reverse is often true. The digital information age— against a backdrop of rising globalization—offers consumers unprecedented access to news, information, democratized credit and much more. Anyone may collect and share information on any subject, corporation, government—or in many cases, other individuals.

Companies from retailers to search engines to software makers all collect consumer data—enough to fill vast server warehouses. Of course, Web sites have long collected and marketed information about visitors. The latest twist is that behavioral marketing firms "watch" our clickstreams to develop profiles or inform categories to better target future advertisements. Unarguably beneficial, the process stokes privacy concerns. Fears abound over the data's security; is any of it personally identifiable? If not, can it conceivably become so? Will personal information fall into the wrong hands? Will it become public? And if a breach occurs, who's punished? While Capitol Hill, beltway regulators or state governments are seen often as the first line of defense, regulatory and legislative proposals, much like the anti-spam law, can fall short of success. Aspirations can exceed actual legislative capability.

Clearly, as a technological phenomenon, mass transactional data tracking and collection are here to stay; and with nascent technologies like biometrics that could fully authenticate users on the horizon, the debates will only intensify.

Along with behavioral advertising, new data-mining and biometrics technologies promise higher levels of convenience and, ultimately, more secure commerce online. Beyond the "merely" commercial, the technologies also hint at greater physical security in the "homeland" and in our workplaces via authentication.

On the upside, online advertising enables today's familiar subscription-fee-free cornucopia of news and information, and the free soapbox enjoyed by bloggers worldwide. It's become cliché to note the commercialized Internet is one of the most important wealth-creating sectors and democratizing technologies ever known. Benefits to society range from frictionless e-commerce, to the democratization of privileges once available only to the rich, to a megaphone for all.

This online bounty has also brought real and imagined privacy vulnerabilities to the forefront, ranging from personal identity theft to exposure of private thoughts and behavior online. Once, we could contend merely with nuisances like spam, cookie-collection practices and the occasional spyware eruption. Since policies today are being formulated in the context of a post-Sept. 11 world, cybersecurity and computerized infrastructure access and security join routine privacy as prime policy issues. Adding complexity is the noted emergence of biometric technologies and highly engineered data mining that could alter the future of behavioral marketing. Thus we must contend not just with run of the mill commercial aspects of privacy policies, but with national security themes and what some consider a dangerous new surveillance state.

The question is, do newfangled data collection techniques threaten fundamental expectations of privacy, and in the case of government data collection, even liberty itself?

What principles distinguish between proper and improper uses of personal information, and what policies maximize beneficial e-commerce and consumer welfare? Business use of behavioral advertising can be irritating, but many have made peace with advertisers' using personal information. One-size-fits-all privacy mandates will undermine e- commerce and the consumer benefits we take for granted. Sweeping regulations can especially harm start-ups that lack the vast data repositories already amassed by their larger competitors. Our policies should be consistent with tomorrow's entrepreneurs (and consumers) starting businesses of their own to compete with the giants of today.

Thus, privacy policies need to be filtered through the lens of the entire society's needs. We must consider the impact on (1) consumers (2) e-commerce and commerce generally (3) broader security, cybersecurity, homeland security and critical infrastructure issues, and finally (3) citizen's 4th amendment protections.

Happily the prospect of billions in economic losses from mistakes incentivize the market's efforts to please consumers and safeguard information and networks.

WEB FUNCTIONALITY CONTINUES TO UNFOLD

The recent emergence of behavioral advertising reinforces the easily forgotten reality that there's more to the Internet than the "Web" at any given juncture; it's only 2008, and there are doubtless more commercially valuable avenues for marketing yet to be discovered in the decades ahead. Targeted, behavioral and contextual advertising make use of heretofore unexploited underlying capabilities of the Internet, possibilities that hadn't yet occurred to anyone else, just as the original banner ad trailblazers first did years ago—and, yes, just as the spammers did.

AT THE OUTSET: POLICY MUST DISTINGUISH BETWEEN PUBLIC AND PRIVATE DATA

Parameters are needed to talk coherently about the treatment of individual's data. Information acquired through the commercial process must be kept separate from that extracted through government mandates. Similarly, private companies generally should not have access to information that government has forced individuals to relinquish (what one might call the "Social Security" problem). Private industry should generate its own marketing-related information (whether "personally identifiable" or not), for purposes limited by consumer acceptance or rejection, rather than piggyback on government IDs. Confidentiality is a value, and should be a competitive feature.

Conversely, for any debate over behavioral advertising to make sense, corporate America needs to be able to make credible privacy assurances to the public. People need to know that the data they relinquish is *confined to an agreed-upon business, transactional or record-keeping purpose*, not incorporated in a government database. If regulators end up routinely requiring banks, airlines, hotels, search engines, software companies, Internet service providers and other businesses to hand over private information (in potentially vulnerable formats), *they will not only undermine evolving commercial privacy standards, including behavioral, but make them impossible,* Government's own information security practices is the elephant in the room when it comes to contemplating e-commerce sector's stance with respect to privacy. It's all too easy to give the online marketing industries a black eye and risk turning society against the technologies, and ensure regulation and politicization. Private data and public data policies are potentially on a collision course, but need not be.

The benefits that personalization brings, like easier, faster shopping experiences, are in their infancy. Sensible data collection improves search, communication, ability to innovate, U.S. competitiveness—all the things we associate with a well-functioning economy and evolution in healthy consumer convenience and power.

PRIVACY LEGISLATION: PREMATURE AND OVERLY COMPLEX

In contemplating government's role with respect to privacy and information security, we must recognize the realities of differing user preferences that preclude one-size-fits-all privacy and security policy. Online, there are exhibitionists and hermits. Some hide behind the equivalent of gated communities; others parade less-than-fully clothed before personal webcams.

Note how we work ourselves up into a lather: policymakers were concerned about privacy when ads were *untargeted and irrelevant* (spam); now a solution—behavioral and contextual marketing—makes ads relevant, and we're hand-wringing about privacy there too. Incidentally, spam was framed as a privacy problem, but in reality the spammer didn't typically know who you were. Likewise, a positive early development in behavioral advertising is that personally identifiable information is not always crucial to the marketer (although sensible uses of personally identifiable information should not be thwarted). Too often, the complaint seems to be *commerce as such*. For example, the Federal Communications Commission recently decided to investigate the "problem" with embedded ads in TV programming.[1]

Policy should recognize privacy is not a single "thing" for government to protect; it is a *relationship* expressed in countless ways. That relationship is best facilitated by emergent standards and contracts—like the Network Advertising Initiative's behavioral advertising principles[2] that predate the Federal Trade Commission's late 2007 principles[3]—and in emergent market institutions like identity theft insurance. Apart from varied privacy preferences, any legislative effort to regulate behavioral advertising gets exceedingly complex:

- If online privacy is regulated, what about offline?
- Should behavioral advertising be opt-in or opt-out? (Why and when?)
- Who defines which advertising is "behavioral"?
- What is the legislative line between sensitive, and non-sensitive, personally identifiable information?
- Should the federal government pre-empt state privacy laws?
- Will the privacy rules apply to government?
- Will government abstain from accessing or seizing private databases?
- What about *non-commercial* information collection? (Will the rules apply to bloggers? Or to Facebook activism?)
- What about consumer harm caused by privacy legislation (Given that in the business world, most transactions occur between strangers.)
- What of practical problems of written privacy notices? (Especially given the declining importance of the desktop, the emergent web-like multi-sourced nature of web-pages themselves, smaller wireless-device screens, and the "thing-tothing" Net that bypasses humans altogether.)
- Could disclosure and reporting mandates create a burdensome paperwork requirements detrimental to small businesses? (A privacy "Sarbanes-Oxley")
- What about the right to remain anonymous; Behavioral marketing appears to be on course to facilitate anonymous transactions; will government permit it? How should tolerance of anonymity differ in commercial and political contexts?

The Internet was designed as an open, non-secure network of semi-trusted users. Thus one interpretation of the nature of the cyberspace is that advertisers may legitimately assemble information on what is clearly a very public network that never offered any real pretense of security. But even assuming one's online pursuits can be tracked, privacy tools nonetheless are emerging, and vendors must be held to commitments. Given legislations complications and the Internet's inherent security limitations, a rational policy prescription should be more limited: *Hold the private sector accountable to the contracts and guarantees it makes, and target identity theft and the criminals who perpetrate it.* If legislation merely does such things as send bad actors overseas, we merely create regulatory hassles for mainstream companies that already follow "best practices," and for small businesses trying to make a go of legitimate e-commerce.

As in spam debate, we face less a legislative problem than a technological one. It's true that social norms and expectations have yet to gel—but those are as varied as individuals are.

MARKETING IS NOT TODAY'S DOMINANT INFORMATION COLLECTION THREAT

The emphasis on online privacy legislation could represent a case of misdirected energy. The most important information collection issues of the day are not related to mere *marketing*; rather, criminals who ignore already existing laws and will ignore any new law, are the ones creating mischief online, abusing the trust we have or would like to have in vendors. Meanwhile, *government* surveillance and information collection threaten liberties and *genuine* privacy—and one cannot "opt out." (One is reminded of the Peanuts cartoon of Snoopy sitting on his doghouse typing, "Dear IRS... Please remove my name from your mailing list."[4])

The stringent opt-in standard some seek in the behavioral marketing debate is not one government tolerates for itself. The post-Sept. 11 push for compulsory national ID cards, warrant-less wiretapping and escalating data retention mandates signify a government more inclined toward infringing privacy than acting as guarantor.

The rise of the information society amid a "homeland security culture" is an unfortunate coincidence, an accident, but one that colors debates over marketing that would otherwise be more pedestrian. The tendency of government to interfere with privacy practices is undeniable: Total Information Awareness, CAPPSII, and a national ID are examples of expansive government efforts that would undermine the private sector's freedom and ability to make privacy assurances in the first place.

Worse, when technology companies contract with government for information services, they would very likely request immunity for data breaches by extension of the Homeland Security Act that grants similar immunities for failed security technologies; so if markets are tempted to repudiate self-regulation and liability for privacy standards, government oversight becomes the default. The "homeland security culture" can undermine the market" s entrepreneurial tendency to resolve the dilemmas created by information sharing.

Deliberations over privacy and online security should start with the recognition that government often doesn't need to protect our privacy, it needs to *allow it in the first place*. Business, whatever missteps happen in behavioral marketing, can deliver. As it stands, nobody's in any position to make ironclad security guarantees given the open nature of the Internet, but the Web is a giant research experiment, and techniques will improve. In fact, as behavioral tracking does begin to employ personally identifiable information, security benefits in ways that people will approve. The Net's governmental origins have left privacy expectations and rights somewhat ill-defined in many online contexts. But we all at times need to identify ourselves and validate the identity of others.

CONSUMERS ARE NOT POWERLESS: THE REDUNDANCY OF FTC STANDARDS

In spite the Net's vulnerabilities, consider how legislation pales compared to unforgiving competitive discipline. An old joke holds that if McDonald's was giving away free Big Macs in exchange for a DNA sample, there would be lines around the block. But consumers do care; and thanks to the Internet itself, they are hardly a voiceless mass.

Every few weeks brings new headlines about government data-handling debacles, such as governmental bodies forcing employees to carry Social Security cards on their person, or the IRS requirement that payment checks feature the SSN.[5] Confidence isnt inspired when the government's information practices lag the private sector's.

Contrast that with what happens to a careless private firm. Google and its recent mergers and alliances put it under scrutiny, but why? (Recall it was Google that in 2006 refused to hand over user search data to the Justice Department; and Google's YouTube division is now being forced by the a New York district court to hand over user viewing records in a video piracy case. Google not unsurprisingly objects.) But imagine if Google suffered a serious data breach. Consumers would lose trust, and Google could lose millions. Examples abound of consumer sovereignty, such as the backlach against Facebook's Beacon that cross-posted users shopping activities on friend's sites,[6] and Comcast's de-prioritizing of certain file sharing transfers. Today's Internet users are empowered to educate the world about business practices of which they disapprove. The blogosphere transforms Web users into citizen-journalists, harnessing the power of collective discontent. The result: *Companies routinely change and improve their information handling procedures without law.*

Policies proposed in the name of what consumers want or should want are all too common, as if the ideas hadn't occurred to anyone in the competitive marketplace already, or as if the markets hadn't been forced to adapt already, or as if issues weren't more complicated than the regulators suppose.

For example, the November 2007 FTC proposal on behavioral advertising offers pedestrian principles that have long been in play:[7] Paraphrasing, sites should declare that info is being collected and used and users can opt out; data should be "reasonably secured," and retained only as long as necessary; affirmative consent be given for privacy policy changes; and sensitive information should not be collected at all, or only with affirmative opt-in.

Where do the real incentives lie? Industry looks at what consumers actually want; industry often already embraces opt-in for sensitive information categories, even when the information is not personally identifiable. And if not so empowered by a benevolent vendor, users can already exercise the choice allegedly sought in privacy legislation; they can simply choose not to disclose sensitive information on certain sites, or employ privacy software that can thwart unwanted data collection and allow anonymous Web browsing. "Anonymizer" is still out there for encrypted, anonymous surfing. People can switch to "Scroogle" to disguise their Google searches; A consumer can use a dedicated tool to nullify his identity prior to a sensitive search like "HIV"; TrackMeNot can send out "white noise" search queries to disguise the real one. No mandates for choice are needed; choice is the default, whether vendors prefer it or not.

In terms of competitive enterprise, the divisiveness of a debate like behavioral marketing implies that *real market opportunities exist in providing online anonymity*. After all, despite all the hand-wringing over personally identifiable information, any given marketer doesn't necessarily need to know who *you are*, but how somebody *like you* acts. (Much like a politician seeking a vote, incidentally.) Again, the worry is less that the market is invading our privacy and more whether that anonymity will be permitted politically when it finally is available to us commercially.

"SELF-REGULATION" IS A MISNOMER

Privacy and security need to be competitive features. We need to foster competition in reputations. And we need flexibility when the inevitable mistakes are made.

Businesses compete; and one area in which they can compete is in the development of technologies that enhance security. Washington's inclination toward regulating online consumer relationships threatens to undermine the markets catering to diverse individual privacy preferences, and hinder the evolution of competitive research and innovation in secure applications. Privacy encompasses innumerable relationships between consumers and businesses, and no single set of privacy safeguards is appropriate. While government demands information disclosure, profit-driven firms compete to offer robust privacy assurances. As businesses respond to evolving consumer preferences, stronger privacy policies will emerge.

Businesses are disciplined by responses of their competitors. Political regulation is premature; but "self-regulation" like that described in the FTC principles is a misnomer; it is *competitive discipline* that market processes impose on vendors. Nobody in a free market is so fortunate as to be able to "self regulate." Apart from the consumer rejection just noted, firms are regulated by the competitive threats posed by rivals, by Wall Street and intolerant investors, indeed by computer science itself.

Neither the government nor private sector has a spotless "self-regulatory" record, but FTC seems unconcerned about the former. Data breaches at businesses, governments and universities rose 69 percent in 2008.[8] Government can contribute to data security by ensuring that its own policieslike data sharing or data retention mandates, or sweeping subpoenas—do not interfere with competitive discipline.

Even governmental calls for self-regulation seem lukewarm. Along with the Federal Trade Commission's Principles on what personally identifiable information firms may collect, a bill in the New York state legislature would impose drastic opt-in standards, preventing companies from gathering personalized information without explicit user permission. When Microsoft bid for Yahoo this year, the Justice Department almost immediately wondered whether the combined firm would possess "too much" consumer data. Canada recently announced an investigation into Facebook's privacy protections. Now the Department of Justice is investigating the Google-Yahoo deal.[9]

Everybody's heard of Google and Microsoft, but fewer have heard of companies like Phorm and NebuAd, which present the more pertinent behavioral marketing issues; their new techniques give ISPs a dog in the fight, since online advertising is a commercial opportunity impossible for ISPs to ignore. ISPs see Google and Microsoft and they want a piece of the online advertising action too. These companies' techniques have been called spyware, but again, they incorporate the Net's underlying capabilities in novel ways, and they too are subject to competitive discipline. One's sympathies will depend upon the "ownership" status one accords to Web pages, and what one regards as online "trespass." The only certainty is a Web page today is not what a Web page tomorrow will be. Was there ever a real reason for publishers and advertisers to think they could control everything a user saw, given the open-ended potential of software's obvious ability to route content to browsers in novel ways? At many sites, like Facebook, each page is a "Web" in its own right, containing widgets drawing information and ads from numerous sources. The debate has really only just begun, and online marketing trade groups are truly the "Battered Business Bureau." But they're battered by competitive discipline, not merely regulators

Lessons from Personally Identifiable Data Use Can Inform Future Online Security Practices

A frontier industry requires the flexibility to learn from mistakes. We must distinguish between proper and improper uses of surveillance by *both* the private and public sectors. Not many want to be tracked by the authorities, or treated like human bar code. Myriad benefits will accrue from the further deployment of identification techniques—even personally identifiable—into various facets of daily life. But where is the line crossed, and who is capable of crossing it?

In private hands, techniques like behavioral marketing, biometric and data-mining technologies enlarge our horizons. They expand the possibilities of a market economy by bolstering security in private transactions ranging from face-to-face authentication to long-distance commerce. The best, most secure technologies are those that *prevent others from posing as us*—that's why the value of personally identifiable data cannot be ruled out. The Web is desperately short of that kind of clarity and authentication, in a world of cyber-risks, identity theft, and the need to conduct ever more sensitive transactions. But nothing is automatic. The marketplace imperative requires private sector experimentation in privacy: It's messy, but necessary.

On the one hand, policy should not create situations where companies are required to ask for personal info that otherwise wouldn't be needed. (Google declares in its comments on the FTC advertising principles that obeying certain rules would require it to collect information it otherwise would not need.) On the other hand, certain forms of identifiable behavioral tracking may prove important in specific contexts and shouldn't be prohibited.

Disallowing personally identifiable information nis the wrong thing to do. We often need to identify those we're dealing with on line, and for them to be able to identify us; such instruments will be governed by heretofore unknown contracts and privacy polices. It's not "self-regulation," but the needs of the world at large driving this evolution. Rather than legislating, it's likely better to keep this a war between computer scientists; between those working on behavioral advertising with personal information and/or authentication, and those working on behavioral without authentication. Being able to sell to a customer but not have that customer identified is a key research area in computer science. The consumer-control ethos—the notion that we don't have to be tracked—puts consumers, not advertisers, in the drivers seat Let the computer scientists duke it out.

In many transactions and contexts, the Web needs better authentication, not the abandonment of personally identifiable information. The private sector should experiment with generating such data in ways that consumers can accept. Some say we must regulate because online risks exist; this report argues for *not* regulating because there are online risks. The firms that reduce risks in ways palatable to consumers offer a great service. New products and institutions still need to emerge around online commerce.

Expanding the Marketplace for Liability and Private Security Insurance

Privacy is one subset of the much broader issues of online security and cybersecurity. It's been noted that a basic problem today is that no one stands in any position to make guarantees to anybody about anything. That doesn't mean improved insurance products and enhanced liability contracts won't develop online, however. Lessons learned from spam, privacy, and preventing piracy of intellectual property will carry over to the security issues of tomorrow.

Government shouldn't grant immunity to software companies for breaches, but at the same time it should not impose liability on them either. It's not so clear whom to sue on an Internet not amenable to authentication, but standards will emerge. Government interference can impede private cyber-insurance innovations

Certain innovations can be sacrificed by regulating. The private sector needs to "practice" now for the really difficult cases like the integration of biometrics into the online world; meanwhile the federal government needs to focus on cyber-crime.

A Positive Agenda for the Federal Government

Policymakers should appreciate the government's inherent limitations as well as the vulnerabilities that can be created by federal policies and procedures.

From lost laptops to hacks into the Pentagon email system, to "D" grades for the Department of Homeland Security's own information security practices, regulators' ability to rationally guide others on privacy is questionable. In many areas it makes sense to circumscribe regulators' sphere of influence, while increasing that of the market.

Recognizing that governments can fail just as markets can, there are numerous ways government within its limitations can *properly* foster private sector innovation in security:

- Foster competitive discipline
- Emphasize protecting government's own insecure networks, not regulating markets. This means many things, including: removing sensitive information from government websites; limit the size and scope of government databases to ensure government doesn't create artificial cybersecurity risks; avoiding data retention mandates and other interventions that undermine private-sector security guarantees.

- Focus on computer criminals, not cyber-regulations
- Assess areas where it's best to *liberalize* private sector data-sharing rules. For example, facilitating private sector medical data sharing could deliver benefits to suffering patients. More broadly, some firms cannot share data among their own divisions because of antitrust and privacy strictures. Enhancing cross-firm coordination can improve reliability and security
- Recognize that commercial anonymity and political anonymity differ; we may need "less" of the former, even as we expand the latter. Research should continue on the seemingly opposed agendas of authentication of users on the one hand, and anonymizing technologies on the other.

CONCLUSION: AFFIRMING PRIVATE SECTOR PRIMACY OVER INFORMATION PRACTICES

Our greatest privacy concern should be government collection of our information, not the emergence of targeted marketing.

In the changing world of e-commerce, the role of government is not to predetermine commercial privacy arrangements, but to enforce information-sharing contracts that companies make between themselves or with individuals. Privacy policies are legally binding. Government's role is not to dictate the structure of privacy contracts through such means as opt-in or opt-out policies; it is to halt deceptive practices and hold private firms accountable to the guarantees they make. Government's other role is to protect citizens from identity theft, which is not a commercial enterprise, but a criminal one.

If anonymity and the inability to exclude bad actors are at the root of genuine online security problems, legislation doesn't make them go away. When contemplating centralized government vs. decentralized market approaches to protection consumers onlie, we must strive, before regulating, to follow the "cybersecurity commandment": *Don't entrench regulation to such a degree that effective private alternatives and institutions, however warranted as conditions change, simply cannot emerge.*

APPENDIX: RELATED READING

Wayne Crews and Ryan Radia, "Rigid Federal Mandates Hinder Privacy Technologies," *San Jose Mercury News*, June 15, 2008, http://www.mercurynews.com/opinion/ci9593341

Wayne Crews, "Cybersecurity Finger-pointing: Regulation vs. Markets for Software Liability, Information Security, and Insurance," *CEI Issue Analysis* 2005 No. 7, May 31, 2005, http://cei.org/pdf/4569.pdf.

Wayne Crews, "Cybersecurity and Authentication: The Marketplace Role in Rethinking Anonymity—Before Regulators Intervene," *CEI Issue Analysis* 2004 No.2, November 8, 2004, http://cei.org/pdf/4281.pdf.

Wayne Crews, Comments to the FTC on email authentication themes, September 30, 2004, http://www.cei.org/pdf/4229.pdf.

Alberto Mingardi and Wayne Crews, EU takes a Swipe at Google, *International Herald Tribune,* March 9, 2007, http://www.iht.com/articles/2007/03/09/opinion/edmingardi.php.

Wayne Crews and Brooke Oberwetter, "Preventing Identity Theft and Data Security Breaches: The Problem With Regulation, *CEI Issue Analysis* 2006 No. 2, May 9, 2006, http://cei.org/pdf/5316.pdf.

Wayne Crews "Giving Chase in Cyberspace: Does Vigilantism Against Hackers and File-sharers Make Sense?" *CEI OnPoint* No. 109, October 2, 2006. http://cei.org/pdf/5569.pdf.

Wayne Crews, "Trespass in Cyberspace: Whose Ether Is It Anyway?" TechKnowledge #19, Cato Institute, September 10, 2001, http://www.cato.org/tech/tk/010910-tk.html.

Wayne Crews, "Human Bar Code: Monitoring Biometrics Technologies In a Free Society," *Cato Institute Policy Analysis* No. 452, September 17, 2002, http://www.cato.org/pubs /pas/pa452.pdf.

END NOTES

[1] Associated Press, "FCC to look into embedded advertising on TV," *MSNBC.com.* June 26, 2008. http://www.msnbc.msn.com/id/25401193/

[2] http://www.networkadvertising.org/networks/principles_comments.asp

[3] Federal Trade Commission, "Behavioral Advertising, Moving the Discussion Forward to Possible Self-Regulatory Principles," December 20, 2007. http://www.ftc.gov/os/2007/12/P859900stmt.pdf

[4] http://www.freerepublic.com/focus/f-news/1384722/posts.

[5] Associated Press, "U.S. Contradicts Itself Over Its Own ID Protection Advice," SiliconValley.com, July 2, 2008. http://www.siliconvalley.com/news/ci_9762027?nclick_check=1.

[6] Caroline McCarthy, "MoveOn.org takes on Facebook's 'Beacon' ads," CNet News.com. November 20, 2007. http://news.cnet.com/8301-13577_3-9821170-36.html

[7] Federal Trade Commission, 2007.

[8] Brian Krebs, "Data Breaches Are Up 69% This Year, Nonprofit Says," *Washington Post.* July 1, 2008. p. D3. http://www.washingtonpost.com/wp-dyn/content/article/2008/06/30/AR2008063002123.html.

[9] Peter Whoriskey, "Google Ad Deal Is Under Scrutiny," *Washington Post*, July 2, 2008. Page D1. http://www.washingtonpost.com/wp-dyn/content/article/2008/07/01/AR2008070102622.html

In: Electronic Breadcrumbs: Issues in Tracking Consumers   ISBN: 978-1-60741-600-5
Editor: Dmitar N. Kovac   © 2010 Nova Science Publishers, Inc.

Chapter 10

PRIVACY & ONLINE ADVERTISING HEARING- DYKES TESTIMONY

Bob Dykes

Chairman Inouye, Ranking Member Stevens, and Members of the Committee, thank you for inviting me to appear today regarding the privacy implications of online advertising. My name is Bob Dykes, CEO of NebuAd, Inc., a recent entrant into the online advertising industry that partners with Internet Service Providers (ISPs). I have spent considerable time over the past year with federal policymakers at the Federal Trade Commission (FTC), Federal Communications Commission, and in Congress — as well as with consumer and privacy advocates -- discussing NebuAd's technology, operations, and privacy protections and welcome the opportunity to discuss all of this further with the Committee.

INTRODUCTION

Online advertising is a phenomenon of the Internet age. It permits advertisers to provide more relevant messages to consumers and in turn fuels the development of website publishers, both large and small. In fact, advertising is the engine for the free Internet. The FTC has found online advertising benefits consumers by enabling "access to newspapers and information around the world, provided free because it is subsidized by online advertising; tailored ads that facilitate comparison shopping for the specific products that consumers want; and, potentially, a reduction in ads that are irrelevant to consumers' interests and that may therefore be unwelcome."[1]

Within this world of online advertising, NebuAd is a newcomer, just entering among industry giants like Google, Yahoo!, Microsoft, Amazon, and countless website publishers. That means we have a steep hill to climb, but it also means we have great opportunities. We are able to learn the lessons of the industry and construct state-of-the-art technology that delivers ads that are more relevant to users while providing them with robust and industry-leading privacy protections. Indeed, as I will discuss, these privacy protections are built into our technology and designed into our policies from the ground up.

Let me explain our privacy motivation more fully. I come from a security background, serving for many years as Executive Vice President of Symantec Corporation, a global leader in providing security solutions for computers and computer networks. When we launched NebuAd several years ago, it was at a time when many people had particularly heightened concerns about data security. Hackers were piercing firewalls, seeking to capture seemingly random strands of data to find the identity of users. The government was ordering ISPs and other network providers to turn over data on their users. As part of its mission, NebuAd sought to address these privacy and security concerns.

The NebuAd service is architected and its operations are based on principles essential to strong privacy protection:

- Provide users with prior, robust notice and the opportunity to express informed choice about whether to participate, both before the service takes effect and persistently thereafter;
- Do not collect or use personally-identifiable information ("PII");
- Do not store raw data linked to identifiable individuals; and
- Provide state-of-the art security for any information stored.

As a result, NebuAd's service is designed so that no one — not even the government — can determine the identity of our users. That means our service for ISP users, including the ad optimization and serving system, does not collect or use any PII. In addition, NebuAd requires its Internet service provider ("ISP") partners to provide robust, advance notice about our operations and our privacy protections to their subscribers, who at any time can exercise their choice not to participate. And, finally, we have located our servers in highly secure data centers.

THE NEBUAD TECHNOLOGY AND ITS ADVERTISING OPERATIONS

Currently, online advertising solutions operate in many locations throughout the Internet ecosystem — from users' computers to individual web-sites to networks of web-sites. When an Internet user visits the sites of web publishers, like Yahoo! or Amazon, these sites typically collect information about the user's activities to target ads based on that information. When an Internet user conducts a search, the search company may collect information from the user's activity, which in turn may be used to improve the relevance of the ads shown. And when a user visits a web-site within an online advertising network, some of which include thousands of sites, the visits help the network advertising company categorize a user for targeted advertising. All of these activities are well-entrenched in the Internet and, given the enormous and growing use of the Internet, have proven to have mutual benefits for users, publishers — large and small —advertisers, and ad-networks.

NebuAd provides online advertising in partnership with ISPs. The NebuAd advertising service has been architected to use only a select set of a user's Internet activities (only a subset of HTTP traffic) to construct anonymous inferences about the user's level of qualification for a predefined set of market segment categories ("anonymous user profiles"), which are then used to select and serve the most relevant advertisements to that user. The NebuAd advertising service does not collect or use any information from password-protected sites (e.g., HTTPS traffic), web mail, email, instant messages, or VOIP traffic. Using only non-PH, NebuAd constructs and continuously updates these unique and anonymous user profiles.[2]

In the course of these business operations, NebuAd's ad optimization and serving system does not collect PH or use information deemed to be sensitive (*e.g.*, information involving a user's financial, sensitive health, or medical matters).[3] In addition, NebuAd requires its ISP partners to provide robust disclosure notices to users prior to initiating any service and permits them to opt-out of having their data collected and receiving targeted ads. Once a user opts-out, NebuAd deletes that user's anonymous user profile and will ignore the user's subsequent web navigation activity.[4]

Finally, NebuAd's ad optimization and serving system operates similar to traditional ad networks. It makes standard use of cookies for accepted ad serving purposes. It makes standard use of pixel tags that operate only within the security framework of the browser to invoke the placement of ad network cookies and that contain no uniquely identifying number, subscriber identifier, or any other subscriber information. In sum, NebuAd's code used for standard ad serving purposes is both clean in its purpose and function.

THE PRIVACY PARADIGM IN THE UNITED STATES AND NEBUAD'S PRIVACY PROTECTIONS

In contrast to the European Community, where omnibus privacy law covers all industries, in the United States, privacy statutes have been developed in a largely sector-specific fashion. This Committee has long been part of that trend, having overseen the creation of privacy statutes generally covering the cable and telecommunications industries, as well as specific statutes addressing online privacy for children, telemarketing, and Spam. Yet, even though these and other privacy statutes have been developed one at a time, there are common threads running through them:

- When more sensitive data is collected, and when the collection and disclosure of the data could harm or embarrass a consumer, more rigorous disclosure and consent requirements tend to be imposed.
- When raw data linked to an identifiable individual is stored for longer periods, there is an emerging trend that more rigorous disclosure, consent, and security requirements should be imposed.

NebuAd supports this privacy paradigm, which provides users with consistent expectations and substantial protections. This paradigm also is technology and business-neutral, and it is the basis upon which NebuAd built its technology and operations. NebuAd urges the Committee to maintain both the paradigm and the principle of technology and business- neutrality.

In implementing this privacy paradigm, NebuAd not only relied on the expertise of its own personnel, it turned to leading privacy experts, including Fran Maier, Executive Director and President of TRUSTe, the consumer privacy organization, Dr. Larry Ponemon of the Ponemon Institute, and Alan Chapel! of Chapel! & Associates. These experts provided important input into NebuAd's initial privacy program. They were particularly stringent in recommending that NebuAd should not collect PH or sensitive information and that it provide consumers with robust notice and choice. NebuAd followed that guidance in developing our privacy program.[5]

The following are the key privacy protections upon which NebuAd has architected into its technology and based its operations:

NebuAd's service does not collect or use P11 from ISP subscribers. The entire ad optimization and serving system does not collect or use any PII, nor does it collect any information from password-protected sites, web mail, e-mail, instant messages, or VOIP traffic.

NebuAd stores only a set of numbers that represent the user's level of qualification for a predefined set of market segment categories ("anonymous user profiles"). NebuAd does not store raw data such as URLs navigated or rp addresses associated with an identifiable individual. Rather, the NebuAd service constructs anonymous inferences about the user's level of qualification for a predefined set of market segment categories, and then discards the raw data that was used to create or update a user's anonymous profile. This mechanism of constructing anonymous inferences about the user's level of qualification and not storing raw data provides a strong additional layer of privacy protection that goes beyond the standards used by many Internet companies today.

NebuAd's ISP Partners are required to provide robust, direct notice in advance of launch of the service. The notice discloses to the user that the ISP is working to ensure that advertisements shown will be more relevant advertisements, that to deliver these ads its partner creates anonymous profiles based on part of the user's web-surfing behavior, which does not include the collection of PH, and that the user may opt-out of the service. For existing subscribers, the notice is required to be delivered 30-days prior to the launch of the service by postal mail, e-mail, or both.[6] For new subscribers, the notice is required to be placed clearly and conspicuously in the new subscriber sign-up flow and outside the privacy policy. All subscribers can opt-out at any time, and on-going disclosure and opportunity to opt-out is required to be provided within the ISP's privacy policy.

NebuAd and its ISP partners offer users advance and on-going choice of opting- out of the service. Users are provided with a clear statement of what opt-out means and the way it operates. Once the opt-out option is chosen, NebuAd honors that choice and ignores the user's subsequent web surfing activity and thus does not serve the user with behaviorally targeted ads .[7]

NebuAd's service only creates anonymous user profiles, which contain no PI1 and no raw data, and its placement of ads is completely anonymous. NebuAd uses proprietary algorithms and techniques, including one-way encryption of data, so that no one — not even NebuAd's engineers who designed the system — can reverse-engineer an anonymous identifier, or the anonymous user profile associated with it, to an identifiable individual.

NebuAd avoids any sensitive websites or product categories. NebuAd does not track or serve ads based on visits related to adult content, sensitive medical information, racial or ethnic origins, religious beliefs or content of a sexual nature, and does not have market segment categories for illegal products.

NebuAd does not permit either complexity of data or narrowness of data to be reverse-engineered into PII. This protection is accomplished because anonymous user profiles are constructed by anonymous inferences about the consumer's level of qualification for a predefined set of market segment categories. Raw data is simply not stored as part of the anonymous user profile. In addition, the NebuAd service does not have narrowly-defined segments. Finally, the anonymous profile identifier is the result of multiple encryptions, and based on multiple data elements including the hashed IP address.

There is no connection or link between the ISP's registration data systems and NebuAd. That means that no user-specific data is exchanged between NebuAd and ISP data systems. This boundary is preserved further and inadvertent disclosure is prevented because NebuAd immediately performs a one-way encryption of the IP address and other anonymous user identifiers used within the NebuAd system.

NebuAd installs no applications on users' computers, has no access to users' hard drives, and has no access to secure transactions. As such, NebuAd does not control a user's computer or web-surfing activity in any way (*e.g.,* by changing computer settings or observing private or sensitive information).

NebuAd's Data Centers are professionally operated and secured. NebuAd's servers are located at secure sites with state-of-the-art protections against any intrusion, electronic or physical.

NebuAd is proud of these protections — all of which were adopted to comply with both the spirit and letter of the government's privacy paradigm — and, it continuously seeks to enhance them.

CONCLUSION

As I stated at the outset, I have spent years seeking to ensure that users have robust and transparent privacy protections. In a very real sense, NebuAd is the product of that work_ It has adopted and implemented state-of-the-art privacy protections, and, equally as important, it has established a process to continuously improve on them. The Internet is a highly dynamic environment, where new technologies are constantly developed to address new challenges, and we both want and need to take advantage of them. NebuAd takes its responsibilities to its users very seriously. It looks forward to continuing to work with government policymakers as they examine online advertising and privacy issues.

END NOTES

[1] It is an axiom that advertising has more value when the advertiser believes the user is more interested in the advertiser's product. Such interest is not obvious when a user visits general-purpose news and information sites, which are some of the very ones noted by the FTC Staff as standing to benefit from online advertising. Accordingly, the online advertising industry is constantly seeking other ways to infer user interest and then bring that knowledge to bear on the placement of ads on these sites. That is, behavioral advertising drives value and supports those sites on the Internet that provide society with great value.

[2] The anonymous user profiles do not contain any original raw data, such as URLs navigated, but only consist of a set of numbers that represent the anonymous inferences about the user's level of qualification for a predefined set of market segment categories.

[3] NebuAd understands that the definition of "sensitive" information will evolve. We stated in our comments to the FTC on the "Staff's Proposed Principles for the Self-Regulation of Behavioral Advertising" that we would adopt the Staff's definition of "sensitive" information, assuming it is not limitless. We also would consider additional reasonable limitations proposed by other stakeholders.

[4] NebuAd has enhanced the industry-standard opt-out "cookie" based system with the use of proprietary techniques. This enables the opt-out to be more persistent. NebuAd's entire enhanced opt-out system is linked to individual computers and browsers, and it informs users of this fact in assisting them in understanding the nature of their opt-out choice.

[5] A just released survey of U.S. Internet users by TRUSTe showed that 71% of online consumers are aware their web-surfing information may be collected for the purpose of advertising and 91% wanted to have the tools to assure they could protect their privacy. NebuAd has strived to provide users with this transparency by educating users about its activities and their choices regarding whether to participate in NebuAd's services.

[6] NebuAd seeks to ensure that users are fully informed of its activities and are given full opportunity to choose whether to participate. To that end, we are developing enhanced notification mechanisms.

[7] The user, of course, will continue to receive ads.

In: Electronic Breadcrumbs: Issues in Tracking Consumers
Editor: Dmitar N. Kovac

ISBN: 978-1-60741-600-5
© 2010 Nova Science Publishers, Inc.

Chapter 11

PRIVACY & ONLINE ADVERTISING HEARING-HARRIS TESTIMONY

Leslie Harris

I. SUMMARY

Chairman Inouye and Members of the Committee:

On behalf of the Center for Democracy & Technology ("CDT"), I thank you for the opportunity to testify today. We applaud the Committee's leadership in examining the privacy impact of new online advertising models.

CDT recognizes that advertising is an important engine of Internet growth. Consumers benefit from a rich diversity of content, services and applications that are provided without charge and supported by advertising revenue. However, as sophisticated new behavioral advertising models are deployed, it is vital that consumer privacy be protected. Massive increases in data processing and storage capabilities have allowed advertisers to track, collect and aggregate information about consumers' Web browsing activities, compiling individual profiles used to match advertisements to consumers' interests. All of this is happening in the context of an online environment where more data is collected – and retained for longer periods – than ever before and existing privacy protections have been far outpaced by technological innovation.

Behavioral advertising represents a small but rapidly growing part of the online advertising market. Market research firm eMarketer reported last year that spending on behaviorally targeted online advertising is expected to reach $1 billion this year and to 2011.[1] quadruple by The recent spate of acquisitions of the online advertising industry's largest players by major Internet companies is powerful evidence that the online advertising marketplace is headed toward more data aggregation tied to a single profile – and one that may be more readily tied to a person's identity.[2] And while we have yet to see evidence that this new advertising model will reap the promised rewards, it is already migrating from individual Web sites to the infrastructure of the Internet itself: In the last year, Internet Service Providers ("ISPs") have begun to form partnerships with ad networks to mine information from individual Web data streams for behavioral advertising. Ad networks that partner with ISPs could potentially collect and record every aspect of a consumer's Web browsing, including every Web page visited, the content of those pages, how long each page is viewed, and what links are clicked. Emails, chats, file transfers and many other kinds of data could all be collected and recorded.

The ISP model raises particularly serious questions. Thus far, implementations appear to defy reasonable consumer expectations, could interfere with Internet functionality, and may violate communications privacy laws.

Notwithstanding the recent growth of behavioral advertising, most Internet users today do not know that their browsing information may be tracked, aggregated and sold. After almost a decade of self-regulation, there is still a profound lack of transparency associated with these practices and an absence of meaningful consumer controls.

There are several efforts underway to respond to the new online advertising environment. First, the Federal Trade Commission staff recently released a draft of proposed principles for self -regulation, which represent a solid step forward. However, it is not clear whether the FTC will formally adopt the principles or put its enforcement power behind them.

The Network Advertising Initiative ("NAI") is also in the process of revising its guidelines. This is a welcome but long-overdue development. Unfortunately, self- regulation has not worked to date and, even if strengthened, will never by itself fully protect consumers' privacy interests.

Congress needs to take a comprehensive look at the current and emerging practices associated with behavioral advertising and the risks those practices pose to consumer privacy and control. We recommend that Congress take the following steps to address the significant privacy concerns raised by behavioral advertising:

- The Committee should hold a series of hearings to examine specific aspects of behavioral advertising, in particular the growing involvement of ISPs, the use of sensitive information, and secondary uses of behavioral profiles.
- The Committee should set a goal of enacting in the next year a simple, flexible baseline consumer privacy law that would protect consumers from inappropriate collection and misuse of their personal information, both online and offline.
- The Committee should strongly urge the Federal Trade Commission to exercise its full enforcement authority over online advertising practices.
- Congress should examine and strengthen existing communications privacy laws to cover new services, technologies and business models with consistent rules. The Electronic Communications Privacy Act ("ECPA") is decades old, and its application in today's online world is often unclear.
- Congress should encourage the FTC to investigate how technology can be harnessed to give consumers better control over their online information. Simple tools that put consumers in controls of their information, such as a "Do Not Track" list, deserve consideration.

II. UNDERSTANDING ONLINE ADVERTISING PRACTICES

Commercial Web sites that supply content to consumers free of charge are often supported by online advertising. These sites – known as "publishers" in the advertising world

– make available certain portions of space on their pages to display ads. That space is sold to advertisers, ad agencies, or online ad intermediaries that find and place advertisements into the space. These intermediaries may also make arrangements to collect information about user visits to the publisher pages. Since very few publishers supply their own advertising, it is common that when a consumer visits a publisher site, the consumer's computer also connects to one or more advertisers, ad agencies, or ad intermediaries to send data about the consumer's visit to the site and receive the advertising on the site.

One type of ad intermediary is known as an "advertising network." At their most basic level, ad networks contract with many different publishers on one side and many different advertisers on the other. Armed with a pool of space in which to display ads on publisher sites, and a pool of ads to display, ad networks are in the business of matching up the two by using the data they collect about consumers' site visits.

A. Contextual Advertising

There are many different ways for an ad network to determine which advertisement should be placed in which space. The two most often discussed are "contextual" advertising and "behavioral" advertising. Contextual advertising, which is often used to generate ads alongside search results, matches advertisements to the content of the page that a consumer is currently viewing – a consumer who visits a sports site may see advertisements for golf clubs or baseball tickets on that site.

The privacy risks associated with contextual advertising vary. If the practice is transparent to the user and data collection and retention is minimal, the practice poses little risk. By contrast, privacy concerns are heightened if the user data is retained in an identifiable or pseudonymous form (i.e., linked to a user identifier) for long periods of time even if it is not immediately used to create advertising profiles.

B. Behavioral Advertising

By contrast, behavioral advertising matches advertisements to the interests of the consumer as determined over time. If a consumer visits several different travel sites before viewing a news site, he or she might see a behaviorally targeted travel advertisement displayed on the news page, even if the news page contains no travel content. A traditional behavioral ad network builds up profiles of individual consumers by tracking their activities on publisher sites in the network (although this model is evolving, as we discuss below). When the consumer visits a site where the ad network has purchased ad space, the ad network collects data about that visit and serves an advertisement based on the consumer's profile. Diagrams illustrating this process are included in Appendix A.

Consumers' behavioral advertising profiles may incorporate many different kinds of data that are in and of themselves not personally identifiable. Many networks avoid linking profiles to what has traditionally been considered "personally identifiable information" ("PII"): names, addresses, telephone numbers, email addresses, and other identifiers. But as the comprehensiveness of consumer advertising profiles increases, the ability of marketers and others to link specific individuals to profiles is also growing. In 2006, for example, AOL released three months' worth of search queries generated by half a million users; in the interest of preserving users' anonymity, AOL replaced individuals' screen names with numbers. Based solely on search terms associated with one number, reporters at the New York Times were able to pinpoint the identity of the user who generated them.[3] The risk of supposedly non-personally identifying data being used to identify individuals has spurred several ad networks to take extra steps to de-identify or remove personal information from their data storage.[4]

Profiles may also be intentionally tied to PII. For example, data collected online by a merchant or by a service provider may permit an advertising profile to be tied to an individual's email account. Offline data may also be merged with online profiles. For years, data service companies have maintained profiles about consumers based on information gleaned from public sources such as property and motor vehicle records, as well as records from sources like catalog sales and magazine subscriptions. These data companies are now also entering the online advertising business, potentially allowing the linking of online and offline profiles.[5]

C. The Evolution of Behavioral Advertising – More Data, More Data Sources

As noted above, recent market consolidation facilitates more comprehensive data collection. Companies that run consumers' favorite Web-based services – Web search, Web mail, maps, calendars, office applications, and social networks – have all purchased behavioral advertising networks within the last year. In the past, major Internet companies could gather information about how an individual used its services and applications such as search, but did not have direct access to information about the user's other Web browsing habits. With the acquisition of behavioral advertising networks, these companies could potentially marry the rich data about an individual's use of one site with a broad view of his or her activities across the Web. The concerns about this aggregation of consumer data are heightened because many online companies retain data for months or years on end in identifiable or pseudonymous form, creating a host of privacy risks.

Finally, ad networks are now turning to the most comprehensive and concentrated source of information about Internet use: the individual Web data streams that flow through ISPs.[6] In this emerging model, the ISP intercepts or allows an ad network to intercept the content of each individual's Web data stream. The ad network then uses this traffic data for behavioral advertising, serving targeted ads to the ISP's customers on publisher sites as the customers surf the Web. We address the unique issues posed by this advertising model in detail below.

III. THE PRIVACY RISKS OF BEHAVIORAL ADVERTISING

Behavioral advertising poses a growing risk to consumer privacy; consumers are largely unaware of the practice and are thus ill equipped to take protective action. They have no expectation that their browsing information may be tracked and sold, and they are rarely provided sufficient information about the practices of advertisers or others in the advertising value chain to gauge the privacy risks and make meaningful decisions about whether and how their information may be used. In a recently released Harris Interactive/Alan F. Westin study, 59% of respondents said they were not comfortable with online companies using their browsing behavior to tailor ads and content to their interests even when they were told that such advertising supports free services.[7] A recent TRUSTe survey produced similar results.[8] It is highly unlikely that these respondents understood that this type of ad targeting is already taking place online every day.

In most cases, data collection for behavioral advertising operates on an opt-out basis. Opt-out mechanisms for online advertising are often buried in fine print, difficult to understand, hard to execute and technically inadequate. Only the most sophisticated and technically savvy consumers are likely to be able to successfully negotiate such opt-out processes. Moreover, in most cases, opt-out mechanisms offered for behavioral advertising only opt the user out of receiving targeted ads, but do not opt the user out of data collection about his or her Internet usage.

For behavioral advertising to operate in a truly privacy-protective way, data collection needs to be limited and data retention limits should be tied to the original purposes for collecting the data. Consumers need to be informed about what data is being collected about their Internet activities, how the information will be used, whether the information will be shared with others, and what measures are being taken to ensure that any transfer of data remains secure. They should be presented with this information in a manner that supports informed choice over their information and that choice should honored persistently over time. Consumers must also have opportunities for legal redress for misuse of the data. As a recent D.C. District Court opinion established, data leakage and the concern for potential abuses of that data are recognizable harms standing alone, without any need to show misuse of the data.[9] Consumers do not need to become victims of identity theft to suffer from an invasion of privacy.

There is also a risk that profiles for behavioral advertising may be used for purposes other than advertising. For example, ad networks that focus on "re-targeting" ads may already be using in pricing. [10] profiles to help marketers engage differential Behavioral profiles, particularly those that can be tied to an individual, may also be a tempting source of information in making decisions about credit, insurance, and employment. While the lack of transparency makes it almost impossible to know whether behavioral profiles are being used for other purposes, the lack of enforceable rules around the collection and use of most personal information leaves the door wide open for a myriad of secondary uses.

Finally, because the legal standards for government access to personal information held by third parties are extraordinarily low, these comprehensive consumer profiles are available to government officials by mere subpoena, without notice to the individual or an opportunity for the individual to object.[11]

IV. THE USE OF SENSITIVE INFORMATION FOR BEHAVIORAL ADVERTISING

The concerns about behavioral advertising practices are heightened because of the increasingly sensitive nature of the information that consumers are providing online in order to take advantage of new services and applications. Two data types of particular concern are health information and location information.

A. Personal Health Information – Increasingly Available Online

Personal health data is migrating online through an ever-expanding array of health information and search sites, online support groups, and personal health record sites. Federal privacy rules under the Health Information Portability and Accountability Act ("HIPAA") do not cover personal health information once it moves online and out of the control of HIPAA-covered entities. Once it is posted online, it may have no more legal protection than any other piece of consumer information. In addition, information provided by consumers that is not part of a "medical record" – such as search terms – may nevertheless reveal highly sensitive information. We do not know the full extent to which personal health data is being collected for behavioral advertising. We do know that the limits placed on its collection by the industry are inadequate and that there is an urgent need to develop a definition for personal health information in the Inte rnet context that is robust enough to protect privacy.

B. Location Information – Not Always Protected by Current Law

As technologies converge and Internet services are provided over cellular phones and other mobile devices, the ability to physically locate consumers is spurring location-based advertising, targeted to where a user is at any given moment. Plans to incorporate location information into behavioral advertising are still in development. Although laws exist to protect location information colle cted by telecommunications carriers, applications providers are increasingly offering location-based services that fall completely out of that legal framework. Standards for government access to location information are also unclear, even as law enforcement has shown a greater interest in such information.[12]

V. THE EMERGING USE OF ISP DATA
FOR BEHAVIORAL ADVERTISING

The use of ISP data for behavioral advertising is one area that requires close scrutiny from lawmakers. The interception and sharing of Internet traffic content for behavioral advertising defies reasonable user expectations, can be disruptive to Internet and Web functionality, and may run afoul of communications privacy laws.

A. How ISP Data Is Used for Behavioral Advertising

In this new model, an ad network strikes a deal with an ISP that allows the network to receive the contents of the individual Web traffic streams of each of the ISP's customers. The ad network analyzes the content of the traffic in order to create a record of the individual's online behaviors and interests. As customers of the ISP surf the Web and visit sites where the ad network has purchased ad space, they see advertisements targeted based on their previous Internet behavior. While the model as it exists today involves an ISP contracting with a third party that operates such an ad network, it would also be possible for ISPs to do the traffic content inspection, categorization, and advertising delivery themselves.

B. Privacy Implications of the Use of ISP Data for Behavioral Advertising

The privacy implications of behavioral advertising at large are amplified in this ISP model. Ad networks that partner with ISPs may potentially gain access to all or substantially all of an individual's Web traffic as it traverses the ISP's infrastructure, including traffic to all political, religious, and other non-commercial sites. While traditional ad networks may be large, few if any provide the opportunity to collect information about an individual's online activities as comprehensively as in the ISP model, particularly with respect to activities involving non-commercial content. And although these ad networks currently inspect predominantly Web traffic, ISPs carry emails, chats, file transfers and many other kinds of data that they could decide to pass on to behavioral ad networks in the future.

Moreover, the use of Internet traffic content for behavioral advertising defies user expectations about what happens when they surf the Web and communicate online. Absent unmistakable notice, consumers simply do not expect their ISP or its partners to be looking into the content of their Internet communications. Finding out that there is a middleman lurking between consumers and the Web sites they visit would come as a unwelcome surprise to most Internet users. ISPs are a critical part of the chain of trust that undergirds the Internet. Giving an unknown third party broad access to all or most consumer communications may undermine that trust.

C. Current Implementations May Interfere with Normal Internet Use

Despite these concerns, several ad network companies are moving forward with plans to use ISP data for behavioral advertising. The two most prominent ad networks engaged in this practice are NebuAd in the United States and Phorm in the UK. Charter Communications, a cable broadband ISP, recently announced – and then delayed – a plan to conduct trials of the advertising technology.[13] NebuAd behavioral Several other ISPs, such as Wide Open West (WOW!), CenturyTel, Embarq and Knology also announced plans with NebuAd to trial or deploy its behavioral advertising technology. Although a number of these ISPs have put their plans on hold in the wake of a firestorm of criticism, NebuAd continues to work with U.S. ISPs and seek new ISP partners. Phorm, which originally announced deals with three of the UK's largest ISPs and has sought partnerships with U.S. ISPs, is also now encountering hesitation from some of its partners.[14]

Independent analyses of both companies' systems have revealed that by virtue of their ability to intercept Internet traffic in the middle of the network – and based on their desire to track individual Internet users – they engage in an array of practices that are inconsistent with the usual flow of Internet traffic. NebuAd reportedly injects computer code into Web traffic streams that causes numerous cookies to be placed on users' computers for behavioral tracking, none of which are related to or sanctioned by the Web sites the users visit.[15] When a user navigates to a particular Web site, Phorm reportedly pretends to be that Web site so that it can plant a behavioral tracking cookie linked to that site on the user's computer.[16] In addition to the privacy implications of tracking all of an individual's Web activities, this kind of conduct has the potential to create serious security vulnerabilities in the network,[17] hamper the speed of users' Internet connections, and interfere with ordinary Web functionality. At a time when many different kinds of companies are working to build a trusted computing platform for the Internet, having ISPs work with partners whose practices undermine trust raises future cyber-security concerns.

D. Current Implementations May Violate Federal Law

Depending on how this advertising model is implemented, it may also run afoul of existing communications privacy laws. The federal Wiretap Act, as amended by the Electronic Communications Privacy Act ("ECPA"), prohibits the interception and disclosure of electronic communications – including Internet traffic content – without consent.[18] Although exceptions to this rule permit interception and disclosure without consent, we seriously doubt that any of them apply to the interception or disclosure of Internet traffic content for behavioral advertising purposes. Accordingly, we believe that the Wiretap Act requires unavoidable notice and affirmative opt-in consent before Internet traffic content may be used from ISPs for behavioral advertising purposes. Certain state laws may take this one step further, requiring consent from both parties to the communication: the consumer and the Web site he or she is visiting. A detailed CDT legal memorandum on the application of the Wiretap Act, ECPA and relevant state wiretap laws to the use of ISP data for behavioral advertising is attached as Appendix B.

As several members of Congress have noted, the Cable Communications Policy Act also applies here.[19] The law prohibits cable operators from collecting or disclosing personally identifiable information prior consent.[20] without   While the term "personally identifiable information" in the law is defined by what it does not include – "any record of aggregate data which does not identify particular persons"[21] – we doubt that a user's entire Web traffic stream, unique to that individual, often containing both PII and non-PII, would be considered aggregate data as that term is commonly understood.

We do not believe that it is possible to shoehorn the collection and disclosure of a subscriber's entire browsing history for advertising purposes into the statute's exception for collection or disclosure of information that is necessary to render service.[22] Thus, we conclude that cable-based ISPs that wish to disclose customer information to advertising networks would also have to meet the consent requirements of the Cable Communications Policy Act.

The ISP models that have been deployed thus far have failed to obtain affirmative, express opt-in consent required by law. Several small U.S. ISPs, for example, have failed to meet this threshold requirement, burying vague information about their deals with NebuAd in the ISPs' terms service.[23] Charter Communications, the largest U.S. ISP that had planned to partner with NebuAd, notified its subscribers that they would be receiving more relevant ads, but did not explain its plans to intercept subscribers' traffic data, and did not provide a way for subscribers to give or withhold consent. Charter has since suspended its plans.

Designing a robust opt-in consent system for ISP-based behavioral advertising presents a formidable challenge. We are less than sanguine that such a system can be easily designed, particularly since it must not only provide a way for consumers to give affirmative consent, but it must also provide a method for them to revoke that consent. The burden is on those who wish to move forward with the model to demonstrate that an express notice and consent regime can work in this context.

VI. THE LIMITS OF SELF-REGULATION

For almost a decade, the primary privacy framework for the behavioral advertising industry has been provided by the Network Advertising Initiative, a self-regulatory group of online advertising networks formed in response to pressure from the Federal Trade Commission and consumer advocates in the wake of privacy concerns over the merger of ad network DoubleClick and Abacus, an offline data broker. NAI members agree to provide consumers with notice and, at minimum, a method to opt out of behavioral advertising. They further pledged to use information collected for only for marketing purposes. While at the time of their release CDT welcomed the NAI principles as an important first step, we also noted then that there were flaws in the approach that needed to be addressed and that self-regulation was not a complete solution. The FTC agreed, concluding in its July 2000 report to Congress that "backstop legislation addressing online profiling is still required to fully ensure that consumers' privacy is protected online."[24] That remains true today.

Eight years after the creation of the principles, few consumers are aware of behavioral advertising and fewer still have been able to successfully navigate the confusing and complex opt-out process.[25] Although individual NAI companies have launched their own consumer awareness initiatives, more work remains to be done.[26] For those consumers who successfully opt out, the NAI's reliance on flawed opt-out cookies means that user preferences are often not persistently honored.

In addition, the NAI's guidelines for the use of sensitive information have never been adequate to guard consumer privacy. Until recently, the definition was limited to a narrowly defined set of PII. While the definition is being revised, it still falls far short of what is needed to address the increasingly sensitive nature of consumer information online.[27]

Finally, the NAI principles only apply to companies that voluntarily join the initiative. The NAI has no way to force companies to join; the current membership is missing numerous behavioral advertising firms, including some key industry players. In addition, measures to ensure compliance and transparency have withered on the vine.[28] The original NAI principles provided for independent audits and enforcement against noncompliant members, but the audit results were never made public, and reporting on compliance with the principles has been inconsistent.[29]

For all these reasons, while we encourage more robust self-regulatory efforts, we continue to have doubts about the effectiveness of the self-regulatory framework. As online advertising becomes increasingly complex and data collection becomes more pervasive, Congress and the FTC must step in to ensure that consumer interests are fully protected.

VII. THE ROLE OF CONGRESS

Congress should take action to address the significant privacy concerns raised by behavioral advertising:

- As a first step, we urge the Committee to hold a series of hearings to examine specific aspects of behavioral advertising. In particular, we believe that further investigation of new models of behavioral advertising using ISP data is warranted, and that the Committee should explore how current laws such as ECPA, the Wiretap Act and the Cable Communications Policy Act apply. Secondary uses of behavioral advertising profiles for purposes other than marketing also deserve additional investigation and scrutiny, as does the use of sensitive information.

- This Committee should set a goal of enacting in the next year general privacy legislation covering both the online and offline worlds. CDT has long argued for simple, flexible baseline consumer privacy legislation that would protect consumers from inappropriate collection and misuse of their personal information while enabling legitimate business use to promote economic and social value. In principle, such legislation would codify the fundamentals of fair information practices, requiring transparency and notice of data collection practices, providing consumers with meaningful choice regarding the use and disclosure of that information, allowing consumers reasonable access to personal information they have provided, providing remedies for misuse or unauthorized access, and setting standards to limit data collection and ensure data security.

- The Federal Trade Commission has played a helpful role in consumer education efforts around behavioral advertising. But it also must exercise its authority under its deception and unfairness jurisdiction to issue enforceable guidelines for behavioral advertising. We ask the Committee to strongly urge the Commission to exercise the full measure of its enforcement authority over online advertising practices.

- Congress should also examine and strengthen existing communications privacy laws to cover new services, technologies and business models with consistent rules. ECPA was passed more than 20 years ago, long before there was a World Wide Web and the Internet became integrated into Americans' daily lives. The application of the law to common online activities including Web search remains unclear and the legal protections it provides for the enormous amounts of personal data stored online are far too low.

- Finally, Congress should encourage the FTC to investigate how technology can be harnessed to give consumers better control over their online information. The lack of effective controls and the difficulty that consumers have in exercising choice about their participation in online tracking and targeting was the motivation behind the "Do Not Track" list idea proposed by CDT and nine other consumer and privacy groups.[30] Although the proposal has been controversial, the idea behind Do Not Track is both simple and important: provide consumers with an easy-to-use, technology-neutral, persistent way to opt out of behavioral advertising. Congress should promote further study of this idea and other innovative ways to put consumers in control of their information.

VIII. Conclusion

I would like to thank the Committee again for holding this important hearing. We believe that Congress has a critical role to play in ensuring that privacy is protected in an increasingly complex online advertising environment. CDT looks forward to working with the Committee as it pursues these issues further.

Appendix A: Simplified Illustration of a Traditional Online Ad Network

Figure 1 below shows a simplified version of a traditional online ad network. Ad networks contract with advertisers on one side and publishers on the other. They take the ads they receive from advertisers and match them to open ad spaces on publisher sites.

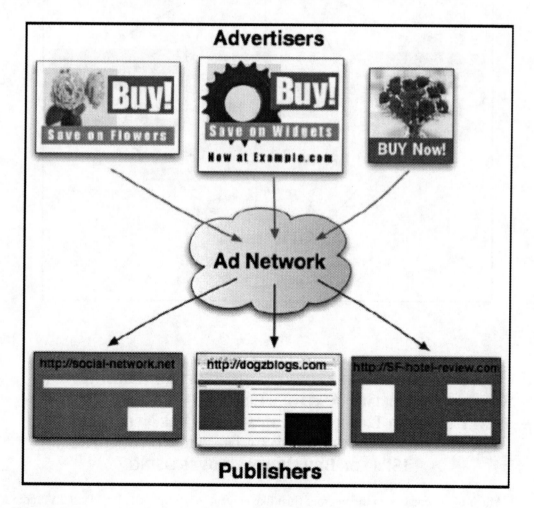

Figure 1.

Figure 2 shows how an ad network collects data about a consumer's Web activities. When the consumer first visits a publisher site in the network (SF-hotel-review.com), the ad network places a cookie with a unique ID (12345) on the consumer's computer. When the user subsequently visits other publisher sites in the network (including dogzblogs.com and social-network.net), the cookie containing the ID is automatically transmitted to the ad network. This allows the ad network to keep track of what sites the consumer has visited and build a behavioral profile based on that information, linked to the cookie ID.

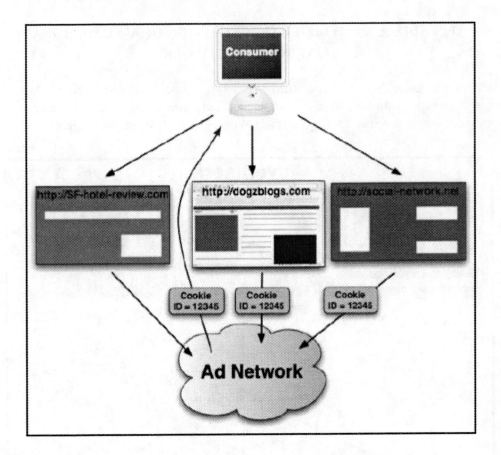

Figure 2.

APPENDIX B: AN OVERVIEW OF THE FEDERAL WIRETAP ACT, ELECTRONIC COMMUNICATIONS PRIVACY ACT, AND STATE TWO-PARTY CONSENT LAWS OF RELEVANCE TO THE NEBUAD SYSTEM AND OTHER USES OF INTERNET TRAFFIC CONTENT FROM ISPS FOR BEHAVIORAL ADVERTISING

Much of the content on the Internet (just like content in newspapers, broadcast TV, radio and cable) is supported in whole or part by advertising revenue. The Internet offers special opportunities to target ads based on the expressed or inferred interests of the individual user.

There are various models for delivering targeted ads online. These range from the purely contextual (everyone who visits a travel site sees the same airline ad) to models that involve compiling information about the online behavior of individual Internet users, to be used in serving them advertisements. For years, Web sites have entered into agreements with advertising networks to use "cookies" to track individual users across Web sites in order to compile profiles. This approach has always been, and remains, a source of privacy concern, in part because the conduct usually occurs unbeknownst to most Internet users. Recent developments, including the mergers between online service providers and some of the largest online advertising networks, have heightened these concerns. The Center for Democracy & Technology has been conducting a major project on behavioral advertising, in which we have been researching behavioral advertising practices, consulting with Internet companies and privacy advocates, developing policy proposals, filing extensive comments at the FTC, and analyzing industry self-regulatory guidelines.

This memo focuses on the implications of a specific approach to behavioral advertising being considered by Internet advertising networks and Internet Service Providers (ISPs). This new approach involves copying and inspecting the content of each individual's Internet activity with the cooperation of his or her ISP.[31] Under this new model, an advertising network strikes a deal with an ISP, and the ISP allows the network to copy the contents of the individual Web traffic streams of each of the ISP's customers. The advertising network analyzes the content of these traffic streams in order to create a record of each individual's online behaviors and interests. Later, as customers of the ISP surf the Web and visit sites where the advertising network has purchased advertising space, they see ads targeted based on their previous Internet behavior.

NebuAd is one such advertising network company operating in the United States. In the past few months, it has come to light that NebuAd was planning to partner with Charter Communications, a cable broadband ISP, to conduct trials of the NebuAd behavioral advertising technology. Several other smaller ISPs, such as Wide Open West (WOW!), CenturyTel, Embarq, and Knology, have also announced plans with NebuAd to trial or deploy its behavioral advertising technology. In response to concerns raised by subscribers, privacy advocates, and policymakers, Charter, CenturyTel and Embarq have delayed these plans, but NebuAd and other similar companies are continuing to seek new ISP partners.

The use of Internet traffic content from ISPs for behavioral advertising is different from the "cookie" -based model in significant ways and raises unique concerns.[32] Among other differences, it copies all or substantially all Web transactions, including visits to sites that do not use cookies. Thus, it may capture not only commercial activity, but also visits to political, advocacy, or religious sites or other non-commercial sites that do not use cookies.

In this memo, we conclude that the use of Internet traffic content from ISPs may run afoul of federal wiretap laws unless the activity is conducted with the consent of the subscriber.[33] To be effective, such consent should not be buried in terms of service and should not be inferred from a mailed notice. We recommend prior, express consent, but we do not offer here any detailed recommendations on how to obtain such consent in an ISP context. Also, we note that that the California law requiring consent of all the parties to a communication has been applied by the state Supreme Court to the monitoring of telephone calls when the monitoring is done at a facility outside California. The California law so far has not been applied to Internet communications and it is unclear whether it would apply specifically to the copying of communications as conducted for behavioral monitoring purposes, but if it or another state's all-party consent rule were applied to use of Internet traffic for behavioral profiling, it would seem to pose an insurmountable barrier to the practice.

I. Wiretap Act

A. Service Providers Cannot "Divulge" The Contents of Subscriber Communications, Except Pursuant to Limited Exceptions

The federal Wiretap Act, as amended by the Electronic Communications Privacy Act, protects the privacy of wire, oral, and electronic communications.[34] "[E]lectronic communication" is defined as "any transfer of signs, signals, writing, images, sounds, data, or intelligence of any nature transmitted in whole or in part by a wire, radio, electromagnetic, photoelectronic or photooptical system. . . . "[35] Web browsing and other Internet communications are clearly electronic communications protected by the Wiretap Act.

In language pertinent to the model under consideration, § 2511(3) of the Act states that "a person or entity providing an electronic communication service to the pubic shall not intentionally divulge the contents of any communications. . . while in transmission on that service to any person or entity other than an addressee or intended recipient . . . ."[36]

There are exceptions to this prohibition on disclosure, two of which may be relevant here. One exception specifies that "[i]t shall not be unlawful under this chapter for an. . . electronic communication service, whose facilities are used in the transmission of a[n] . . . electronic communication, to intercept, disclose, or use that communication in the normal course of his employment while engaged in any activity which is a *necessary incident to the rendition of his service* or to the protection of the rights or property of the provider of that service."[37] We will refer to this as the "necessary incident" exception. The second exception is for disclosures with the consent of one of the parties.[38] We will discuss both exceptions below. We conclude that only the consent exception applies to the disclosure of subscriber content for behavioral advertising, and we will discuss preliminarily what "consent" would mean in this context.

B. With Limited Exceptions, Interception Is Also Prohibited

The Wiretap Act regulates the "interception" of ele ctronic communications. The Act defines "intercept" as the "acquisition of the contents of any. . . electronic. . . communication through the use of any electronic, mechanical, or other device."[39]

The Wiretap Act broadly bars all intentional interception of electronic communications.[40] The Act to this prohibition.[41] specific enumerates exceptions Law enforcement officers, for example, are authorized to conduct interceptions pursuant to a court order. For ISPs and other service providers, there are three exceptions that might be relevant. Two we have mentioned already: the "necessary incident" exception and a consent exception. [42]

A third exception, applicable to interception but not to disclosure, arises from the definition of "intercept," which is defined as acquisition by an "electronic, mechanical, or other device," which in turn is defined as "any device or apparatus which can be used to intercept a[n] . . . electronic communication *other than*—(a) any telephone or telegraph instrument, equipment or facility, or any component thereof. . . (ii) being used by a provider of. . . electronic communication service in the *ordinary course of its business. .. .*"[43] This provision thus serves to limit the definition of "intercept," providing what is sometimes called the "telephone extension" exception, but which we will call the "business use" exception.

C. The Copying of Internet Content for Disclosure to Advertising Networks Constitutes Interception

When an ISP copies a customer's communications or allows them to be copied by an advertising network, those communications have undoubtedly been "intercept[ed]."[44] Therefore, unless an exception applies, it seems likely that placing a device on an ISP's network and using it to copy communications for use in developing advertising profiles would constitute illegal interception under § 2511(1)(a); similarly, the disclosure or use of the intercepted communications would run afoul of § 2511 (1)(c) or § 2511 (1)(d), respectively.

D. The "Necessary Incident" Exception Probably Does Not Permit the Interception or Disclosure of Communications for Behavioral Advertising Purposes

The Wiretap Act permits interception of electronic communications when the activity takes place as "a necessary incident to the rendition of [the ISP's] service or to the protection of the rights or property of the provider of that service.[45] "The latter prong covers anti-spam and anti-virus monitoring and filtering and various anti-fraud activities, but cannot be extended to advertising activities, which, while they may enhance the service provider's revenue, do not "protect" its rights. Courts have construed the "necessary incident" prong quite strictly, requiring a service provider to show that it *must* engage in the activity in order to carry out its b·usiness.[46] It is unlikely that the copying, diversion, or disclosure of Internet traffic content for behavioral advertising would be construed as a "necessary incident" to an ISP's business. Conceivably, an ISP could argue that its business included copying its subscribers communications and providing them to third parties for purposes of placing advertisements on Web sites unaffiliated with the ISP, but the ISP would probably have to state that that business existed and get the express agreement of its cust omers that they were subscribing to that business as well as the basic business of Internet access, which leads anyhow to the consent model that we conclude is necessary.

E. While It Is Unclear Whether the "Business Use" Exception Would Apply to the Use of a Device Installed or Controlled by a Party Other than the Service Provider, the Exception Does Not Apply to the Prohibition Against Divulging a Subscriber's Communications

The "business use" exception, § 251 0(5)(a), constricts the definition of "device" and thereby narrows the definition of "intercept" in the Wiretap Act. There are two questions involved in assessing applicability of this exception to the use of Internet traffic content for behavioral advertising: (1) whether the device that copies the content for delivery to the advertising network constitutes a "telephone or telegraph instrument, equipment or facility, or any component thereof," and (2) whether an ISP's use of the device would be within the "ordinary course of its business."

We will discuss the "business use" exception at some length, because there has been considerable discussion already about whether copying of an ISP subscriber's communications for behavioral advertising is an "interception" under § 2511(1) of the Wiretap Act. However, even if the business use exception applied, an ISP would only avoid liability for the *interception* of electronic communications. It would still be prohibited from divulging the communications of its customers to an advertising network under the separate section of the Wiretap Act, § 2511(3), which states that a service provider "shall not intentionally divulge the contents of any communication. . . while in transmission on that service to any person or entity other than an addressee or intended recipient. . . ."[47] The business use exception does not apply to this prohibition against divulging.[48]

At first glance, it would seem that the business use exception is inapplicable to the facilities of an ISP because the exception applies only to a "telephone or telegraph instrument, equipment or facility, or any component thereof." However, the courts have recognized that ECPA was motivated in part by the "dramatic changes in new computer and telecommunications technologies"[49] and therefore was intended to make the Wiretap Act largely neutral with respect to its treatment of various communications technologies. The Second Circuit, for example, concluded in a related context that the term "telephone" should broadly include the "instruments, equipment and facilities that ISPs use to transmit e-mail."[50] Therefore, as a general matter, it should be assumed that the business use exception is available to ISPs.

However, it is not certain that the device used to copy and divert content for behavioral advertising would be considered to be a component of the service provider's equipment or facilities. In some of the behavioral advertising implementations that have been described, the monitoring device or process is not developed or controlled by the ISP but rather by the advertising network.

The second question is whether an ISP's use of a device to copy traffic content for behavioral advertising falls within the "ordinary course of its business." There are a number of cases interpreting this exception, but none of them clearly addresses a situation where a service provider is copying all of the communications of its customers. Many of the cases arise in situations where employers are monitoring the calls of their employees for purposes of supervision and quality assurance. "These cases have narrowly construed the phrase 'ordinary course of business.'"[51] Often such cases also involve notice to the employees and implied consent.[52] One court has stated that, even if an entity could satisfy the business use exception, notice to one of the parties being monitored would be required.[53] Other cases involve the monitoring of prisoners.

Some cases have interpreted "ordinary course" to mean anything that is used in "normal" operations. The D.C. Circuit, for instance, has suggested that monitoring "undertaken normally" qualifies as being within the "ordinary course of business."[54] In the context of law enforcement taping of the phone calls of prisoners, the Ninth and Tenth Circuits have concluded that something is in the "ordinary course" if it is done routinely and consistently.[55] It might be that courts would give equal or greater latitude to service providers in monitoring their networks than they would give to mere subscribers or users.

Other circuit courts have used a more limited interpretation, concluding that "ordinary course" only applies if the device is being used to intercept communications for "legitimate business reasons."[56] Although the courts have not been entirely clear as to what that means, some have suggested that it is much closer to necessity than to mere profit motive.[57] One frequently-cited case explicitly holds that the business use exception does not broadly encompass a company's financial or other motivations: "The phrase 'in the ordinary course of business' cannot be expanded to mean anything that interests a company."[58]

Normal principles of statutory interpretation would require that some independent weight be given to the word "ordinary," so that the exception does not encompass anything done for business purposes. It is unclear, however, how much weight courts would give to the word "ordinary" in a rapidly changing market. It does not seem that the phrase "ordinary course of business" should preclude innovation, but courts might refer to past practices and normal expectations surrounding a line of business and specifically might look to what customers have come to expect.

Viewed one way, it is hard to see how the copying of content for behavioral advertising is part of the "ordinary course of business" of an ISP. After all, the ISP is not the one that will be using the content to develop profiles of its customers; the profiling is done by the advertising network, which does not even disclose to the ISP the profiles of its own subscribers. (The profiles are proprietary to the advertising network and it is careful not to disclose them to anyone.) Very few (if any) of the ads that are placed using the profiles will be ads for the ISP's services; they will be ads for products and services completely unrelated to the ISP's "ordinary course of business." Moreover, the ads will be placed on Web sites having no affiliation with the ISP. On the other hand, the ISP could argue that part of its business model—part of what keeps its rates low —is deriving revenue from its partnership with advertising networks.

The legislative histories of the Wiretap Act and ECPA weigh against a broad reading of the business use exception. Through these laws, Congress intended to create a statutory regime generally affording strong protection to electronic communications. Congress included limited, specific and detailed exceptions for law enforcement access to communications, and other limited, specific and detailed exceptions to allow companies providing electronic communications service to conduct ordinary system maintenance and operational activities. Congress gave especially high protection to communications content. If the business use exception can apply any time an ISP identifies a new revenue stream that can be tapped though use of its customers' communications, this careful statutory scheme would be seriously undermined.

F. The Consent Exception: The Context Weighs Heavily in Favor of Affirmative, Opt-In Consent from ISP Subscribers

Consent is an explicit exception both to the prohibition against intercepting electronic communications under the Wiretap Act and to the Act's prohibition against disclosing subscriber communications. The key question is: How should consent be obtained for use of Internet traffic content for behavioral advertising? Courts have held in telephone monitoring cases under the Wiretap Act that consent can be implied, but there are relatively few cases specifically addressing consent and electronic communications. However, in cases involving telephone monitoring, one circuit court has stated that consent under the Wiretap Act "is not to cavalierly implied." [59] be Another circuit court has noted that consent "should not casually be inferred"[60] and that consent must be "actual," not "constructive."[61] Yet another circ uit court has stated: "Without actual notice, consent can only be implied when the surrounding circumstances *convincingly* show that the party knew about and consented to the interception.[62] "Furthermore, "knowledge of the *capability* of monitoring alone cann ot be considered implied consent."[63] The cases where consent has been implied involve very explicit notice; many of them involve the monitoring of prisoners' phone calls.[64]

Consent is context-based. It is one thing to imply consent in the context of a prison or a workplace, where notice may be presented as part of the daily log-in process. It is quite another to imply it in the context of ordinary Internet usage by residential subscribers, who, by definition, are using the service for personal and often highly sensitive communications. Continued use of a service after a mailed notice might not be enough to constitute consent. Certainly, mailing notification to the bill payer is probably insufficient to put all members of the household who share the Internet connection on notice.

Thus, it seems that an assertion of implied consent, whether or not users are provided an opportunity to opt out of the system, would most likely not satisfy the consent exception for the type of interception or disclosure under con sideration here. Express prior consent (opt-in consent) is clearly preferable and may be required. While meaningful opt-in consent would be sufficient, courts would likely be skeptical of an opt-in consisting merely of a click-through agreement—i.e., a set of terms that a user agrees to by clicking an on-screen button—if it displays characteristics typical of such agreements, such as a large amount of text displayed in a small box, no requirement that the user scroll through the entire agreement, or the opt-in provision buried among other terms of service.[65]

In regards to consent, the model under discussion here is distinguishable from the use of "cookies," which were found to be permissible by a federal district court in a 2001 case involving DoubleClick.[66] In that case, the Web sites participating in the DoubleClick advertising network were found to be parties to the communications of the Internet users who visited those sites. As parties to the communications, the Web sites could consent to the use of the cookies to collect information about those communications. Here, of course, the ISPs are not parties to the communications being monitored and the interception or disclosure encompasses communications with sites that are not members of the advertising network. Therefore, the source of consent must be the IPS's individual subscribers, as it would be impossible to obtain consent from every single Web site that every subscriber may conceivably visit.

II. State Laws Requiring Two-Party Consent to Communication Interception

A. Summary

In addition to the federal Wiretap Act, a majority of states have their own wiretap laws, which can be more stringent than the federal law. Most significantly, twelve states[67] require all parties to consent to the interception or recording of certain types of communications when such interception is done by a private party not under the color of law.

In several of these states—for example, Connecticut—the all-party consent requirement applies only to the recording of oral conversations. In others, the all-party consent rule extends to both voice and data communications. For example, Florida's Security of Communications Act makes it a felony for any individual to intercept, disclose, or use any wire, oral, or electronic communication, unless that person has obtained the prior consent of all parties.[68] Similarly, the Illinois statute on criminal eavesdropping prohibits a person from "intercept[ing], retain[ing], or transcrib[ing an] electronic communication unless he does so. . . with the consent of all of the parties to such. . . electronic communication."[69]

The most important all-party consent law may be California's, because the California Supreme Court held in 2006 that the law can be applied to activity occurring outside the state.

B. California

The 1967 California Invasion of Privacy Act makes criminally liable any individual who "intentionally taps, or makes any unauthorized connection. . . or who willfully and without the consent of all parties to the communication.. . reads, or attempts to read, or to learn the contents or meaning of any message. . . or communication while the same is in transit or passing over any wire, line, or cable, or is being sent from, or received at any place" in California.[70] It also establishes liability for any individual "who uses, or attempts to use, in any manner. . . any information so obtained" or who aids any person in doing the same.[71] The law has a separate section creating liability for any person eavesdropping upon or recording a confidential communication "intentionally and without the consent of all parties," whether the parties are present in the same location or communicating over telegraph, telephone, or other device (except a radio).[72]

Consent can be implied only in very limited circumstances. The California state Court of Appeals held in *People v. Garber* that a subscriber to a telephone system is deemed to have consented to the telephone company's monitoring of his calls if he uses the system in a manner that reasonably justifies the company's belief that he is violating his subscription rights, and even then the company may only monitor his calls to the extent necessary for the investigation.[73] An individual can maintain an objectively reasonable expectation of privacy by explicitly withholding consent for a tape recording, even if the other party has indicated an intention to record the communication.[74]

In *Kearney v. Salomon Smith Barney, Inc.*, the state Supreme Court addressed the conflict between the California all -party consent standard and Georgia's wiretap law, which is modeled after the federal one-party standard.[75] It held that, where a Georgia firm recorded calls made from its Georgia office to residents in California, the California law applied. The court said that it would be unfair to impose damages on the Georgia firm, but prospectively the case effectively required out-of-state firms having telephone communications with people in California to announce to all parties at the outset their intent to record a communication. Clear notice and implied consent are sufficient. "If, after being so advised, another party does not wish to participate in the conversation, he or she simply may decline to continue the communication."[76]

C. The Implications of Kearney

The Kearney case arose in the context of telephone monitoring, and there is a remarkable lack of case law addressing whether the California statute applies to Internet communications. If it does, or if there is one other state that applies its all-party consent rule to conduct affecting Internet communications across state lines, then no practical form of opt -in, no matter how robust, would save the practice of copying Internet content for behavioral advertising. That is, even if the ISP only copies the communications of those subscribers that consent, and the monitoring occurs only inside a one-party consent state, as soon as one of those customers has a communication with a non -consenting person (or Web site) in an all-party consent state that applies its rule to interceptions occurring outside the state, the ISP would seem to be in jeopardy. The ISP could not conceivably obtain consent from every person and Web site in the all-party consent state. Nor could it identify (for the purpose of obtaining consent) which people or Web sites its opted-in subscribers would want to communicate with in advance of those communications occurring.

A countervailing argument could be made that an all-party consent rule is not applicable to the behavioral advertising model, since the process only copies or divulges one half of the communication, namely the half from the consenting subscriber.

CONCLUSION

The practice that has been described to us, whereby an ISP may enter into an agreement with an advertising network to copy and analyze the traffic content of the ISP's customers, poses serious questions under the federal Wiretap Act. It seems that the disclosure of a subscriber's communications is prohibited without consent. In addition, especially where the copying is achieved by a device owned or controlled by the advertising network, the copying of the contents of subscriber communications seems to be, in the absence of consent, a prohibited interception. Affirmative express consent, and a cessation of copying upon withdrawal of consent, would probably save such practices under federal law, but there may be state laws requiring all-party consent that would be more difficult to satisfy.

END NOTES

[1] "Behavioral Advertising on Target É to Explode Online," *eMarketer* (Jun. 2007), http://www.emarketer.com/Article.aspx?id=1004989.

[2] No fewer than five major mergers and acquisitions have been completed in the last 18 months: Google purchased online advertising company DoubleClick, Inc.; WPP Group, a large ad agency, acquired the online ad company 24/7 Real Media; Yahoo! acquired ad firm RightMedia; Microsoft acquired online ad service provider aQuantive; AOL purchased Tacoda, a pioneering firm in the area of behavioral advertising.

[3] Michael Barbaro and Tom Zeller, Jr., "A Face Is Exposed for AOL Searcher No. 4417749," *The New York Times* (Aug. 2006),
http://www.nytimes.com/2006/08/09/technology/09aol.html?_r=1&ex=1312776000&adxnnl=1&oref=slogi n&adxnnlx=12 1502181 6-j7kbrLxHU1hCdcMyNqHEbA.

[4] See, e.g., Microsoft, *Privacy Protections in Microsoft's Ad Serving System and the P rocess of "De-identification"* (Oct. 2007), http://download.microsoft.com/download/3/1/d/31df6942-ed99-4024-a0e0-594b9d27a3 1 a/Privacy%20Protections%20in%20Microsoft%27s%20Ad%20Serving%20System%20and% 20the%20Process%20of%20De-Identification.pdf.

[5] Acxiom runs Relevance-X, an online ad network. Last year Experian acquired the online data analysis company Hitwise. *See* Acxiom, *Acxiom: Relevance-X* (last visited Jul. 2008), http://www.acxiom.com/Relevance-X; Experian, "Acquisition of Hitwise" (Apr. 2007),
http://www.experiangroup.com/corporate/news/releases/2007/2007-04-1 7b/.

[6] *See, e.g.,* Peter Whoriskey, "Every Click You Make," *The Washington Post* (Apr. 2008), http://www.washingtonpost.com/wp - dyn/content/article/2008/04/03/AR2008040304052.html?nav=hcmodule; Saul Hansell, "I.S.P. Tracking: The Mother of All Privacy Battles," *The New York Times: Bits Blog* (Mar. 2008) at http://bits.blogs.nytimes.com/2008/03/20/isp-tracking-the-mother-of-all-privacy-battles/?scp=1-b&sq=the+mother+of+all+privacy+battles&st=nyt.

[7] Alan F. Westin, *How Online Users Feel About Behavioral Marketing and How Adoption ofPrivacy and Security Policies Could Affect Their Feelings* (Mar. 2008).

[8] TRUSTe, "TRUSTe Report Reveals Consumer Awareness and Attitudes About Behavioral Targeting" (Mar. 2008), http://www.marketwire.com/mw/release.do?id=837437&sourceType=1 ("71 percent of online consumers are aware that their browsing information may be collected by a third party for advertising purposes. . ... 57 percent of respondents say they are not comfortable with advertisers using that browsing history to serve relevant ads, even when that information cannot be tied to their names or any other personal information.").

[9] *Am. Fed'n of Gov't Employees v. Hawley*, D.D.C., No. 07 -00855, 3/31/08 (ruling, *inter alia*, that concerns about identity theft, embarrassment, inconvenience, and damage to financial suitability requirements after an apparent data breach constituted a recognizable "adverse effect" under the Privacy Act, 5 U.S.C. § 552(a) (citing *Kreiger v. Dep't of Justice*, 529 F.Supp.2d 29, 53 (D.D.C. 2008)).

[10] See Louise Story, "Online Pitches Made Just For You," *The New York Times* (Mar. 2008), http://www.nytimes.com/2008/03/06/business/media/06adco.html.

[11] See Center for Democracy & Technology, *Digital Search and Seizure: Updating Privacy Protections to Keep Pace with Technology* (2006), http://www.cdt.org/publications/digital-search-and-seizure.pdf at 7-9; Deirdre K. Mulligan, "Reasonable Expectations in Electronic Communications: A Critical Perspective on the Electronic Communications Privacy Act," 72 Geo. Wash. L. Rev. 1557 (Aug. 2004); Daniel J. Solove, "Digital Dossiers and the Dissipation of Fourth Amendment Privacy," 75 S. Cal. L. Rev. 1083, 1135 (2002).

[12] *See* Center for Democracy & Technology, *Digital Search & Seizure: Updating Privacy Protections to Keep Pace with Technology* (2006), http://www.cdt.org/publications/digital-search-and-seizure.pdf at 23- 29.

[13] Saul Hansell, "Charter Suspends Plan to Sell Customer Data to Advertisers," *The New York Times: Bits Blog* (Jun. 2008), http://bits.blogs.nytimes.com/2008/06/24/charter-suspends-plan-to-sell-customer-data-to-advertisers/?scp=3-b&sq=charter+nebuad&st=nyt.

[14] Chris Williams, "CPW builds wall between customers and Phorm," *The Register* (Mar. 2008), http://www.theregister.co.uk/2008/03/11/phorm_shares_plummet/

[15] Robert M. Topolski, *NebuAd and Partner ISPs: Wiretapping, Forgery and Browser Hijacking*, Free Press and Public Knowledge (Jun 2008), http://www.publicknowledge.org/pdf/nebuad-report2008061 8.pdf.

[16] Richard Clayton, *The Phorm "Webwise" System* (May 2008), http://www.cl.cam.ac.uk/~rnc1/080518-phorm.pdf.

[17] These types of behaviors have much in common with well-understood online security threats, and parts of the Internet security community are already investigating how to respond. See Anti-Spyware Coalition, "Anti-Spyware Coalition Aims to Address Behavioral Targeting" (Apr. 2008), http://antispywarecoalition.org/newsroom/20080425press.htm.

[18] 18 U.S.C. § 2511.

[19] House Representative Edward Markey and House Representative Joe Barton, *Letter to Charter Communications CEO in Regards to the Charter-NebuAd Data Collection Scheme* (May 2008) http://markey.house.gov/docs/telecomm/letter_charter_comm_privacy.pdf. A 1992 amendment adding the phrase "other services" to the Cable Act's privacy provision made it clear that the law covers Internet services provided by cable operators.

[20] 47 U.S.C. § 551(b)-(c).

[21] Id. § 551(a)(2)(A).

[22] Id. § 551(a)(2)(B).

[23] *See* Mike Masnick, "Where's The Line Between Personalized Advertising And Creeping People Out?," *TechDirt* (Mar. 2008), http://www.techdirt.com/articles/20080311/121305499.shtml; Peter Whoriskey, "Every Click You Make," *The Washington Post* (Apr. 2008), http://www.washingtonpost.com/wp-dyn/content/article/2008/04/03/AR2008040304052.html?nav=hcmodule.

[24] Federal Trade Commission, *Online Profiling: A Report to Congress* (Jul. 2000), http://www.ftc.gov/os/2000/07/onlineprofiling.htm.

[25] The drawbacks of opt-out cookies have been well documented: they are confusing for the majority of consumers who do not understand the technology and counter-intuitive to those who are accustomed to deleting their cookies to protect their privacy. Cookies are susceptible to accidental deletion and file corruption. While the NAI is in the process of updating the principles , it has not proposed changes to the opt-out regime. See Center for Democracy & Technology, *Applying the FTC's Spyware Principles to Behavioral Advertising: Comments of the Center for Democracy & Technology in regards to the FTC Town Hall, "Ehavioral Advertising: Tracking, Targeting, and Technology"* (Oct. 2007), http://www.cdt.org/privacy/20071019CDTcomments.pdf at 8.

[26] See, e.g., AOL, *Mr. Penguin* (last visited Jul. 2008), http://corp.aol.com/o/mr-penguin/; Yahoo!, *Customized Advertising* (last visited Jul. 2008), http://info.yahoo.com/relevantads/; Google, *The Google Privacy Channel* (last visited Jul. 2008), http://youtube.com/user/googleprivacy.

[27] Center for Democracy & Technology, Comments Regarding the NAI Principles 2008: The Network Advertising Initiative's Self-Regulatory Code of Conductfor Online Behavioral Advertising (June 2008), http://www.cdt.org/privacy/20080612_NAI_comments.pdf at 6-9.

[28] CDT testing has revealed that only a tiny fraction of companies that collect data that could be used for behavioral advertising are NAI members. *See* Center for Democracy & Technology, *Statement of The Center for Democracy & Technology before The Antitrust, Competition Policy and Consumer Rights Subcommittee of the Senate Committee on the Judiciary on "An Examination of the Google-DoubleClick Merger and the Online Advertising Industry: What Are the Risks for Competition and Privacy?"* (Sept. 2007), *http://www.cdt.org/privacy/20070927committee-statement.pdf.*

[29] *See* Pam Dixon, *The Network Advertising Initiative: Failing at Consumer Protection and at Self - Regulation* (Nov. 2007), *http://www.worldprivacyforum.org/pdf/WPF_NAI_report_Nov2_2007fs.pdf at 16-17.*

[30] See Pam Dixon et al, Consumer Rights and Protections in the Behavioral Advertising Sector (Oct. 2007), http://www.cdt.org/privacy/20071031consumerprotectionsbehavioral.pdf.

[31] *See, e.g.,* Peter Whoriskey, *Every Click You Make*, WASH. POST (Apr. 3, 2008),
http://www.washingtonpost.com/wp -
dyn/content/article/2008/04/03/AR2008040304052.html?nav=hcmodule; Saul Hansell, *I.S.P. Tracking: The Mother ofAll Privacy Battles*, N.Y. TIMES: BITS BLOG (Mar. 20, 2008),
http://bits.blogs.nytimes.com/2008/03/20/isp-tracking-the-mother-of-all-privacy-battles/?scp=1-
b&sq=the+mother+of+all+privacy+battles&st=nyt.

[32] Privacy concerns also apply to advertising-based models that have been developed for services, such as email, that ride over ISP networks. *See* CDT Policy Post 10.6, *Google GMail Highlights General Privacy Concerns,* (Apr. 12, 2004), http://www.cdt.org/publications/policyposts/2004/6 (recommending express prior opt-in for advertising-based email service).

[33] Additional questions have been raised under the Cable Communications Policy Act. *See* Rep. Edward Markey and Rep. Joe Barton, *Letter to Charter Communications CEO in Regards to the Charter -NebuAd Data Collection Scheme* (May 2008),
http://markey.house.gov/docs/telecomm/letter_charter_comm_privacy.pdf. In this memo, we focus on issues arising under the federal Wiretap Act, as amended by the Electronic Communications Privacy Act.

[34] 18 U.S.C. §§ 25 10-2522.

[35] *Id.* § 2510(12).

[36] *Id.* § 2511 (3)(a). Lest there be any argument that the disclosure does not occur while the communications are "in transmission," we note that the Stored Communications Act (SCA) states that "a person or entity providing an electronic communication service to the public shall not knowingly divulge to any person or entity the contents of a communication while in electronic storage by that service."*Id.* § 2702(a)(1). We do not comment further here on the SCA because, in our judgment, the approach that has been described so far clearly involves the divulging of communications "while in transmission."

[37] *Id.* § 2511 (2)(a)(i) (emphasis added). This analysis focuses on the capture of electronic communications and definitions are abridged accordingly.

[38] *Id.* § 2511(3)(b)(ii).

[39] *Id.* § 2510(4).

[40] *Id.* § 2511(1).

[41] *Id.* § 2511(2).

[42] Separate from the consent provision for disclosure, the consent exception for interception is set forth in 18 U.S.C. § 2511 (2)(d): "It shall not be unlawful under this chapter for a person not acting under color of law to intercept a[n] . . . electronic communication where such person is a party to the communication or where one of the parties to the communication has given prior consent to such interception. . . ."

[43] *Id.* § 2510(5) (emphasis added).

[44] *See, e.g.,* United States v. Rodriguez, 968 F.2d 130, 136 (2d Cir. 1992) (holding in context of telephone communications that "when the contents of a wire communication are captured or redirected in any way, an interception occurs at that time" and that "[r]edirection presupposes interception"); *In re* State Police Litig., 888 F. Supp. 1235, 1267 (D. Conn. 1995) (stating in context of telephone communications that "it is the act of diverting, and not the act of listening, that constitutes an 'interception'").

[45] 18 U.S.C. § 2511(2)(a)(i).

[46] *See* United States v. Councilman, 418 F.3d 67, 82 (1st Cir. 2005) (en banc) (holding that service provider's capture of emails to gain commercial advantage "clearly" was not within service provider exception); Berry v. Funk, 146 F.3d 1003, 1010 (D.C. Cir. 1998) (holding in context of telephone communications that switchboard operators' overhearing of a few moments of phone call to ensure call went through is a "necessary incident," but anything more is outside service provider exception).

[47] 18 U.S.C. § 2511(3)(a).

[48] By adopting two different exceptions—"necessary incident" and "ordinary course"—Congress apparently meant them to have different meanings. Based on our reading of the cases, the necessary incident exception is narrower than the ordinary course exception. It is significant that the "necessary incident" exception applies to both interception and disclosure while the "ordinary course" exception is applicable only to interception. This suggests that Congress meant to allow service providers broader latitude in examining (that is, "intercepting" or "using") subscriber communications so long as they did not disclose the communications to third parties. This permits providers to conduct a range of in-house maintenance and service quality functions that do not involve disclosing communications to third parties.

[49] S. Rep. No. 99-541, at 1(1986), *reprinted in* 1986 U.S.C.C.A.N. 3555.

[50] Hall v. Earthlink Network, Inc., 396 F.3d 500, 505 (2d Cir. 2005) (quoting S. Rep. No. 99-541 at 8).

[51] United States v. Murdock, 63 F.3d 1391. 1396 (6th Cir 1995).

[52] *E.g.,* James v. Newspaper Agency Corp., 591 F.2d 579 (10th Cir. 1979).

[53] *See, e.g.,* Adams v. City of Battle Creek, 250 F.3d 980, 984 (6th Cir. 2001).

[54] Berry v. Funk, 146 F.3d 1003, 1009 (D.C. Cir. 1998) (workplace monitoring).

[55] *See* United States v. Van Poyck, 77 F.3d 285, 292 (9th Cir. 1996); United States v. Gangi, 57 Fed. Appx. 809, 814 (10th Cir. 2003).

[56] *See* Arias v. Mutual Central Alarm Serv., Inc., 202 F.3d 553, 560 (2d Cir. 2000) (monitoring calls to an central alarm monitoring service).

[57] *See id.* (concluding that alarm company had legitimate reasons to tap all calls because such businesses "are the repositories of extremely sensitive security information, including information that could facilitate access to their customers' premises"); *see also* Firstv. Stark County Board of Comm'rs, 234 F.3d 1268, at *4 (6th Cir. 2000) (table disposition).

[58] Watkins v. L.M. Berry & Co., 704 F.2d 577, 582 (11th Cir. 1983). Watkins states: "We hold that a personal call may not be intercepted in the ordinary course of business under the exemption in section 251 0(5)(a)(i), except to the extent necessary to guard against unauthorized use of the telephone or to determine whether a call is personal or not. In other words, a personal call may be intercepted in the ordinary course of business to determine its nature but never its contents." 704 F.2d at 583. This language supports the conclusion that the business use exception could not cover wholesale interception of ISP traffic, no more than switchboard operators can perform wholesale monitoring of telephone traffic.

[59] Watkins. 704 F.2d at 581 ("Consent under title III is not to be cavalierly implied. Title III expresses a strong purpose to protect individual privacy by strictly limiting the occasions on which interception may lawfully take place.").

[60] Griggs-Ryanv. Smith,904F.2d 112, 117 (1st Cir. 1990).

[61] *In re* Pharmatrak, Inc. Privacy Litig., 329 F.3d 9, 20 (1st Cir. 2003); *see also* United States v. Corona- Chavez, 328 F.3d 974, 978 (8th Cir. 2003).

[62] Berry v. Funk, 146 F.3d 1003, 1011 (D.C. Cir. 1998) (internal quotation omitted).

[63] Watkins, 704 F.2d at 581; *see also* Deal v. Spears, 980 F.2d 1153, 1157 (8th Cir. 1992) (holding that consent not implied when individual is aware only that monitoring might occur, rather than knowing monitoring is occurring).

[64] The circumstances relevant to an implication of consent will vary from case to case, but the compendium will ordinarily include language or acts which tend to prove (or disprove) that a party knows of, or assents to, encroachments on the routine expectation that conversations are private. And the ultimate determination must proceed in light of the prophylactic purpose of Title III-a purpose which suggests that consent should not casually be inferred." Griggs-Ryan, 904 F.2d at 117.

[65] *See, e.g.,* Specht v. Netscape Commc'ns Corp., 306 F.3d 17 (2d Cir. 2002) (rejecting online arbitration agreement because, among other things, site permitted customer to download product without having scrolled down to arbitration clause and agreement button said only "Download"); United States v. Lanoue, 71 F.3d 966, 981 (1st Cir. 1995) ("Deficient notice will almost always defeat a claim of implied consent.").

[66] *In re* DoubleClick Inc. Privacy Litig., 154 F.Supp.2d 497 (S.D.N.Y. 2001).

[67] The twelve states are California, Connecticut, Florida, Illinois, Maryland, Massachusetts, Michigan, Montana, Nevada, New Hampshire, Pennsylvania, and Washington.

[68] Fla. Stat. § 934.03(1).

[69] Ill. Comp Stat. 5/14-1(a)(1).

[70] Cal. Pen. Code § 63 1(a).

[71] *Id.*

[72] *Id.* § 632(a). The statute explicitly excludes radio communications from the category of confidential communications.

[73] 275 Cal. App. 2d 119 (Cal. App. 1st Dist. 1969).

[74] Nissan Motor Co. v. Nissan Computer Corp., 180 F. Supp. 2d 1089 (C.D. Cal. 2002).

[75] 39 Cal. 4th 95 (2006).

[76] Id.at118.

In: Electronic Breadcrumbs: Issues in Tracking Consumers
Editor: Dmitar N. Kovac
ISBN: 978-1-60741-600-5
© 2010 Nova Science Publishers, Inc.

Chapter 12

PRIVACY & ONLINE ADVERTISING HEARING-HINTZE TESTIMONY

Michael D. Hintze

Chairman Inouye, Ranking Member Stevens, and honorable Members of the Committee, my name is Michael Hintze, and I am an Associate General Counsel of Microsoft Corporation. Thank you for the opportunity to share Microsoft's views on the important privacy issues presented by advertising on the Internet. We appreciate the initiative that this Committee has taken in holding this hearing, and we are committed to working collaboratively with you, the Federal Trade Commission, consumer groups, and other stakeholders to protect consumers' privacy interests online.

Much is at stake with respect to the issues we will be considering today. Online advertising has become the very fuel that powers the Internet and drives the digital economy. It supports the ability of websites to offer their content and services online; it has created new opportunities for businesses to inform consumers about their products and services; and it allows consumers to receive ads they are more likely to find relevant. Simply stated, the Internet would not be the diverse and useful medium it has become without online advertising.

At the same time, online advertising is unique because it can be tailored automatically to a computer user's online activities and interests. An online ad can be served based on the website a user is visiting, the searches a user is conducting, or a user's past Internet browsing behavior, among other things. In each instance, serving the online advertisement involves the collection of information about consumers' Internet interactions. And this data collection has implications for consumer privacy.

The objective we face is to maintain the growth of online advertising while protecting consumer privacy. This is a commitment Microsoft embraces. We recognize that consumers have high expectations about how we and other Internet companies collect, use, and store their information. Consumers must *trust* that their privacy will be protected. If the Internet industry fails to meet that standard, consumers will make less use of online technologies, which will hurt them and industry alike.

It also could hurt the U.S. economy. E-commerce sales reached $136.4 billion in 2007, an increase of 19% from 2006, according to the U.S. Census Bureau.[1] In comparison, total retail sales in 2007 increased only 4% from 2006. If consumers feel that Internet companies are not protecting their privacy, the Internet's ability to serve as an engine of economic growth will be threatened. This means that Microsoft, and all companies operating online, must adopt robust privacy practices that build trust with consumers.

Microsoft has a deep and long-standing commitment to consumer privacy. Microsoft was one of the first companies to appoint a chief privacy officer, an action we took nearly a decade ago, and we currently employ over 40 employees who focus on privacy full-time, and another 400 who focus on it as part of their jobs. We have a robust set of internal policies and standards that guide how we do business and how we design our products and services in a way that respects and protects user privacy.[2] And we have made significant investments in privacy in terms of training and by building our privacy standards into our product development and other business processes.

In general, three key principles have guided our approach to privacy issues:

- *Transparency.* We believe consumers should be able to easily understand what information will be collected about them and when. They also should know how such information will be used and whether it will be combined with other information collected from or about them.
- *Control.* We believe consumers should be able to control whether their personal information is made available to others and should have a choice about whether information about their online activities is used to create profiles for targeted advertising.
- *Security.* Consumers and their information should be protected against outside threats and from unwanted disclosure. Data that directly identifies individual consumers, such as name and email address, should not be stored in direct association with search terms or data about Web surfing behavior used to deliver ads online. And strict data retention policies should apply to search data.

Today, I will discuss why we believe these principles are important, how we have put each of these principles into action, and how they underlie Microsoft's approach to privacy in online advertising. But first I would like to provide an overview of how online advertising works, the role that consumer data plays in serving online ads, and the online advertising market.

I. ONLINE ADVERTISING AND THE ROLE OF USER DATA

Consumers today are able to access a wealth of information and a growing array of services online for free. Websites can offer this content and these services for free because of the income they receive from advertising.[3] Just as newspapers and TV news programs rely on traditional advertising, online news sites and other commercial websites rely on online advertising for their economic survival. Online advertising is particularly critical for the thousands of smaller websites that do not publish through offline channels and thus depend entirely on the revenue they receive from selling space on their websites to serve ads online. It is also critical for smaller businesses that serve niche markets (e.g., out-of-print books on European history) who rely on online advertising to reach those niche audiences cost-effectively; indeed, many of these businesses could not survive without it.

The importance of online advertising is evident from its growing share of the overall advertising market. It accounted for $21 billion of the market in 2007 and is expected to grow to $50 billion in the next three years.[4] In the United States, online advertising spending already exceeds spending for advertising through radio, magazines, and cable television.[5]

One reason for this rapid growth is the ability to target online ads to Internet users. Newspaper, magazine, and television advertisements can, of course, be targeted based on the broad demographics of readers or viewers. But the Internet is interactive, and this interaction yields a wealth of data about users' activities and preferences. Each search, click, and other user action reveals valuable information about that user's likely interests. The more information an entity collects, the greater that entity's ability to serve an advertisement that is targeted to the user's interests. This targeting benefits users, not only because it enables the free services and content they enjoy, but also because the ads they see are more likely to be relevant. And it benefits advertisers because users are more likely to respond to their ads.[6]

There are a variety of ways in which data can be collected about users to serve targeted ads on the Internet. Users reveal information about what they are looking for when they search online, and ads can be targeted to their search queries.[7] Advertising networks enter into agreements with websites that allow them to display ads; to deliver and target those ads, data is gathered about the pages users view and the links users click on within those sites.[8] And new business models are emerging where data about users' online activities can be collected through a user's Internet service provider, and ads can be served based on that information. In general, most data collection happens in connection with the display of ads. This means the entity that serves the most ads (search and/or non- search ads) will also collect the most data about users.

II. THE ONLINE ADVERTISING ENVIRONMENT

The online advertising ecosystem has undergone significant changes in the past few years. There continue to be millions of websites that display online ads and thousands of advertisers who use online advertising. However, there is a relatively small number of so-called advertising networks, or "middlemen," to bring advertisers and websites together to buy and sell online ad space. And the number of companies playing this intermediary role has decreased significantly in recent months as a result of consolidation in the industry.[9]

This market consolidation impacts the privacy issues we are discussing today in several ways. First, it is important to recognize that in the past, advertising networks typically did not have direct relationships with consumers. Today, however, the major ad networks are owned by entities — such as Microsoft, Google, and Yahoo! — that provide a wide array of Web-based services and, therefore, often have direct relationships with consumers. This increases the potential that data collected through online advertising will be combined with personally identifiable information. While Microsoft has designed its online advertising system to address this concern,[10] no ad network is required to do so.

Further, as noted above, there is a direct connection between the market share of an advertising network or an online search provider and the amount of data collected about a user's online activity. For example, the larger the share of search ads a company delivers, the larger number of users' online search queries it collects and stores. Similarly, the larger the share of non-search ads an advertising network delivers across the Web, the larger number of users' page views it collects and stores, and the more complete picture of individuals' online surfing behavior it is able to amass. Today, Google AdWords is the leading seller of search advertising.[11] Google also has the leading non-search ad network, AdSense. Google recently expanded its reach into non-search by acquiring DoubleClick.[12] By comparison, Microsoft is a relatively small player in search ads, and its reach in non- search advertising is also smaller than Google's.[13] Google's growing dominance in serving online ads means it has access to and collects an unparalleled amount of data about people's online behavior.[14]

There also is a critical relationship between competition and privacy that must not be overlooked in this discussion. Competition ensures companies have an incentive to compete on the basis of the privacy protections they offer. On the other hand, a dominant player who is insulated from competitive pressure has little reason to heed consumer demand for stronger privacy protections and faces no significant competitive pressure from other firms offering superior privacy practices. Indeed, if a dominant player could generate additional profits by diluting its privacy practices, there is a significant risk it may do so. This could bring about a "race to the bottom" on privacy as other companies weaken their privacy practices in an effort to catch up to the market leader.

Yahoo! and Google's recently announced agreement raises important questions in this regard. Under the agreement, Yahoo! will outsource to Google the delivery of ads appearing alongside Yahoo!'s search engine results.[15] This has the potential to give Google, the market leader, further control over the sites and services where ads are served, enabling Google to collect even more data about computer users and potentially to combine that data with the personal information it has on those users.[16] It also will reduce competition in the search advertising market, and thereby weaken Google's incentives to compete on the quality of its privacy practices. Both of these outcomes have implications for consumer privacy.[17]

III. MICROSOFT'S COMMITMENT TO PRIVACY IN ONLINE ADVERTISING

Microsoft recognizes the role that data plays in online advertising and the corresponding importance of protecting consumer privacy. To guide our approach to data collection for online advertising, we released Microsoft's Privacy Principles for Live Search and Online Ad Targeting last July.[18] We are deeply committed to these principles, which focus on bringing the benefits of transparency, control and security to the protection of consumers' data and privacy online.

A. Transparency

I want to first touch upon the importance of transparency. Transparency is significant because it provides consumers with an informed understanding of a company's data collection practices, of how their data might be used, and the privacy controls available to users. Without transparency, consumers are unable to evaluate a company's services, to compare the privacy practices of different entities to determine which online products and services they should use, or to exercise the privacy controls that may be available to them. Transparency also helps ensure that when consumers are dealing with a company that has adopted responsible privacy practices, they do not needlessly worry about unfounded privacy concerns, which could prevent them from taking advantage of new technologies.

Transparency is also essential to ensure accountability. Regulators, advocates, journalists and others have an important role in helping to ensure that appropriate privacy practices are being followed. But they can only examine, evaluate and compare practices across the industry if companies are transparent about the data they collect and how they use and protect it.

Transparency is especially important with respect to online advertising. This is because consumers may not understand the types of information that entities collect or log in providing advertisements online. For example, many consumers may not realize that information about the pages they are viewing, the searches they are conducting, or the services they are using may be collected and used to deliver online ads.

For this reason, Microsoft believes that *any* entity that collects or logs *any* information about an individual or computer for the purpose of delivering advertisements online should provide clear notice about its advertising practices. This means posting a conspicuous link on the home page of its website to a privacy statement that sets forth its data collection and use practices related to online advertising. Consumers should not be required to search for a privacy notice; it should be readily available when they visit a website. This obligation should apply to entities that act as ad networks, as well as to websites on which ads appear — whether they display ads on their own or rely on third parties to deliver online advertising.

In addition to being easy to find, the privacy notice must be easy to understand. While many websites have publicly posted a privacy notice, this alone is not enough. Too often, the posted privacy notice is complex, ambiguous and/or full of legalese. These notices make privacy practices more opaque, not more transparent. Instead, short and simple highlights are essential if consumers are to easily understand a company's information practices. It helps avoid the problem of information overload, while enabling consumer awareness.

Finally, to ensure that the consumer can be fully informed, the privacy notice should also describe the website's data collection and use activities in detail. This includes, at a minimum, descriptions of the types of information collected for online advertising; whether this information will be combined with other information collected from or about consumers; and the ways in which such information may be used, including whether any non-aggregate information may be shared with a third party.

Microsoft has embraced these obligations. We post a link to our privacy notice on every page of our websites, including the home page. We also were one of the first companies to develop so-called "layered" privacy notices that give clear and concise bullet- point summaries of our practices in a short notice, with links to the full privacy statement for consumers and others who are interested in more detailed information. And our privacy statement is clear about the data we collect and use for online advertising. Further, we have released more detailed information about our practices, such as a white paper that describes the methods we use to "de-identify" data used for ad targeting.[19] To illustrate our efforts to be transparent about our practices, we have included in Appendix 2 screen shots of the privacy link available on the home page of our Windows Live search service and of our layered privacy notice, including both the short notice and our full online privacy statement.

B. Control

The second core principle Microsoft looks to in protecting our customers' privacy is user control. Consumers should have a choice about how information about their online activities is used, especially when that information can be aggregated across multiple websites or combined with personal information. Microsoft has made consumer control a key component of our practices online.

As an example, Microsoft has recently deployed a robust method to enable users to opt out of behavioral ad targeting. As background, most industry players that offer consumers a choice about having information about their online activities used to serve behaviorally targeted ads do so by offering consumers the ability to place an "opt-out" cookie on their machines. In general, this process works well, but it does have some inherent limitations. For example, opt-out cookies are computer-specific — if a consumer switches computers, he or she will need to specify any opt-out preferences again. Further, if cookies are deleted from the user's PC, that user's opt-out choice is no longer in effect. To address these limitations, Microsoft now gives consumers the option to tie their opt-out choice to their Windows Live ID. This means that even if they delete cookies on their machine, when they sign back in their opt-out selection will persist. It also means that a single choice can apply across multiple computers that they use. This will help ensure that consumers' choices are respected.[20]

Microsoft also has committed to respecting consumers' opt-out choice on all sites where it engages in behavioral advertising. This means that consumers are offered a choice about receiving behaviorally targeted ads across both third-party websites on which Microsoft delivers behaviorally targeted ads, as well as Microsoft's own websites. This is important because consumers reasonably expect that the opt-out choice offered by a company would apply on all websites where that company engages in behavioral advertising practices. This is another example of where we have committed to going beyond standard industry practice to better protect the interests of consumers.

We also recognize it is appropriate that the level of consumer control may vary depending on the data that will be used to serve an online ad. For example, many consumers have serious reservations about the receipt of targeted advertising based on the use of certain categories of personally identifiable information, particularly those that may be considered especially sensitive. Thus, we have proposed that companies should obtain additional levels of consent for the use of such information for behavioral advertising — including affirmative opt-in consent for the use of sensitive personally identifiable information.[21]

C. Security

The third principle we look to in protecting consumers' privacy is that strong, simple, and effective security is needed to strengthen consumers' trust in our products, the Internet, and all information technologies. Security has been fundamental at Microsoft for many years as part of our Trustworthy Computing initiative. And it plays a key role with respect to our online advertising practices.

We have taken a broad approach to protecting the security of computer users with respect to serving ads online. This approach includes implementing technological and procedural protections to help guard the information we maintain. We also have taken steps to educate consumers about ways to protect themselves while online, and we have worked closely with industry members and law enforcement around the world to identify security threats, share best practices, and improve our coordinated response to security issues.

In addition, we have designed our systems and processes in ways that minimize their privacy impact from the outset while simultaneously promoting security. For example, we use a technical method (known as a one-way cryptographic hash) to separate search terms from account holders' personal information, such as name, email address, and phone number, and to keep them separated in a way that prevents them from being easily recombined. We have also relied on this method to ensure that we use only data that does not personally identify individual consumers to serve ads online. As a result of this "de- identification" process, search query data and data about Web surfing behavior used for ad targeting is associated with an anonymized identifier rather than an account identifier that could be used to personally and directly identify a consumer.[22]

Finally, we have implemented strict retention policies with respect to search query data. Our policy is to anonymize all such data after 18 months, which we believe is an appropriate timeframe in our circumstances to enable us to maintain and improve the security, integrity and quality of our services. We intend to continue to look for ways to reduce this timeframe while addressing security, integrity and quality concerns. In addition, unlike other companies, our anonymization method involves irreversibly removing the *entire* IP address and other cross-session identifiers, such as cookies and other machine identifiers, from search terms. Some companies remove only the last few digits of a consumer's IP address, which means that an individual search query may still be narrowed down to a small number of computers on a network. We think that such partial methods do not fully protect consumer privacy, so we have chosen an approach that renders search terms truly and irreversibly anonymous.

IV. MICROSOFT'S SUPPORT FOR SELF-REGULATION AND PRIVACY LEGISLATION

Microsoft believes that these core principles of transparency, control, and security are critical to protecting consumers' privacy interests online. These principles form the basis for our support of robust self-regulation in the online advertising market and for baseline privacy legislation.

We have been an active participant in self-regulatory efforts. Microsoft has been engaging with the Network Advertising Initiative ("NAI"), a cooperative of online marketing and advertising companies that addresses important privacy and consumer protection issues in emerging media.[23] The NAI is currently in the process of revising its guidelines to address changes in the online advertising industry. The NAI's efforts have been critical to understanding the privacy issues associated with online advertising, and we will continue to work with them as they finalize their draft proposal.

We also filed comments responding to the Federal Trade Commission's request for input on a proposed self-regulatory framework for online advertising. In our comments, we explained the need for a broad self-regulatory approach since all online advertising activities have potential privacy implications and some may be contrary to consumers' expectations. To this end, we proposed a tiered approach to self regulation that is appropriately tailored to account for the types of information being collected and how that information will be used. It would set a baseline set of privacy protections applicable to all online advertising activity and would establish additional obligations for those companies that engage in practices that raise additional privacy concerns. We are attaching a copy of our comments to the FTC for your convenience.[24]

In addition to supporting self-regulatory efforts, we have long advocated for legislation as a component of effective privacy protections. We were one of the first companies to actively call for comprehensive federal privacy legislation.[25] More recently, we have supported balanced and well-crafted state legislation on privacy in online advertising that would follow the general structure proposed in our FTC comments.[26] And we would be glad to work with the Committee on similar national privacy standards that would protect both privacy and opportunities for innovation in the online advertising industry.

Our support of self regulation in the online advertising market and prudent privacy legislation is only a part of our comprehensive approach to protecting consumer privacy. We will continue to support consumer education efforts to inform users of how to best protect themselves and their information online. And we will persist in our efforts to develop technology tools that promote the principles of transparency, control, and security. In short, we are prepared to work collaboratively on all fronts to maintain the growth of online advertising while fostering consumer trust online.

V. CONCLUSION

Microsoft recognizes that the protection of consumer privacy is a continuous journey, not a single destination. We can and will continue to develop and implement new privacy practices and protections to bring the benefits of transparency, choice, and security to consumers. Thank you for giving us the opportunity to testify today. We look forward to working with you to ensure consumers' privacy interests are protected as they continue to enjoy the proliferation of free services and information that online advertising supports.

APPENDIX 1: MICROSOFT'S PRIVACY PRINCIPLES FOR LIVE SEARCH AND ONLINE AD TARGETING

Microsoft's Privacy Principles for Live Search and Online Ad Targeting represent the continuing evolution of Microsoft's long-standing commitment to privacy. They build on our existing policies and practices, as reflected in our privacy statements. They also complement our other privacy efforts, such as the public release of our Privacy Guidelines for Developing Software Products and Services and our work to advocate for comprehensive federal privacy legislation in the US and strong public policies worldwide to protect consumer privacy. Some parts of these principles reflect current practices, while other aspects describe new practices that will be implemented over the next 12 months.

In addition to guiding our own practices in the areas of Live Search and online ad targeting, we hope that these principles will be even more valuable in helping to advance an industry dialogue about the protection of privacy in these areas. We also recognize that these are dynamic technologies that are rapidly developing and changing. As such, we will continue to examine and update our privacy approach to ensure that we are striking the right balance for our customers.

Principle I: User Notice

We will be transparent about our policies and practices so that users can make informed choices. For example:

- Our current Microsoft Online Privacy Statement provides clear disclosures in an easy to navigate format that is readily accessible from every page of each major online service that we operate.
- We will regularly update the Microsoft Online Privacy Statement to maintain transparency as our services evolve or our practices change.
- In addition, we will shortly update our privacy statement to provide more detail on online advertising and search data collection and protection.

Principle II: User Control

We will implement new privacy features and practices as we continue to develop our online services. For example:

- We will continue to offer controls that help users to manage the types of communications they receive from Microsoft.
- Once we begin to offer advertising services to third party websites, we will offer users the ability to opt-out from behavioral ad targeting by Microsoft's network advertising service across those websites, in conformity with the Network Advertising Initiative (NAI) Principles.
- We will continue to develop new user controls that will enhance privacy. Such controls may include letting individuals use our search service and surf Microsoft sites without being associated with a personal and unique identifier used for behavioral ad targeting, or allowing signed-in users to control personalization of the services they receive.

Principle III: Search Data Anonymization

We will implement specific policies around search query data, be explicit with users about how long we retain search terms in an identifiable way, and inform users of when and how we may "anonymize" such data. Specifically:

- We will anonymize all Live Search query data after 18 months, unless we receive user consent for a longer time period. This policy will apply retroactively and worldwide, and will include irreversibly removing the entirety of the IP address and all other cross-session identifiers, such as cookie IDs or other machine identifiers, from the search terms.
- We will ensure that any personalized search services involving users choosing a longer retention period are offered in a transparent way with prominent notice and consent.
- We will follow high standards for protecting the privacy and security of the data as long as it is retained, as described in Part IV below.

Principle IV: Minimizing Privacy Impact and Protecting Data

We will design our systems and processes in ways that minimize the privacy impact of the data we collect, store, process and use to deliver our products and services. For example:

- We will store our Live Search service search terms separately from account information that personally and directly identifies the user, such as name, email address, or phone numbers ("individually identifying account information"). We will maintain and continually improve protections to prevent unauthorized correlation of this data. Moreover, we will ensure that any services requiring the connection of search terms to individually identifying account information are offered in a transparent way with prominent notice and user consent.
- We have also designed our online ad targeting platform to select appropriate ads based only on data that does not personally and directly identify individual users, and we will store clickstream and search query data used for ad targeting separately from any individually identifying account information, as described above.
- We will continue to implement technological and process protections to help guard the information we collect and maintain.

Principle V: Legal Requirements and Industry Best Practices

We will follow all applicable legal requirements as well as leading industry best practices in the markets where we operate. For example:

- We adhere to the standards set forth in the Organization for Economic Cooperation and Development (OECD) privacy guidelines.

- We follow the Online Privacy Alliance (OPA) guidelines.
- We are a member of the TRUSTe Privacy Program.
- We abide by the safe harbor framework regarding the collection, use, and retention of data from the European Union.
- As we begin to offer advertising services on third party websites, we plan to follow applicable Network Advertising Initiative (NAI) Principles, for example:

  We will give users the opportunity to opt out of behavioral targeting on third party websites (including the delivery of behaviorally targeted ads on third party websites and the usage of data collected on third party websites for behavioral targeting).

  We will not associate Personally Identifiable Information with clickstream data collected on third party websites without user notice and consent.

APPENDIX 2: MICROSOFT'S PRIVACY NOTICE

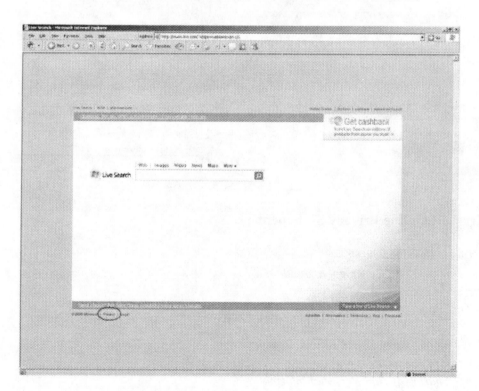

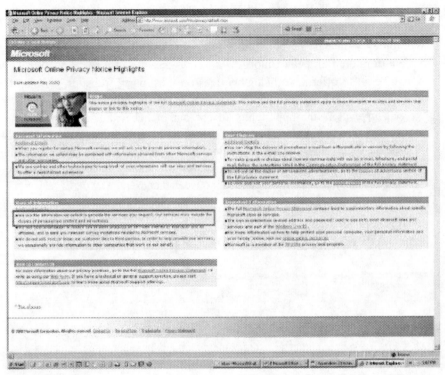

Search Microsoft.com for:

[ ] Go

Microsoft Online Privacy Statement

(last updated May 2008)
view the privacy statement highlights

On This Page

- *Collection of Your Personal Information*
- *Use of Your Personal Information*
- *Sharing of Your Personal Information*
- *Accessing Your Personal Information*
- *Communication Preferences*
- *Display of Advertising*
- *Security of Your Personal Information*
- *Collection and Use of Children's Personal Information*
- *Use of Cookies*
- *Use of Web Beacons*
- *Controlling Unsolicited E-mail ("Spam")*
- *TRUSTe Certification*
- *Enforcement of This Privacy Statement*

- *Changes to This Privacy Statement*
- *Contacting Us*

Supplemental Privacy Information

- *CRM Online*
- *Messenger*
- *MSN*
- *Office Live*
- *Office Online*
- *Search and Maps*
- *Support Services*
- *Windows Live*
- *Windows Live ID / Passport*
- *Windows Marketplace*
- *Windows Live OneCare*
- *WindowsMedia.com*
- *Xbox LIVE, Games for Windows LIVE and Xbox.com*
- *Zune*

Related Links

- *Silverlight Privacy Statement*
- *Security at Home*
- *Trustworthy Computing*
- *FTC Privacy Initiatives*

Microsoft is committed to protecting your privacy. Please read the Microsoft Online Privacy Statement below and also any supplemental information listed to the right for additional details about particular Microsoft sites and services that you may use.

This Microsoft Online Privacy Statement applies to data collected by Microsoft through the majority of its Web sites and services, as well as its offline product support services. It does not apply to those Microsoft sites, services and products that do not display or link to this statement or that have their own privacy statements. Some products and services mentioned in this statement may not be available in all markets at this time.

Collection of Your Personal Information

At some Microsoft sites, we ask you to provide personal information, such as your e-mail address, name, home or work address, or telephone number. We may also collect demographic information, such as your ZIP code, age, gender, preferences, interests and favorites. If you choose to make a purchase or sign up for a paid subscription service, we will ask for additional information, such as your credit card number and billing address, which is used to create a Microsoft billing account.

In order to access some Microsoft services, you will be asked to sign in with an e-mail address and password, which we refer to as your *Windows Live ID or Microsoft Passport Network* credentials. You can use the same credentials to sign in to many different Microsoft sites and services, as well as those of select Microsoft partners.

By signing in on one Microsoft site or service, you may be automatically signed into other Microsoft sites and services. If you access our services via a mobile phone, you may also use your telephone number and a PIN as an alternative credential to your username and password. As part of creating your credentials, you may also be requested to provide questions and secret answers, which we use to help verify your identity and assist in resetting your password, as well as an alternate e-mail address. Some services may require added security, and in these cases, you may be asked to create an additional security key. Finally, a unique ID number will be assigned to your credentials which will be used to identify your credentials and associated information.

We may collect information about your interaction with Microsoft sites and services. For example, we may use website analytics tools on our site to retrieve information from your browser, including the site you came from, the search engine(s) and the keywords you used to find our site, the pages you view within our site, your browser add-ons, and your browser's width and height. We may also use technologies, such as cookies and web beacons (described *below*), to collect information about the pages you view, the links you click and other actions you take on our sites and services. Additionally, we collect certain standard information that your browser sends to every website you visit, such as your IP address, browser type and language, access times and referring Web site addresses. We also deliver advertisements (see the *Display of Advertising* section below) and provide Web site analytics tools on non-Microsoft sites and services, and we may collect information about page views on these third party sites as well.

When you receive newsletters or promotional e-mail from Microsoft, we may use web beacons (described below), customized links or similar technologies to determine whether the e-mail has been opened and which links you click in order to provide you more focused e-mail communications or other information.

In order to offer you a more consistent and personalized experience in your interactions with Microsoft, information collected through one Microsoft service may be combined with information obtained through other Microsoft services. We may also supplement the information we collect with information obtained from other companies. For example, we may use services from other companies that enable us to derive a general geographic area based on your IP address in order to customize certain services to your geographic area.

Use of Your Personal Information

Microsoft collects and uses your personal information to operate and improve its sites and services. These uses may include providing you with more effective customer service; making the sites or services easier to use by eliminating the need for you to repeatedly enter the same information; performing research and analysis aimed at improving our products, services and technologies; and displaying content and advertising that are customized to your interests and preferences. For more information about the use of information for advertising, see the *Display of Advertising* section below.

We also use your personal information to communicate with you. We may send certain mandatory service communications such as welcome letters, billing reminders, information on technical service issues, and security announcements. Some Microsoft services, such as Windows Live Hotmail, may send periodic member letters that are considered part of the service. We may also occasionally send you product surveys or promotional mailings to inform you of other products or services available from Microsoft and its affiliates.

Personal information collected on Microsoft sites and services may be stored and processed in the United States or any other country in which Microsoft or its affiliates, subsidiaries or service providers maintain facilities. Microsoft abides by the safe harbor framework as set forth by the U.S. Department of Commerce regarding the collection, use, and retention of data from the European Union.

Sharing of Your Personal Information

Except as described in this statement, we will not disclose your personal information outside of Microsoft and its controlled subsidiaries and affiliates without your consent. Some Microsoft sites allow you to choose to share your personal information with select Microsoft partners so that they can contact you about their products, services or offers. Other sites, such as MSN, do not share your contact information with third parties for marketing purposes, but instead may give you a choice as to whether you wish to receive communications from Microsoft on behalf of external business partners about a partner's particular offering (without transferring your personal information to the third party). See the Communication Preferences section below for more information.

Some Microsoft services may be co-branded and offered in conjunction with another company. If you register for or use such services, both Microsoft and the other company may receive information collected in conjunction with the co-branded services.

We occasionally hire other companies to provide limited services on our behalf, such as handling the processing and delivery of mailings, providing customer support, hosting websites, processing transactions, or performing statistical analysis of our services. Those service providers will be permitted to obtain only the personal information they need to deliver the service. They are required to maintain the confidentiality of the information and are prohibited from using it for any other purpose. However, for credit card processing, our fraud detection vendors may use aggregate data to help improve their service. This helps them more accurately detect fraudulent uses of credit cards. We may access or disclose information about you, including the content of your communications, in order to: (a) comply with the law or respond to lawful requests or legal process; (b) protect the rights or property of Microsoft or our customers, including the enforcement of our agreements or policies governing your use of the services; or (c) act on a good faith belief that such access or disclosure is necessary to protect the personal safety of Microsoft employees, customers or the public.

Accessing Your Personal Information

You may have the ability to view or edit your personal information online. In order to help prevent your personal information from being viewed by others, you will be required to sign in with your credentials (e-mail address and password). The appropriate method(s) for accessing your personal information will depend on which sites or services you have used.

- **Microsoft.com** - You can access and update your profile on microsoft.com by visiting the *Microsoft.com Profile Center.*
- **Microsoft Billing and Account Services** - If you have a Microsoft Billing account, you can add to or update your information at the *Microsoft Billing Web site* by clicking on the "Personal Information" or "Billing Information" links.
- **Microsoft Connect** - If you are a registered user of Microsoft Connect, you can access and edit your personal information by clicking *Manage Your Connect Profile* at the Microsoft Connect Web site.
- **MSN & Windows Live** - If you have used MSN or Windows Live services, you can update your profile information, change your password, view the unique ID associated with your credentials, or close certain accounts by visiting MSN / Windows Live *Account Services.*
- **MSN Public Profile** - If you have created a public profile on MSN, you may also edit or delete information in your public profile by going to the *MSN Member Directory.*
- **MSN Keyword Advertising** - If you buy MSN Keyword advertising, you can review and edit your personal information at the *Microsoft adCenter Web site.*
- **Microsoft Partner Programs** - If you are registered with Microsoft Partner Programs, you can review and edit your profile by clicking *Manage Your Account* on the Partner Program Web site.
- **Xbox** - If you are an Xbox Live or Xbox.com user, you can access and edit your personal information on the *My Xbox* page on Xbox.com or on your console by selecting Privacy Settings under Edit Gamer Profile on Xbox 360, or selecting the Info Sharing option in Account Management for the Original Xbox Live dashboard.
- **Zune** - If you have a Zune account or a Zune Pass subscription, you can view and edit your personal information at *Zune.net* (click Manage My Account from your profile page) or through the Zune software (sign in, click your Zune tag, then click My Account or Privacy Settings to go to the appropriate page at Zune.net).

Some Microsoft sites or services may collect personal information that is not accessible via the links above.

However, in such cases, you may be able to access that information through alternative means of access described by the service. Or you can write us by using our *Web form*, and we will contact you within 30 days regarding your request.

Communication Preferences

You can stop the delivery of future promotional e-mail from Microsoft sites and services by following the specific instructions in the e-mail you receive.

You may also have the option of proactively making choices about the receipt of promotional e-mail, telephone calls, and postal mail from particular Microsoft sites or services by visiting and signing into the following pages:

- The *Microsoft.com Profile Center* allows you to choose whether you wish to receive marketing communications from Microsoft.com, to select whether Microsoft.com may share your contact information with selected third parties, and to subscribe or unsubscribe to newsletters about our products and services.
- The *MSN & Windows Live Communications Preferences* page allows you to choose whether you wish to receive marketing material from MSN or Windows Live. You may subscribe and unsubscribe to MSN Newsletters by going to the *MSN Newsletters website.*
- If you have an Xbox.com or Xbox Live account, you can set your contact preferences and choose whether to share your contact information with Xbox partners on the *My Xbox* page on Xbox.com or on your console by selecting Privacy Settings under Edit Gamer Profile on Xbox 360, or selecting the Info Sharing option in Account Management on the Original Xbox Live dashboard.
- If you are registered with Microsoft Partner Programs, you can set your contact preferences or choose to share your contact information with other Microsoft partners by clicking *Manage Your Account* on the Partner Program Web site.
- If you have a Zune account or a Zune Pass subscription, you can set your contact preferences and choose whether to share your contact information with Zune partners at *Zune.net* (click Manage My Account, Newsletter Options from your profile page) or through the Zune software (sign in, click your Zune tag, then click My Account, Newsletter Options to go to the appropriate page at Zune.net).

These choices do not apply to the display of online advertising. Nor do they apply to the receipt of mandatory service communications that are considered part of certain Microsoft services, which you may receive periodically unless you cancel the service.

Display of Advertising

Many of the Web sites and online services we offer, as well as those of our partners, are supported by advertising. Through the Microsoft Advertising Platform, we may display ads on our own sites and the sites of our advertising partners.

When we display online advertisements to you, we will place a persistent cookie on your computer in order to recognize your computer each time we display an ad to you. Because we may serve advertisements on many different Web sites, we are able to compile information over time about where you, or others who are using your computer, saw and/or clicked on the advertisements we display. We use this information to make predictions about your characteristics, interests or preferences and to display targeted advertisements that we believe may be of interest to you. We may also associate this information with your subsequent visit, purchase or other activity on participating advertisers' Web sites in order to determine the effectiveness of the advertisements.

While we may use some of the information we collect in order to personalize the ads we show you, we designed our systems to select ads based only on data that does not personally and directly identify you. For example, we may select the ads we display according to certain general interest categories or segments that we have inferred based on (a) demographic or interest data, including any you may have provided when creating an account (e.g. age, zip or postal code, gender), demographic or interest data acquired from other companies, and a general geographic location derived from your IP address, (b) the pages you view and links you click when using Microsoft's and its advertising partners' Web sites and services, and (c) the search terms you enter when using Microsoft's Internet search services, such as Live Search.

When we display personalized ads, we take a number of steps designed to protect your privacy. For example, we store page views, clicks and search terms used for ad personalization separately from your contact information or other data that directly identifies you (such as your name, e-mail address, etc.). Further, we have built in technological and process safeguards designed to prevent the unauthorized correlation of this data. We also give you the ability to opt-out of personalized ads. For more information or to use the opt-out feature, you may visit our *opt-out page.*

We also provide third party ad delivery through our Atlas subsidiary, and you may read the Atlas privacy statement at http://www.atlassolutions.com/privacy.aspx.

Although the majority of the online advertisements on Microsoft sites are displayed by Microsoft, we also allow third-party ad serving companies, including other ad networks, to display advertisements on our sites. These companies currently include, but are not limited to: *24/7 Real Media, Advertising.com, Bidclix, BlueStreak, Burst Media, DoubleClick, EuroClick, Eyeblaster, EyeWonder, Falk, Interpolls, Kanoodle, Mediaplex, Pointroll, TangoZebra, Yahoo! Publisher Network,* and *Zedo.*

These companies may offer you a way to opt out of ad targeting based on their cookies. You may find more information by clicking on the company names above and following the links to the Web sites of each company. Some of these companies are members of the *Network Advertising Initiative,* which offers a single location to opt out of ad targeting from member companies.

Security of Your Personal Information

Microsoft is committed to protecting the security of your personal information. We use a variety of security technologies and procedures to help protect your personal information from unauthorized access, use, or disclosure. For example, we store the personal information you provide on computer systems with limited access, which are located in controlled facilities. When we transmit highly confidential information (such as a credit card number or password) over the Internet, we protect it through the use of encryption, such as the Secure Socket Layer (SSL) protocol.

If a password is used to help protect your accounts and personal information, it is your responsibility to keep your password confidential. Do not share this information with anyone. If you are sharing a computer with anyone you should always log out before leaving a site or service to protect access to your information from subsequent users.

Collection and Use of Children's Personal Information

Many Microsoft sites and services are intended for general audiences and do not knowingly collect any personal information from children. When a Microsoft site does collect age information, and users identify themselves as under 13, the site will either block such users from providing personal information, or will seek to obtain consent from parents for the collection, use and sharing of their children's personal information. We will not knowingly ask children under the age of 13 to provide more information than is reasonably necessary to provide our services.

Please note that if you grant consent for your child to use Microsoft services, this will include such general audience communication services as e-mail, instant messaging, and online groups, and your child will be able to communicate with, and disclose personal information to, other users of all ages. Parents can change or revoke the consent choices previously made, and review, edit or request the deletion of their children's personal information. For example, on MSN and Windows Live, parents can visit Account Services, and click on "Permission for kids." If we change this privacy statement in a way that expands the collection, use or disclosure of children's personal information to which a parent has previously consented, the parent will be notified and we will be required to obtain the parent's additional consent.

If you have an MSN Premium, MSN Plus, or MSN 9 Dial-Up account, and use MSN Client software version 9.5 or below, you can choose to set up MSN Parental Controls for the other users of that account. Please read the supplemental privacy information for MSN for further information. For users of *MSN* Client software version 9.6 and above, we recommend the use of *Windows Live OneCare Family Safety*. We also offer an area that is specifically designed for children at http://kids.msn.com/ which has a special privacy statement that informs children and parents about the MSN Kids area, describes the additional privacy protections provided in this area, and provides children with tips on how to protect themselves online.

We encourage you to talk with your children about communicating with strangers and disclosing personal information online. You and your child can visit our *online safety resources* for additional information about using the Internet safely.

Use of Cookies

Microsoft Web sites use "cookies" to enable you to sign in to our services and to help personalize your online experience. A cookie is a small text file that is placed on your hard disk by a Web page server. Cookies contain information that can later be read by a Web server in the domain that issued the cookie to you. Cookies cannot be used to run programs or deliver viruses to your computer.

One of the primary purposes of cookies is to store your preferences and other information on your computer in order to save you time by eliminating the need to repeatedly enter the same information and to display your personalized content and appropriate advertising on your later visits to these sites. Microsoft Web sites also use cookies as described in the *Collection of your Information* and *Display of Advertising* sections of this privacy statement.

When you sign in to a site using your Windows Live ID or Microsoft Passport Network credentials, we store your unique ID number, and the time you signed in, in an encrypted cookie on your hard disk. This cookie allows you to move from page to page at the site without having to sign in again on each page. When you sign out, these cookies are deleted from your computer. We also use cookies to improve the sign in experience. For example, your e-mail address may be stored in a cookie that will remain on your computer after you sign out. This cookie allows your e-mail address to be pre-populated, so that you will only need to type your password the next time you sign in. If you are using a public computer or do not otherwise want this information to be stored, you can select the appropriate radio button on the sign-in page, and this cookie will not be used.

You have the ability to accept or decline cookies. Most Web browsers automatically accept cookies, but you can usually modify your browser setting to decline cookies if you prefer. If you choose to decline cookies, you may not be able to sign in or use other interactive features of Microsoft sites and services that depend on cookies, and some advertising preferences that are dependent on cookies may not be able to be respected.

If you choose to accept cookies, you also have the ability to later delete cookies that you have accepted. In Internet Explorer 7, you can delete cookies by selecting "Tools", "Delete browsing history" and clicking the "Delete Cookies" button. If you choose to delete cookies, any settings and preferences controlled by those cookies, including advertising preferences, will be deleted and may need to be recreated.

Use of Web Beacons

Microsoft Web pages may contain electronic images known as Web beacons - sometimes called single-pixel gifs - that may be used to assist in delivering cookies on our sites and allow us to count users who have visited those pages and to deliver co-branded services. We may include Web beacons in promotional e-mail messages or our newsletters in order to determine whether messages have been opened and acted upon.

Microsoft may also employ Web beacons from third parties in order to help us compile aggregated statistics regarding the effectiveness of our promotional campaigns or other operations of our sites. We prohibit Web beacons on our sites from being used by third parties to collect or access your personal information.

Finally, we may work with other companies that advertise on Microsoft sites to place Web beacons on their sites in order to allow us to develop statistics on how often clicking on an advertisement on a Microsoft site results in a purchase or other action on the advertiser's site.

Controlling Unsolicited E-mail ("Spam")

Microsoft is concerned about controlling unsolicited commercial e-mail, or "spam." Microsoft has a strict *Anti-Spam Policy* prohibiting the use of a Windows Live Hotmail or other Microsoft-provided e-mail account to send spam. Microsoft will not sell, lease or rent its e-mail subscriber lists to third parties. While Microsoft continues to actively review and implement new technology, such as expanded filtering features, there is no currently available technology that will totally prevent the sending and receiving of unsolicited e-mail. Using junk e-mail tools and being cautious about the sharing of your e-mail address while online will help reduce the amount of unsolicited e-mail you receive.

TRUSTe Certification

Microsoft is a member of the TRUSTe Privacy Program. TRUSTe is an independent, non-profit organization whose mission is to build trust and confidence in the Internet by promoting the use of fair information practices. To demonstrate our commitment to your privacy, we have agreed to disclose our information practices and have our privacy practices reviewed for compliance by TRUSTe. The TRUSTe program covers only information that is collected through Microsoft's Web sites, and does not cover information that may be collected through software downloaded from such sites.

Enforcement of This Privacy Statement

If you have questions regarding this statement, you should first contact us by using our *Web form*. If you do not receive acknowledgement of your inquiry or your inquiry has not been satisfactorily addressed, you should then contact TRUSTe at http://www.truste.org/consumers/watchdogcomplaint.php. TRUSTe will serve as a liaison with Microsoft to resolve your concerns.

Changes to This Privacy Statement

We will occasionally update this privacy statement to reflect changes in our services and customer feedback. When we post changes to this Statement, we will revise the "last updated" date at the top of this statement. If there are material changes to this statement or in how Microsoft will use your personal information, we will notify you either by prominently posting a notice of such changes prior to implementing the change or by directly sending you a notification. We encourage you to periodically review this statement to be informed of how Microsoft is protecting your information.

Contacting Us

Microsoft welcomes your comments regarding this privacy statement. If you have questions about this statement or believe that we have not adhered to it, please contact us by using our *Web form*. If you have a technical or general support question, please visit http://support.microsoft.com to learn more about Microsoft Support offerings.

Microsoft Privacy, Microsoft Corporation, One Microsoft Way, Redmond, Washington 98052 USA • 425-882-8080

To find the Microsoft subsidiary in your country or region, see http://www.microsoft.com/worldwide/.

© 2008 Microsoft Corporation. All rights reserved. *Anti-Spam Policy*
Manage Your Profile | Contact Us | Microsoft This Week! Newsletter | Legal
© 2008 Microsoft Corporation. All rights reserved. *Contact Us | Terms of Use | Trademarks | Privacy Statement*

APPENDIX 3: PRIVACY PROTECTIONS IN MICROSOFT'S AD SERVING SYSTEM AND THE PROCESS OF "DE-IDENTIFICATION"

As part of its strong commitment to protecting individual privacy, by design Microsoft bases its ad selection solely on data that does not personally and directly identify individual users.

The information contained in this document represents the current view of Microsoft Corp. on the issues discussed as of the date of publication. Because Microsoft must respond to changing market conditions, it should not be interpreted to be a commitment on the part of Microsoft, and Microsoft cannot guarantee the accuracy of any information presented after the date of publication.

This white paper is for informational purposes only. MICROSOFT MAKES NO WARRANTIES, EXPRESS OR IMPLIED, IN THIS DOCUMENT.

Complying with all applicable copyright laws is the responsibility of the user. Without limiting the rights under copyright, no part of this document may be reproduced, stored in or introduced into a retrieval system, or transmitted in any form or by any means (electronic, mechanical, photocopying, recording or otherwise), or for any purpose, without the express written permission of Microsoft.

Microsoft may have patents, patent applications, trademarks, copyrights or other intellectual property rights covering subject matter in this document. Except as expressly provided in any written license agreement from Microsoft, the furnishing of this document does not give you any license to these patents, trademarks, copyrights or other intellectual property.

© 2007 Microsoft Corp. All rights reserved.

Microsoft, Hotmail, MSN, Windows, Windows Live and Windows Vista are either registered trademarks or trademarks of Microsoft Corp. in the United States and/or other countries. The names of actual companies and products mentioned herein may be the trademarks of their respective owners.

Microsoft Corp.
One Microsoft Way
Redmond, WA 98052-6399
USA

Introduction

As the Internet has matured, online advertising has become the means by which many Web sites offer users rich content and services for free. Online advertising has also become an increasingly sophisticated vehicle for targeting users' interests—based on context (such as car ads on a car Web site) or based on user behavior on a site. The serving of relevant ads benefits advertisers, who are more likely to find customers for their products. It also benefits consumers, who are less likely to see ads that do not interest them. The key is making sure that users' privacy is protected in the process.

As part of its strong commitment to protecting individual privacy, by design Microsoft bases its ad selection solely on data that does not personally and directly identify individual users. The vast majority of ads that Microsoft serves online are not targeted to specific known users—they are based on context or are untargeted. For individually targeted ads, Microsoft's ad serving platform stores the data used for ad personalization separate from contact information or any other data that directly identifies the user. The system also has strong built-in safeguards against unauthorized correlation of these sets of data. The key to these important privacy protections is the use of an "Anonymous" ID (ANID) to enable recording of relevant online user activity without correlating it with data that can be used to personally and directly identify a user. This paper describes how Microsoft uses the ANID as a part of the de-identification process it uses to achieve robust individual privacy protections while still serving relevant targeted ads to users of its Web sites and online services, including MSN® and Windows Live™ sites.

Overview of Ad Targeting

Generally, online ad targeting providers try to correlate the interests of users, as implied by their past behavior or demographics, with the ads those users are served. Users' perceived interests are inferred over time based on information they provide when they register with a Web site or service or actions they take and information they provide when interacting with the site or service. In some cases, their interests are also inferred using publicly available information supplied by third parties. Based on this collection of data, users are assigned to different targeting segments and are accordingly served segment-specific ads. Users can be targeted in this way without the advertiser having any information that might personally and directly identify an individual person. (Similar kinds of behavioral targeting have existed in the offline direct mail and telemarketing industries for years, although they generally require indentifying information such as names, mailing addresses and telephone numbers.)

A generic per-computer ad targeting scenario typically works in the following way: A user visits a Web site, and the site places a cookie on the user's computer. A cookie is a tiny text file into which a Web site stores information called a cookieID that it can later use to recognize the user. The cookieID is also recorded in a database at the Web site. Let's assume that the user is visiting the site for the first time and that he has not and will not register at the site or provide the site with any information that could personally and directly identify him. The user is therefore unknown to the site. Each time the user visits that site, the site reads the cookieID and logs his actions on the site. These actions are stored in the database by the Web server and associated with the cookieID. Over time, the cookieID entries in the database might build up a significant record of actions taken by the unknown user on the site.

When sufficient data has been collected, the Web site's business rules might place the cookieID into one or more segments based on the user actions logged in the database. For example, if a user visits the hotel portion of a travel Web site often enough, the cookieID associated with his computer might be placed into a "Hotel Seekers" buying segment. From that point until the business rules dictate differently, the user might be shown hotel ads when he visits that site. Such behavioral targeting has been shown to significantly increase click-through and conversion rates for advertisers.

Clearing the cookie on the user's computer disassociates that computer from the cookieID and the logs of the user's behaviors and segments on the Web site's database. If the user never clears the cookie, the cookie will persist on his computer and the site can continue to accrue information until the cookie's expiration date or until the computer is recycled or the operating system is reinstalled or replaced.

This scenario becomes somewhat more complicated if a computer or computer user account is shared by two or more people. In general, a separate set of cookies is created for each user account (an account with a separate username and password) on a computer. In the case of Microsoft® Windows Vista® or Windows® XP, if all users of a PC share a single user account, the cookies stored on that PC may represent the totality of all their actions on that computer. So, for example, the records that a Web site attributes to a single unknown user might actually represent the actions of an entire family that shares the same computer account or the actions of all users of a public computer. If each user of the PC uses a separate account, each user will have a separate set of cookies.

Third-party ad networks—service providers that provide ads to a number of Web sites—serve targeted ads to computers in a manner similar to that just described. However, they differ in two significant ways. First, ad networks generally have broader reach because they serve ads across a variety of (often unrelated) Web sites rather than on a single site. Second, they may aggregate information about a user's behavior across multiple sites on which they serve ads, so they might capture a broader range of user activity.

Ad Targeting at MSN and Windows Live[27]

As a matter of policy, Microsoft takes steps to separate any information that can be used to personally and directly identify a user—such as name, e-mail address or phone number—from the information in its ad selection system. This de-identification adds an important layer of privacy protection while still allowing Microsoft to serve targeted ads based on user behavior. In other words, the MSN and Windows Live sites do not need to correlate personally and directly identifying data with user behavior online in order to take full advantage of behavioral targeting. For example, MSN can target ads to a person who likes coffee, lives in Seattle and is male without knowing the name, e-mail address or any other personally identifying information that the user might have provided when registering for particular services on MSN or Windows Live.

Microsoft uses three different cookies—the Machine Unique ID (MUID), the Windows Live User ID (LiveID) and the "Anonymous" ID (ANID)—in its ad targeting infrastructure.[28] The latter two are part of the process that segregates data used for ad personalization from information that could personally and directly identify a user. We'll look at each of these in turn.

The Machine Unique ID (MUID)

When a user first visits an MSN or Windows Live site, a standard cookie with a randomly generated unique identifier called the Machine Unique ID (MUID) is placed on the user's computer (the "machine"). For the purpose of ad targeting, that cookieID may behave in the same manner as the cookieID described earlier in the generic example. This means that the MUID may be used to target ads based on the behaviors of an unknown user. This behavior is illustrated in Figure 1. Information that could personally and directly identify a user is not associated with the MUID.

The Windows Live User ID (LiveID)

The example of the MUID involves a cookieID that is assigned per computer account to users who are not known to the Web site. Now we'll discuss cookieIDs that are assigned on a "per- login" basis to users who have established a relationship with the Web site.

In general, Web sites that require a user to log in to access a user-specific service, such as Web- based e-mail, use a user-based cookieID as a part of their system for granting access. At MSN and Windows Live, the core user-based ID is the Windows Live ID (LiveID). When a user first registers at the site, she typically chooses a username and password and provides Microsoft with a first and last name, plus a few pieces of non-identifying demographic information such as country, Zip code, age, gender and language. In scenarios where a user is creating a billing account, additional pieces of personal information might also be collected at this point. A unique LiveID is then generated and associated with this data. The LiveID is the unique ID number specific to that user account.

The LiveID is stored on the Windows Live ID servers and, once the user has presented a valid username and password, is placed in a cookie on her computer. The presence of the LiveID cookie is the signal to an MSN or Windows Live service that it should continue to grant access— for example, to the user's e-mail in the case of Windows Live Hotmail. When the user logs out of the service or ends the session, the LiveID cookie expires (unless the user has opted to make the cookie permanent by clicking "Save My Password" so she does not have to log in each time she accesses the service). Granting a user access to her Hotmail e-mail is an example of when the LiveID needs to be associated with personal information. Other Windows Live services that require this type of authentication via a LiveID include Windows Live Messenger and Windows Live Spaces.

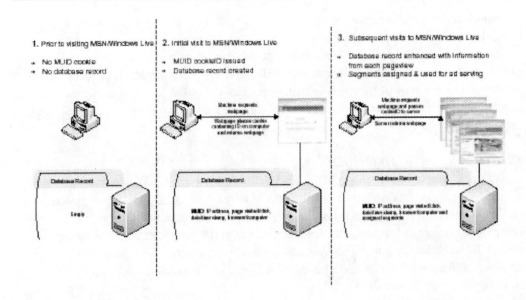

Figure 1. The Machine Unique ID (MUID).

Because the LiveID database contains data that could be used to personally and directly identify individual users, by design Microsoft's advertising system *does not* use the LiveID to select and serve ads—even though it would be technically far simpler to have it do so. One of Microsoft's *online advertising principles* is that its ad targeting platform can select appropriate ads based *only* on data that does not personally and directly identify individual users.[29]

The "Anonymous" ID (ANID)

One of Microsoft's goals is to serve targeted ads in a manner that protects user privacy. To avoid using the LiveID cookie to serve per-user ads—because, as described earlier, it is directly associated with information that could personally identify the user—Microsoft has created an "Anonymous" ID, called the ANID, on which its ad serving capabilities are based.

When a user first registers with Windows Live or MSN, a LiveID and an ANID are created simultaneously. The ANID is derived by applying a one-way cryptographic hash function to the LiveID. A one-way cryptographic hash function ensures that there is no practical way of deriving the original value from the resulting hash value—that is, the process cannot be reversed to obtain the original number.

What this means in practical terms is that each time a registered user logs in, Microsoft's system applies the hash function to the LiveID to generate an ANID, and each ID is put in a separate cookie on the computer. The advantage of using a one-way cryptographic hash function is that although the same number is guaranteed to be generated each time it is applied to a given LiveID, it is virtually impossible to reverse the process. In other words, it is extremely difficult to use a given ANID (with or without knowing the hashing algorithm) to derive the original LiveID value. Because all personally and directly identifying information about a user is stored on servers in association with a LiveID rather than an ANID, there is no practical way to link data stored in association with an ANID back to any data on Microsoft servers that could personally and directly identify an individual user. Figure 2 illustrates this relationship between the two IDs.

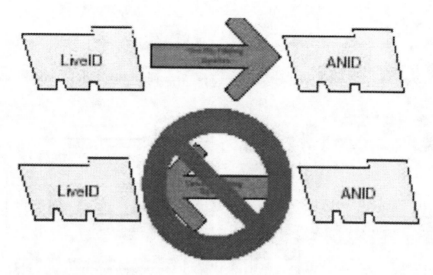

Figure 2. One-way cryptographic hash.

As mentioned earlier, a user might input particular pieces of demographic information when a LiveID is created. When the LiveID and ANID are created, the demographic information that cannot be used to personally and directly identify the user is copied to a database that is indexed on only the ANID. Microsoft's ad serving infrastructure consumes data associated with the ANID but not the LiveID, so copying the demographic data in this way allows Microsoft to make it available to the ad serving infrastructure. As a user with an ANID cookie on her computer navigates around the Microsoft sites, data associated with her online behaviors, such as searches and pageviews, is associated with the AN ID. All of this information can then be used to assign ad targeting segments to the ANID in the same manner as described previously in the generic description of ad targeting. (Figure 3 illustrates this process.) Most importantly, because of the one-way hash used in creating the ANID, none of the specific behaviors associated with the ANID or the ad targeting segments consequently assigned to the ANID are linked back to the personal information associated with the LiveID.

When a user logs out of a Windows Live account, the LiveID cookie is deleted from her computer. However, the ANID cookie remains on the user's system until a different Windows Live account is accessed from that computer account (which would replace the old ANID cookie with a different one), until the user takes steps to delete the ANID cookie or until the cookie expires.

Privacy protections tend to be strongest when implemented as a part of the fundamental architecture of a computer system. Microsoft's ad serving system was designed expressly to work with the AN ID, and the ANID was designed expressly to enhance user privacy. These safeguards help ensure that information associated with a LiveID will not leak into the ad serving environment.

Of course, the ANID infrastructure itself does not guarantee complete and irreversible anonymity. But it does provide strong technical protection, which, combined with stringent internal policies, is designed to keep the data used for ad serving separated from information that identifies an individual.

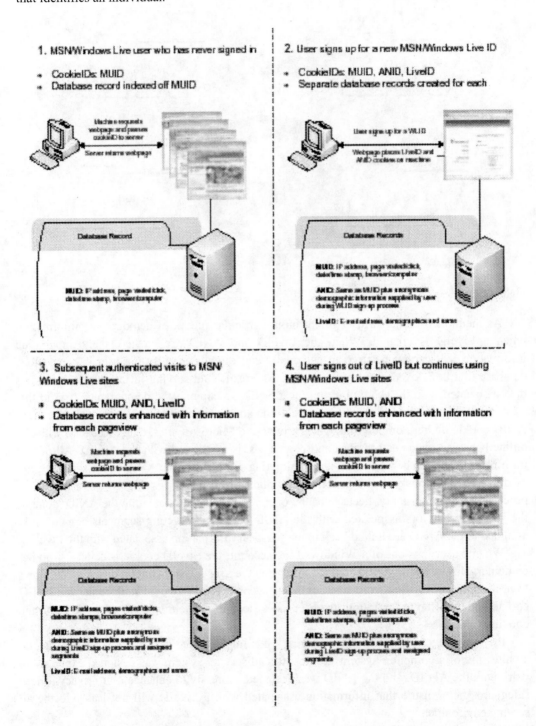

Figure 3. Sample MUID, ANID and LiveID interactions.

For example, because the system is AN ID-based, Microsoft employees with access to the company's ad serving system alone cannot identify users who are served ads based on the data in the system. Furthermore, to associate any of the ANID-based data in the Microsoft ad system with an individual user, an internal or external attacker would not only need access to the ad serving system (to access the data), the Windows Live ID system (to access all LiveIDs ever issued) and the hashing algorithm but would also need a massive computing infrastructure to run the algorithm on each and every LiveID ever created to try to find the ANID in question. Each of these components is separately protected with strong internal security measures, rendering this scenario virtually impossible.

Further, the use of the ANID is part of the company's overall approach to protecting user privacy, which includes strong and meaningful protections from the time that behavioral data is first collected. These protections also include the recently announced policy of anonymizing search query data after 18 months. (This includes the complete and irreversible deletion of full IP addresses and cookieIDs—including ANIDs—from search terms.)

CONCLUSION

Microsoft's use of the ANID enables the delivery of relevant ads to users while basing ad selection solely on data that does not personally and directly identify individual users. As a fundamental element of Microsoft's ad targeting infrastructure, the ANID underscores the company's strong commitment to privacy. It is complemented by the recent announcement of Microsoft's *Privacy Principles for Live Search and Online Ad Targeting,*[30] the public release of the company's *Privacy Guidelines for Developing Software Products and Services*[31] and its advocacy for comprehensive federal privacy legislation in the United States and strong public policies worldwide to protect consumer privacy. In a dynamic industry where rules and best practices are continually evolving, Microsoft is committed to ensuring that its current and future products and services implement industry-leading technologies and processes that protect individual privacy.

APPENDIX 4: MICROSOFT'S COMMENTS TO THE FEDERAL TRADE COMMISSION

Microsoft

Via Hand And Email Delivery

Mr. Donald S. Clark
Secretary
Federal Trade Commission
Room H-135 (Annex N) 600 Pennsylvania Avenue, NW
Washington, DC 20580

Re. Online Behavioral Advertising. Moving the Discussion Forward to Possible Self-Regulatory Principles

Dear Secretary Clark:

Microsoft submits these comments in response to the Commission's request for feedback on its proposed self-regulatory principles for online behavioral advertising. Microsoft commends the Commission for releasing these principles and for its successful November Town Hall, "Ehavioral Advertising: Tracking, Targeting, and Technology." The Commission's efforts have raised awareness and fostered an important dialogue among stakeholders about the privacy issues associated with online advertising.

I. Executive Summary

Microsoft recognizes the need for self-regulatory principles governing online advertising that provide consumers with greater transparency and control. Microsoft's own online advertising practices include commitments to user notice, user control, anonymization, security, and best practices. These principles are generally tailored to account for the types of information we collect and how we intend to use that information. Microsoft suggests that the Commission adopt a similarly nuanced approach to its self-regulatory principles that impose increasing obligations depending on the type of online advertising activity involved:

- Any entity that logs page views or collects other information about consumers for the purpose of delivering ads or providing advertising-related services ("online advertising") within its own site should inform consumers of its advertising practices in a privacy notice that is available through a clear and conspicuous link on its site's homepage, implement reasonable security procedures, and retain data only as long as necessary to fulfill a legitimate business need or as required by law.
- hird parties that collect information about consumers for online advertising across multiple, unrelated third-party sites ("multi-site advertising") should take reasonable steps to ensure consumers receive notice of their activities.
- Third parties that seek to develop a profile of consumer activity to deliver advertising across multiple, unrelated third-party sites ("behavioral advertising") should additionally offer consumers a choice about the use of their information for such purposes.
- Third parties seeking to merge personally identifiable information with information collected through multi-site or behavioral advertising should be subject to additional obligations.
- Third parties should be required to obtain affirmative express consent before using sensitive personally identifiable information for behavioral advertising.

The increasing obligations that should flow from the type of advertising activity involved can be summarized as follows:

Type of Advertising	Definition	Obligation
Sensitive Personally Identifiable Information Advertising	The use of sensitive personally identifiable information for the purpose of behavioral advertising.	Opt-in consent
Personally Identifiable Advertising	The merger of information that, by itself, can be used to identify someone – such as name, e-mail address, physical address, or telephone number – with data collected through multi-site or behavioral advertising for the purpose of ad targeting.	Prospective use: Opt-out choice Retroactive use: Opt-in consent
Behavioral Advertising	The tracking of a consumer's activities online across multiple, unrelated sites – including the searches the consumer has conducted, the web pages visited, and the content viewed – by a third party in order to deliver advertising across multiple, unrelated sites targeted to the individual consumer's interests.	Opt-out choice
Multi-site Advertising	Online advertising across multiple, unrelated third-party sites.	Pass-through notice: make reasonable efforts to require website operators to link to a privacy notice on their home page
Online Advertising	The logging of page views or the collection of other information about an individual consumer or computer for the purpose of delivering ads or providing advertising-related services.	Link to privacy notice on home page; follow reasonable security and data retention obligations

In addition, with respect to material changes, the Commission should clarify that the level of notice and consumer consent required depends on various factors, including the materiality of the change and whether it would apply retroactively or prospectively.

II. Introduction

Online advertising has assumed a large and growing significance in global economies. As the Commission recognizes, online advertising enables advertisers to target their ads to specific consumers and allows consumers to receive ads that they are more likely to find useful. This facilitates comparison shopping, reduces the number of irrelevant ads received by consumers, and subsidizes the wide variety of free content and services available to consumers online. Consumers value these benefits, but, as the Commission notes, they may not fully appreciate the role that data collection plays in providing them. They also may not appreciate other elements of online advertising that may impact their privacy — most notably that third parties may be involved in delivering online ads and collecting information about them.

In light of these concerns, Microsoft announced five fundamental privacy principles last July for online search and ad targeting. These principles touch upon many of the same themes as those addressed by the Commission and include commitments to user notice, user controls, anonymization, security, and best practices. These principles are discussed in greater detail below, and a full copy of the principles is attached to these comments. Late last year, Microsoft also began the process of joining the Network Advertising Initiative ("NAI"), a cooperative of online marketing and advertising companies that addresses important privacy and consumer protection issues in emerging media.[32]

Microsoft's efforts in the online advertising area are just one aspect of our broader commitment to protecting consumer privacy. We were one of the first companies to advocate for comprehensive federal privacy legislation in the United States. We have led the industry in adopting privacy notices that are clear, concise, and understandable. We have released a set of privacy guidelines designed to help developers build meaningful privacy protections into their software programs and online services.[33] And we have made significant investments in privacy in terms of dedicated personnel and training and by building robust privacy standards into our product development and other business processes.

Microsoft welcomes the opportunity to provide comment on the Commission's proposed self-regulatory framework. Our comments begin by providing an overview of the online advertising principles Microsoft has committed to follow. We then propose a multi-tiered self-regulatory approach that should apply to all entities engaged in advertising online, and we discuss the reasonable security and limited data retention procedures that such entities should follow. We also provide input on the Commission's proposal around material changes and finally respond to the Commission's request for additional information about using tracking data for purposes other than online advertising.

III. Microsoft's Online Advertising Practices

Microsoft's efforts to protect consumer privacy in the online advertising space are reflected in Microsoft's Privacy Principles for Live Search and Online Ad Targeting. These principles build upon existing policies and practices, as reflected in Microsoft's privacy statements, and will help shape the development of our new product offerings. We hope that the insight we have developed in formulating and implementing these principles is of use to the Commission as it contemplates a self-regulatory framework for online advertising.

A. Principle I: User Notice

Microsoft has long believed that providing transparency about its policies and practices is critical to enable consumers to make informed choices. To this end, Microsoft's Online Privacy Statement is readily accessible from every page of each major online service that we operate. It also is written in clear language and offered in a "layered" format that provides consumers with the most important information about our privacy practices upfront, followed by additional layers of notice that provide a more comprehensive examination of our general privacy practices.[34] We recently updated our U.S. privacy statement to provide additional detail about the use of information collected through search and page views for ad targeting, and we intend to further update our privacy statement in the near term to provide more information about online advertising and our search data retention practices.

B. Principle II: User Control

Microsoft currently offers consumers a series of controls that enable users to manage the types of communications they receive. As an initial matter, we have built user controls — including control over third-party cookies — into our Internet Explorer product. We also allow users to easily access and edit their stored personal information and to choose the types of e-mail, phone or fax communications they wish to receive from Microsoft.

In addition, we currently offer users the ability to opt out from receiving behaviorally targeted ads through our Atlas subsidiary.[35] We will soon offer users a choice about receiving targeted ads across both third-party websites and Microsoft-operated websites. We also will enable users to tie their opt-out choice to their Windows Live ID so that their opt-out selection will apply across multiple computers, and if their cookies are deleted, their choice will be reset when they sign in with their ID.

C. Principle III: Search Data Anonymization

Microsoft has committed to make search query data anonymous after 18 months by permanently removing cookies, the entire IP address, and other identifiers from search logs, unless the user has provided consent for us to retain data for a longer period of time. We made the decision early on that partial approaches — such as removing only portions of an IP address — are inadequate. A partially redacted IP address can still narrow down the field of computers from which an associated search originated. Moreover, an IP address is unlikely to be the only unique identifier associated with search data. Depending upon how the search service is designed, there are likely to be other cookie or machine-based identifiers linked to search data, and some of these identifiers may directly or indirectly correlate to user accounts or other personally identifiable information. The presence of cross-session identifiers could permit the correlation of sufficient search data related to an individual user to make it possible to identify such an individual even without an IP address or without what would traditionally be considered personally identifiable information.[36] Thus, we believe that, in order to fully protect privacy and make search query data truly anonymous, all cross-session identifiers must be removed in their entirety from the data.

D. Principle IV: Minimizing Privacy Impact and Protecting Data

Microsoft strives to design all systems and processes in a manner that minimizes their negative privacy impact from the outset, while simultaneously promoting security. Microsoft collects (and will continue to collect) only a limited amount of information from Windows Live users — specifically, name, e-mail, password, and demographic data (gender, birth year, country/region, and zip).

We also take steps to separate the data used for ad targeting from any personally identifiable information before using it to serve ads — a process we refer to as "de-identification." Specifically, for users who have created Windows Live accounts, rather than using the account ID as the basis for our ad systems, we use a one-way cryptographic hash to create a new anonymized identifier. We then use that identifier, along with the non-identifiable demographic data, to serve ads online. Search query data and web surfing behavior used for ad targeting is associated with this anonymized identifier rather than an account identifier that could be used to personally and directly identify a user. In short, user privacy is not only protected through the de-identification process at the outset, but after 18 months, the information is completely and irreversibly anonymized. We believe this multifaceted approach to protecting search query data demonstrates Microsoft's strong commitment to consumer privacy. A white paper describing Microsoft's "de-identification" process is attached to these comments.

Finally, we have implemented robust security protections to prevent the unauthorized correlation of this information and to help protect the information we collect and maintain.

E. Principle V: Legal Requirements and Industry Best Practices

Microsoft adheres to all applicable legal requirements as well as leading industry best practices regarding consumer privacy in all markets where we operate. To this end, Microsoft currently abides by the standards set forth in the Organization for Economic Cooperation and Development (OECD) privacy guidelines, the Online Privacy Alliance (OPA) guidelines, the EU-US Safe Harbor Framework, and the TRUSTe Privacy Program. Microsoft also has advocated for comprehensive federal privacy legislation as an additional pillar of the foundation needed to protect consumer privacy.

IV. Self-Regulatory Principles Should Apply to All Types of Online Advertising

Microsoft supports the Commission's intent to encompass a wide variety of activities through its definition of behavioral advertising. We also agree with the Commission that behavioral advertising raises "unique" concerns that may necessitate heightened transparency and control obligations. That said, we believe that the Commission's focus on behavioral advertising is too narrow because it fails to capture the full array of online advertising activities, all of which have potential privacy implications and some of which may be contrary to consumers' expectations. Microsoft suggests a more nuanced approach to self regulation, one that recognizes the varied forms of online advertising and is appropriately tailored to account for the types of information being collected and how that information will be used. To this end, we propose that certain baseline obligations apply to any entity engaged in online advertising, with additional obligations applying if the entity is engaged in multi-site advertising, behavioral advertising, personally identifiable advertising, or sensitive personally identifiable information advertising.

A. Entities Engaged in Online Advertising Activities Should be Transparent about Their Practices and Protect the Data They Collect

Consumers may not understand the types of information that entities rely upon to provide advertisements online. For example, many consumers may not realize that information about the pages they are viewing, the searches they are conducting, or the services they are using may be collected and used to deliver online ads. Therefore, Microsoft believes that any entity that logs page views or collects other information about an individual consumer or computer for the purpose of delivering advertisements online should be transparent about its practices.

To this end, the self-regulatory principles should impose some minimal obligations on any entity engaged in "online advertising." We suggest defining online advertising as "the logging of page views or the collection of other information about an individual consumer or computer for the purpose of delivering ads or providing advertising- related services." The following obligations should be imposed on an entity that engages in online advertising:

- Post a clear and conspicuous link on the home page of its website to a privacy notice that sets forth its data collection and use practices related to online advertising. Such notice should describe, at a minimum, the types of information collected for online advertising; whether this information will be combined with other information collected; and the ways in which such information may be used, including whether any non-aggregate information may be shared with a third party.

- Take reasonable steps to protect the security of the data it collects for online advertising and retain data only as long as is necessary to fulfill a legitimate business need or as required by law.[37]

B. Third Parties Engaged in Online Advertising Across Multiple, Unrelated Sites Should Ensure Consumers Receive Notice of Their Activities

Many websites rely on third parties to deliver online advertising. Where third parties deliver ads online, the same transparency concerns discussed above are intensified. This is because the collection of data (e.g., page(s) visited, day and time of visit, IP address, or unique identifier) by a third party with whom they may not have a relationship may not be expected or understood by consumers. If the consumer is not able to determine whether a third party will collect information on a particular site, the consumer cannot make a meaningful decision as to whether to continue using the website. Therefore, consumers should be provided with notice anytime a third party will be collecting information about them to deliver advertisements online.

For these reasons, Microsoft urges the Commission to consider an additional tier of online advertising — *"multi-site advertising"* — and to define it as *"online advertising across multiple, unrelated third-party sites."* To ensure consumers receive notice of these activities, a third party engaged in multi-site advertising should:

Make reasonable efforts to require that those websites on which it engages in online advertising post a link on their sites' homepage to a privacy notice that discloses the use of a third party for online advertising.[38] This "pass-through notice" approach will have the additional benefit of obligating entities engaged in multi-site online advertising to take some basic steps to require that their website partners at least adhere to the minimal privacy practice of having a privacy notice available via their home pages.

Ensure that all pass-through notices describe consumers' right to opt out to the extent the third party engages in behavioral advertising or personally identifiable advertising (as defined below).

C. Third Parties Engaged in Behavioral Advertising Should Offer Consumers a Choice About the use of Their Information for Such Purposes

Microsoft agrees with the Commission that the collection of information about consumers to generate a profile of their behavior upon which ads can be targeted raises heightened concerns that warrant additional levels of user control. That said, we believe those concerns are most pronounced when a third party engages in targeting ads based on a behavioral profile developed across multiple, unrelated sites. In its 2000 Report to Congress on issues associated with online profiling, the Commission noted the "widespread concern" regarding profiling practices by companies with whom users do not have a "known, direct relationship."[39] Proposed state legislative efforts around behavioral advertising have similarly focused on third parties,[40] and State Attorneys General have set parameters around the development of behavioral profiles by companies with whom consumers lack an established relationship.[41]

In contrast, the delivery of advertising by a company on its own website, or within a closely-related family of websites,[42] based on information collected within that site raises limited privacy concerns.[43] Certainly this online advertising activity should be disclosed in the privacy policy posted on the site's homepage, as required by the principles around online advertising noted above. But it is simply less invasive than the collection of information across multiple, unrelated sites by a third party with whom the consumer may not have a relationship in an effort to generate a profile of user behavior upon which ads can be targeted. Consumers should be able to choose whether or not to have their information collected and used for such purposes.

Accordingly, Microsoft urges the Commission to modify its definition of "*behavioral advertising*" to focus on third-party tracking across multiple, unrelated sites:

> "The tracking of a consumer's activities online *across multiple, unrelated sites* — including the searches the consumer has conducted, the web pages visited, and the content viewed — *by a third party* in order to deliver advertising *across multiple, unrelated sites* targeted to the individual consumer's interests."

We believe a third party engaged in behavioral advertising should take the following additional steps:

Enable consumers to choose not to have their information used for behavioral advertising.

Respect consumers' opt-out choice on all sites where it engages in behavioral advertising. This is important because consumers acting reasonably under the circumstances would expect that the opt-out choice offered by the third party would apply in all circumstances where the third party engages in behavioral advertising practices — not just on sites the third party does not own or control. Indeed, to offer consumers a choice about having their information collected for behavioral advertising but limit that choice to only those sites the third party does not own or control would likely mislead consumers as to the effect of their opt-out choice.[44]

Ensure that all privacy notices include clear descriptions of the procedure for consumers to opt out of having their information used for behavioral advertising (including a description of the circumstances that would make it necessary for a consumer to renew the opt out, such as when a consumer changes computers, changes browsers, or deletes relevant cookies) and a link to a place where consumers can exercise such choice. This includes pass-through notices, which means third parties should take reasonable steps to require website operators to notify consumers of their ability to exercise choice about the use of their information for behavioral advertising.

D. Third Parties Seeking to Merge Personally Identifiable Information with Data Collected Through Multi-Site or Behavioral Advertising Should be Subject to Additional Obligations.

The merger of personally identifiable information with other information collected about consumers through multi-site or behavioral advertising for the purposes of ad targeting presents further privacy risks. This is because consumers are unlikely to expect that a third party may combine such pieces of information and use it to deliver ads (whether online or offline). These risks are particularly salient when considered in light of the evolving relationship between consumers and third parties who engage in multi-site and behavioral advertising. Today, unlike in the past, the majority of these companies are owned by entities that provide a wide array of Web-based services and, therefore, often have direct relationships with consumers. This increases the potential that data collected through multi-site or behavioral advertising will be combined or associated with personally identifiable information.

Accordingly, self-regulatory principles should impose heightened obligations on any third party seeking to engage in *"personally identifiable advertising,"* which should be defined as *"the merger of information that, by itself, can be used to identify someone — such as name, e-mail address, physical address, or telephone number — with data collected through multi-site advertising or behavioral advertising for the purposes of ad targeting."* A third party planning to use data associated with personally identifiable information for ad targeting (either online or offline) should either de-identify such data or take additional steps to notify consumers and obtain appropriate consent. More specifically:

Third parties should de-identify information before using it for the purpose of serving ads or connecting it with data collected through multi-site or behavioral advertising. Consumers are best served when upfront steps are taken to ensure that information that can be used to personally and directly identify them is separated from information collected through multi-site or behavioral advertising before that information is used to deliver targeted ads. Microsoft, as described in the attached white paper, applies a one- way cryptographic hash function to remove personally identifiable elements from the set of information collected from consumers and to create an anonymized identifier that it uses to serve ads online.

If the data is not de-identified, third parties should ensure that all privacy notices include clear descriptions of the procedure for consumers to opt out of having personally identifiable information combined with non- personally identifiable information collected on a prospective basis for ad targeting (including a description of the circumstances that would make it necessary for a consumer to renew the opt out, such as when a consumer changes computers, changes browsers, or deletes relevant cookies) and a link to a place where consumers can exercise such choice. This includes pass-through notices, which means third parties should take reasonable efforts to require that website operators notify consumers of the procedure for opting out of having personally identifiable information merged with non-personally identifiable information collected on a prospective basis for ad targeting and a link to a place where consumers can exercise such choice.

Third parties should obtain affirmative opt-in consent before combining previously collected non-personally identifiable information with personally identifiable information for either online or offline ad targeting.

E. Third Parties Should be Required to Obtain Affirmative Express Consent before Using Sensitive Personally Identifiable Information for Behavioral Advertising

Microsoft agrees with the Commission that the use of sensitive personally identifiable information to target online ads demands heightened protection. Sensitive personally identifiable information about users — such as their health or medical conditions, sexual behavior or orientation, or religious beliefs — requires special protection. Again, privacy concerns are most pronounced when a third party uses sensitive personally identifiable information for behavioral advertising.

Microsoft therefore urges the Commission to consider a final tier for "*sensitive personally identifiable information advertising*"—and to define it as "*the use of sensitive personally identifiable information for the purpose of behavioral advertising.*"[45] To address the need for greater transparency and consumer control with respect to these activities, a third party seeking to engage in sensitive personally identifiable information advertising should either de- identify sensitive personally identifiable information before using it for the purpose of serving ads, or obtain consent as follows:

Obtain affirmative express consent before using sensitive personally identifiable information for behavioral advertising.

Provide a mechanism for revoking such consent on a prospective basis.

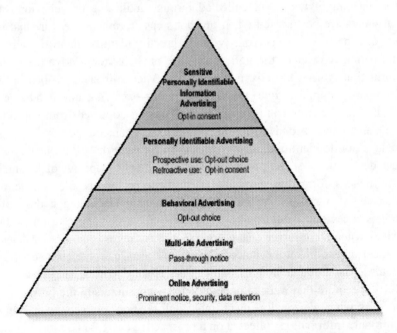

In short, self-regulatory principles for online advertising should be calibrated to the particular type of online advertising activity undertaken by an entity. In all instances, an entity engaged in online advertising or multi-site advertising should be required to ensure consumers receive notice about their advertising activities. As the information upon which ads are delivered becomes more personal or sensitive, additional obligations should follow. This tiered and nuanced approach appropriately recognizes the different privacy concerns posed by different forms of online advertising. It can be briefly summarized graphically in the above figure.

V. Reasonable Security and Limited Data Retention Obligations Should Apply to all Data Collected by Entities Engaged in Online Advertising

Microsoft agrees with and supports the Commission's proposed self-regulatory principles around security and data retention. These principles should apply to any entity engaged in online advertising. The proposed principles recognize that appropriate and effective security and retention practices will depend on a number of factors, and that entities should have the flexibility to adopt practices responsive to the level of risk presented.

A. Reasonable Security

Microsoft is committed to protecting the security of information we collect and maintain. We have adopted strong data security practices, implemented meaningful data protection and security plans, and undertaken detailed third-party audits. We also have taken steps to educate consumers about ways to protect themselves while online, and we have worked closely with industry members and law enforcement around the world to identify security threats, share best practices, and improve our coordinated response to security issues.

Microsoft's data security efforts extend to information we collect through online advertising. As described above, we have designed our systems and processes in ways that minimize the privacy impact of the data we collect and use to deliver ads online. Our online ad targeting platform selects appropriate ads based only on data that does not personally and directly identify individual users, and we store clickstream and search query data used for ad targeting separately from individually identifying account information. We also have committed to continue to implement technological and process protections to help guard the information we maintain.

The Commission's proposed self-regulatory principle around security is appropriately based on a reasonableness standard. Such an approach recognizes that security is an ongoing process, that the threats to data security are constantly changing, and that the degree and type of risk can vary from one situation to another. We agree with the factors identified by the Commission as relevant to determining whether an entity has taken reasonable security measures, including (1) the sensitivity of the data at issue, (2) the nature of a company's business operations, (3) the types of risks a company faces, and (4) the reasonable protections available to a company. This approach gives entities engaged in online advertising — which are in the optimal position to assess the particular security measures that are best suited to the different types of information they maintain — the discretion to implement the most appropriate technologies and procedures for their respective environments.

B. Limited Data Retention

Microsoft agrees with the Commission that entities that collect data through online advertising "should retain data only as long as is necessary to fulfill a legitimate business or law enforcement need." As the Commission notes, there are often sound and legitimate business reasons for retaining data collected from users. These reasons include enhancing fraud detection efforts, helping guard consumers against security threats, understanding website usage, improving the content of online services, and tailoring features to consumer demands.

Microsoft's policy around retaining search query data provides a good example of the careful balance of interests that must be taken into account when analyzing retention periods. As noted above, Microsoft has committed to make all Live Search query data completely and irreversibly anonymous after 18 months, unless the company receives user consent for a longer time period. This policy will apply retroactively and worldwide, and will include permanently removing the entirety of the IP address and all other cross-session identifiers, such as cookie IDs and other machine identifiers, from the search terms.

Of course, the factors involved may be complex and will vary from one company to the next. For Microsoft, we believe that retaining search data for 18 months strikes an appropriate balance and, in the context of the other factors involved, provides a strong approach to protecting user privacy. Especially in light of our stringent approach to anonymization, we determined 18 months was appropriate based on the need to store some data about users to protect against security threats and improve our services.[46] However, what is deemed "necessary" will differ depending on the circumstances, and flexibility is preferable to hard and fast deadlines.

VI. The Commission Should Clarify That Material Changes May Warrant Different Levels of Notice and Consent

Microsoft recognizes the importance of privacy policies as both a tool for consumers to make informed choices about whether to interact with a business or to take advantage of a particular service offering, and as a means to promote accountability among businesses. This is true whether the privacy policy is intended to inform consumers about online advertising activities or other data handling practices. Microsoft takes all of its privacy commitments seriously and seeks to ensure consumers understand these commitments both at the outset and as our business practices change over time.

Microsoft further appreciates that material changes to privacy practices may warrant heightened forms of notice and consumer consent. That said, there appears to be some confusion around what types of changes should be considered material. In general, we believe material changes should be considered those that a consumer, acting reasonably under the circumstances, would deem important to his or her decision to visit a particular website or use a particular online service.[47] For example, a website operator's decision to start selling personally identifiable information to third parties would constitute a material change in most circumstances. There may be other changes that are less significant that, depending upon the representations previously set forth in a privacy notice, could also still be considered material to a reasonable consumer.

In light of the different types of changes that could be deemed material, we believe a nuanced approach to notice about such changes and consumer consent is warranted. More specifically, we urge the Commission to clarify that the following additional factors are relevant to determining the appropriate level of consumer notice and consent in a particular circumstance: (1) whether the change will be applied retroactively or prospectively, (2) the extent to which the change conflicts with a previous promise in a privacy notice, and (3) the likely significance or importance of the change (e.g., whether it involves an internal use of information within the company, or whether it involves a disclosure to a third party). The following two sections discuss the rationale behind this approach and how each factor could be applied in practice.

A. Retroactive Changes

Where a company seeks to apply a change to its privacy policy retroactively, the potential arises that it will alter promises it made at the time the data was originally collected, necessitating a heightened level of notice and choice. In those instances where a proposed retroactive change (1) is material and (2) involves a new practice that explicitly conflicts with a practice or promise set forth in the original privacy policy, the Commission has found individual notice and affirmative express (opt-in) consent to be warranted.[48]

In contrast, in those instances where a proposed retroactive change (1) is material but (2) does not directly conflict with a prior promise, notice and a meaningful opportunity to avoid the practice should be deemed generally sufficient. The exact level of notice and choice, however, should vary with the significance of the change. Thus, a particularly invasive practice — e.g., a company's decision to sell personal information to third parties — should necessitate individual e-mail notice to all affected consumers and require that each customer affirmatively opt in to the disclosure. A less invasive practice — e.g., a company's decision to use personal information to market its own products — should require notice to consumers with the opportunity to opt out of the new practice.

B. Prospective Changes

Where material changes are applied only to information collected following the change in policy (i.e., prospectively), there is less danger of consumer deception or other harm. Users tend to be aware that privacy policies are subject to change and typically receive notice of this potentiality in the privacy policies posted online. Accordingly, a prospective change is more likely to be anticipated by consumers. Nevertheless, some form of heightened notice alerting regular users of a service or website to a change is warranted.

Microsoft believes a nuanced, fact-specific analysis should be employed to determine the appropriate level of heightened notice for prospective privacy policy changes. For example, a website operator might place a notice next to a link to the website's amended privacy policy on its homepage, as well as a notation on the privacy policy informing the reader that the policy has been recently amended and stating the new effective date. Such notice should be sufficient to inform a reasonable consumer that a material change in the website's privacy policy has occurred and should afford the consumer the opportunity to learn more about the details of the change.

Additional levels of notice may be warranted depending on the significance or importance of the prospective change and whether it directly contradicts an existing statement in the policy. A material change involving a highly invasive privacy practice — such as a decision to begin selling personal information — would clearly warrant additional protections. Similarly, a material and prospective change in privacy practices is more likely to defeat consumer expectations where the new policy directly contradicts the superseded policy regarding the use, collection, or disclosure of personal information. In these circumstances, a more prominent notice, such as a pop-up message or similarly visible text, may be appropriate.

VII. Microsoft Does Not Use Data about Users' Online Activities for Purposes That Raise Privacy Concerns

The Commission has requested additional information about the potential "secondary" uses of information gathered about users' online activities and whether any of these uses raise concerns. We cannot speak for other companies, but as described in our privacy statement, Microsoft currently collects information to operate and improve its sites and to deliver the services or carry out the transactions our users have requested. These uses may include providing users with more effective customer service; making the sites or services easier to use by eliminating the need for users to repeatedly enter the same information; performing research and analysis aimed at improving our products, services and technologies; and displaying content and advertising that are customized to our users' interests and preferences. The information we collect is not used for purposes outside of those disclosed to users in our privacy statement. Thus, the use of this information for these purposes should not raise additional privacy concerns that warrant notice or consent beyond those already provided.

VIII. Conclusion

Microsoft appreciates the opportunity to comment on the Commission's proposed self-regulatory principles for online advertising and applauds the Commission's focus on this important set of issues. We hope that our comments help clarify the scope and application of the principles. With these changes, the Commission's principles provide sound guidance to online advertisers and will help ensure that consumers' privacy interests are protected as they continue to enjoy the proliferation of free services and information that online advertising supports.

If you have any questions about our comments, please do not hesitate to let me know. Microsoft looks forward to working with you and other stakeholders to protect consumers' privacy online.

Sincerely,

Michael H. Hintze
Associate General Counsel
Microsoft Corporation

Attachments

- Privacy Protections in Microsoft's Ad Serving System and the Process of "De-identification"
- Microsoft's Privacy Principles for Live Search and Online Ad Targeting

END NOTES

[1] U.S. Census Bureau, *Quarterly Retail E-Commerce Sales: 4th Quarter 2007*, Feb. 15, 2008, *available at* http://www.census.gov/mrts/www/data/html/07Q4.html.

[2] Some of these standards are set forth in Microsoft's Privacy Principles for Live Search and Online Ad Targeting, attached as Appendix 1. This document is also available at http://www.microsoft.com/privacy. Additionally, Microsoft's Privacy Guidelines for Developing Software Products and Services, which are based on our internal privacy standards, are available at http://www.microsoft.com/privacy.

[3] It has become a standard approach to the online economy that there is a value exchange in which companies provide online content and services to consumers without charging a fee and, in return, consumers see advertisements that may be targeted.

[4] *See* Interactive Advertising Bureau, *IAB Internet Advertising Revenue Report*, 7, May 2008, *available at* http://www.iab.net/media/file/IAB_PwC_2007_full_year.pdf; Yankee Group, *Yankee Group Forecasts US Online Advertising Market to Reach $50 Billion By 2011*, Jan. 18, 2008, *available at* http://www.yankeegroup.com/pressReleaseDetail.do?actionType=getDetailPressRelease&ID=1805.

[5] *See* Brian Morrissey, *IAB: Web Ad Spend Tops Cable, Radio*, ADWEEK, May 15, 2008, *available at* http://www.adweek.com/aw/content_display/news/digital/e3ibcf6d45fc7a036dff28457a85c838ff1.

[6] It is for this reason advertisers are willing to pay more for targeted ads. For example, although Merrill Lynch has reported that the average cost per 1000 impressions ("CPM") is $2.50, entities engaged in behavioral targeting have reported average CPMs as high as $10. *See* Brian Morrissey, *Aim High: Ad Targeting Moves to the Next Level*, ADWEEK, Jan. 21, 2008, *available a* http://www.adweek.com/aw/magazine/article_display.jsp?vnu_content_id=1003695822. Data also shows that 57% of 867 search engine advertisers and search engine marketing agencies polled "were willing to spend more on demographic targeting, such as age and gender." Search Engine Marketing Professional Organization, *Online Advertisers Are Bullish on Behavioral Targeting*, May 15, 2008, *available at* http://www.sempo.org/news/releases/05-15-08.

[7] Search ads are selected based on the search term entered by a user and sometimes on data that has been collected about the user, such as the user's history of prior searches. Search ads generally appear either at the top of the search results or along the right-hand side of the page. They often are displayed as text, but they may include graphics as well. Advertisers bid against each other for the right to have their ads appear when a specific search term is entered (known as a "keyword").

[8] These non-search ads are what users see when they visit virtually any site on the Internet other than a search engine site. They can be based on the content of the page the user is viewing (typically referred to as "contextual" ads) or on a profile of a user's activities that has been collected over time (referred to as "behavioral" ads). But in either case, the company serving the ad would log the pages users view – typically in association with a cookie ID from the user's computer and/or an IP address.

[9] Three examples of this are Microsoft's acquisition of aQuantive, Yahoo!'s acquisition of RightMedia and Google's acquisition of DoubleClick. For more information about the key players in the advertising market and the impact of consolidation in the market, see the testimony of Microsoft General Counsel Brad Smith before the Senate Judiciary Committee, *available at* http://www.microsoft.com/presspass/exec/bradsmith/09-27googledoubleclick.mspx.

[10] *See* section III.C below.

[11] Based on comScore's Core Search Report, in May of this year, 62% of searches were performed in the U.S. on Google, amounting to roughly 6.7 billion searches. comScore, *comScore Releases May 2008 U.S. Search Engine Rankings*, June 19, 2008, *available at* http://www.comscore.com/press/release.asp?press=2275. Google also has strategic agreements with AOL and Ask that allow Google to serve ads to those companies' search engine sites. Adding AOL's (4.5%) and Ask.com's (4.5%) share of the search queries, Google's share rises to 71%. *See id.*

[12] Following its acquisition of DoubleClick, Google now serves in the range of 70% of all non-search advertisements. *See, e.g.*, *Lots of Reach in Ad . . .*, April 1, 2008, *available at* http://battellemedia.com/archives/004356.php.

[13] Microsoft's Live Search has approximately 8.5% of Core Search queries in the United States. comScore, *comScore Releases May 2008 U.S. Search Engine Rankings*, June 19, 2008, *available at* http://www.comscore.com/press/release.asp?press=2275.

[14] Concerns have been raised about this dominance as well as the privacy protections surrounding the enormous amount of information about users' online behavior that this dominance enables. *See, e.g.*, Electronic Privacy Information Center, *Supplemental Materials in Support of Pending Complaint and Request for Injunction, Request for Investigation and for Other Relief*, June 6, 2007, *available at* http://epic.org/privacy/ftc/google/supp_060607.pdf ("The combination of Google (the world's largest Internet search engine) with DoubleClick (the world's largest Internet advertising technology firm) would allow the combined company to become the gatekeeper for Internet content. . . . The detailed profiling of Internet users

raises profound issues that concern the right of privacy. . . ."); *see also*, Jaikumar Vijayan, *Google Asked to Add Home Page Link to Privacy Policies*, COMPUTERWORLD, June 3, 2008, *available at* http://www.computerworld.com/action/article.do?command=viewArticleBasic&articleId=9092838; Privacy International, *A Race to the Bottom: Privacy Ranking of Internet Service Companies*, Sept. 6, 2007, *available at* http://www.privacyinternational.org/article.shtml?cmd%5B347%5D=x-347-553961 (We "witnessed an attitude to privacy within Google that at its most blatant is hostile, and at its most benign is ambivalent.").

[15] *See* http://www.google.com/intl/en/press/pressrel/20080612_yahoo.html.

[16] With Google's 71% search query share in the U.S. based on its relationship with AOL and Ask.com (*see supra* fn. 11), in combination with Yahoo's 20.6% share of the core search query market, Google will be able to gather information on up to 92% of online searches. *See* comScore, *comScore Releases May 2008 U.S. Search Engine Rankings*, June 19, 2008, *available at* http://www.comscore.com/press/release.asp?press=2275.

[17] *See* Jeff Chester, *A Yahoo! & Google Deal Is Anti-Competitive, Raises Privacy Concerns*, May 22, 2008, *available at* http://www.democraticmedia.org/jcblog/?p=596.

[18] *See* Appendix 1. Microsoft's Privacy Principles for Live Search and Online Ad Targeting are also available at http://www.microsoft.com/privacy.

[19] *See* section III.C below.

[20] Microsoft's personalized advertising opt-out page is available at https://choice.live.com/advertisementchoice/Default.aspx.

[21] See, for example, Microsoft's comments to the Federal Trade Commission's proposed self-regulatory framework for online advertising, included as Appendix 4 and available at http://www.ftc.gov/os/comments/behavioraladprinciples/080411microsoft.pdf.

[22] A white paper describing Microsoft's "de-identification" process is attached to these comments as Appendix 3. It is also available at http://www.microsoft.com/privacy.

[23] Atlas, which was part of Microsoft's recent acquisition of aQuantive, was a founding member of NAI.

[24] *See* Appendix 4. Our comments are also available at http://www.ftc.gov/os/comments/behavioraladprinciples/080411microsoft.pdf.

[25] *See* http://www.microsoft.com/presspass/download/features/2005/PrivacyLegislationCallWP.doc.

[26] A. 9275-C, 2007-2008 Reg. Sess. (N.Y. 2008), *available at* http://assembly.state.ny.us/leg/?bn=A09275&sh=t (imposing minimum notice and choice obligations on certain website publishers and advertising networks); S. 6441-B, 2007-2008 Reg. Sess. (N.Y. 2008), *available at* http://assembly.state.ny.us/leg/?bn=S06441&sh=t (imposing baseline notice, choice, security, and consumer access obligations on certain third-party advertising networks); H.B. 5765, 2008 Gen. Assem., Feb. Sess. (Conn. 2008), *available at* http://www.cga.ct.gov/2008/FC/2008HB-05765-R000148-FC.htm (imposing minimum notice, choice, security, and use limitations on third-party advertising networks).

[27] This paper does not cover Microsoft's newly acquired Atlas ad serving technology.

[28] Microsoft sites might set other cookies for other purposes, but they are not relevant to the online advertising topics described here and are therefore not discussed in this paper.

[29] Microsoft's online advertising principles can be found at http://download.microsoft.com/download/3/7/f/37f14671-ddee-499b-a794-077b3673f186/Microsoft's%20Privacy%20Pri nci ples%20for%20Live%20Sea rch%20a nd%20On li ne%20Ad%20Ta rget ing.doc.

[30] Available at http://download.microsoft.com/download/3/7/f/37f14671-ddee-499b-a794-077b3673f186/Microsoft's Privacy Principles for Live Search and Online Ad Targeting.doc.

[31] Available at http://www.microsoft.com/downloads/details.aspx?FamilyId=C48CF80F-6E87-48F5-83EC 18D1AD2FC1F&displaylang=en.

[32] Atlas, a Microsoft subsidiary, was a founding member of NAI and remains a member.

[33] Microsoft's Privacy Guidelines for Developing Software Products and Services are available at http://www.microsoft.com/privacy.

[34] For a layered privacy notice to be effective, the top layer should set forth, in plain terms, all important information pertaining to the use, collection, or disclosure of data, including that data is used for behavioral advertising purposes. For example, the Microsoft Online Privacy Notice Highlights informs users that Microsoft "use[s] cookies and other technologies to keep track of your interactions with our sites and services to offer a personalized experience" and that Microsoft's services "may include the display of personalized content and advertising." Not all companies purporting to follow a layered approach disclose this kind of important information in the initial layer.

[35] The Atlas opt out is a standard cookie-based opt out.

[36] Reporters have demonstrated the potential ease with which a series of search queries, linked together by a common identifier, can be associated with specific users. See Michael Barbaro & Tom Zeller Jr., "A Face is Exposed for AOL Searcher No. 4417749," N.Y. Times, Aug. 9, 2006, at A1 (reporting that "[i]t did not take much investigating" to identify a specific user from the search log entries that AOL released).

[37] These security and retention obligations are discussed in more detail in section V below.

[38] Obviously, an entity that has a direct contractual relationship with the website on which the ads are served should include the "pass-through notice" as part of the contract. There are other scenarios in which there is not a direct contractual relationship between the entity serving the ads and the website on which the ads are served. In these less direct scenarios, "reasonable efforts" may be accomplished through other means of encouraging best practices among website publishers. Microsoft is committed to working with others in industry to ensure best practices become part of the online advertising ecosystem. In the meantime, references to "pass-through notice" in these comments should be understood to recognize this distinction.

[39] *See* Online Profiling: A Report to Congress, June 2000, *available at* http://www.ftc.gov/os/2000/06/onlineprofilingreportjune2000.pdf; *see also* FTC Statement Before the Committee on Commerce, Science, and Transportation, United States Senate, "Online Profiling: Benefits and Concerns," June 13, 2000, *available at* http://www.ftc.gov/os/2000/06/onlineprofile.htm (noting "persistent concern[s]" regarding the "extensive and sustained scope of the monitoring").

[40] *See, e.g.*, Assemb. 9275-B, 2007-2008 Reg. Sess. (N.Y. 2008) ("Third Party Internet Advertising Consumers' Bill of Rights").

[41] *See* DoubleClick Consent Order, *available at* http://www.oag.state.ny.us/press/2002/aug/aug26a_02_attach.pdf (requiring companies engaged in online preference monitoring across multiple sites to disclose their activities to consumers).

[42] Websites should be considered "closely related" where a reasonable consumer would understand that the sites are owned and operated by the same entity.

[43] The Commission should consider whether there are some online advertising activities even within the scope of a single website or online service — such as serving ads based on the content of email communications or documents stored on consumers' hard drives — that are so personal or sensitive as to require additional obligations (such as requiring entities to offer users choice before using the contents of email communications to serve ads). Although this issue is outside the Commission's request for feedback, we would be happy to engage in a discussion with the Commission on these other scenarios.

[44] This may not be true in every case. There may be discrete programs for which receiving behaviorally targeted ads is a clear condition of using the service and treating the program separately from the third party's general opt-out opportunity would not confuse consumers. In general, Microsoft believes a third party engaged in behavioral advertising should only determine not to offer consumers an opt-out opportunity from behavioral advertising with respect to its own sites or services in those instances where a reasonable consumer would expect (based on notices received or other factors) that their general decision to opt out of behavioral advertising from the third party would not apply.

[45] We recognize that there may be concerns about the use of sensitive categories of data for behavioral advertising, whether or not the data constitutes personally identifiable information. However, for targeting activities that do not involve personally identifiable information — for example, where the entity engaged in targeting does not have a direct relationship with the individual, it may be impractical or impossible to obtain express opt-in consent. Thus, we propose an express opt-in requirement only for the use of sensitive personally identifiable information. Third parties that use sensitive non-personally identifiable information for behavioral advertising would be required to offer opt-out choice.

[46] More specifically, because normal search behavior varies on a seasonal or annual basis, 18 months of data enables us to create a reliable baseline, which can then be used to identify various security threats, including botnet attacks, spam, click fraud, and worms. In addition, to improve the search experience for customers, it is important to have a sufficient amount of data to account for seasonal variation in search behavior.

[47] The FTC's Deception Policy Statement specifies that to determine whether a representation, omission, or practice contained in an advertisement is material, "[t]he basic question is whether the act or practice is likely to affect the consumer's conduct or decision with regard to a product or service." *See* FTC Policy Statement on Deception, Oct. 1983, *available at* http://www.ftc.gov/bcp/policystmt/ad-decept.htm. More generally, this accords with FTC guidance that, in the advertising context, materiality is to be assessed from the perspective of the consumer. *Id.*

[48] *Cf.* Consent Order, *In the Matter of Gateway Learning, available at* http://www.ftc.gov/os/caselist/0423047/040707agree0423047.pdf. (finding express consent necessary to sell personal information where respondent's prior privacy policy stated that the company would neither sell, rent, or loan to third parties any personal information absent explicit consent, nor provide to any third party for any purpose any personal information about children under the age of thirteen).

In: Electronic Breadcrumbs: Issues in Tracking Consumers
Editor: Dmitar N. Kovac

ISBN: 978-1-60741-600-5
© 2010 Nova Science Publishers, Inc.

Chapter 13

PRIVACY & ONLINE ADVERTISING HEARING- HORVATH TESTIMONY

Jane Horvath

Chairman Inouye, Vice Chairman Stevens, members of the Committee.

I'm pleased to appear before you this morning to discuss online advertising and the ways that Google protects our users' privacy. My name is Jane Horvath, and I am Google's Senior Privacy Counsel. In that role I am responsible for working with our product teams and other privacy professionals at Google to ensure compliance with privacy laws and develop best practices for protecting our users' privacy.

Google's mission is to organize the world's information and make it universally accessible and useful. The best known way that we do this today is through our search engine, which is available for free to internet users throughout the world. The availability of Google search and our other products – and the improvements that we make to our products on a daily basis – is funded by online advertising, by far our primary source of revenue.

Online advertising is relatively young and a very small piece of the advertising market as a whole. It is a dynamic business characterized by strong competition, significant innovation, and continuing growth. Online advertising has succeeded because it helps businesses find customers more efficiently and effectively than through other media. It has also helped to create entirely new and innovative small businesses that generate revenue through advertising, often in partnership with Google.

At Google we believe that our online advertising business has succeeded because our most important advertising goal is to deliver ads that benefit our users. From its inception, Google has focused on providing the best user experience possible. We do this, for example, by ensuring that advertising on our site delivers relevant content that is not a distraction. In fact, our goal is to make our ads just as useful to Google's users as search results themselves.

We've also made a commitment to never compromise the integrity of our search results, for example by manipulating rankings to place our partners higher in our search results. And advertising on Google is always clearly identified as a "Sponsored Link" to ensure that our users know the difference between our search results and any advertising that we provide.

Putting our users first also means that we are deeply committed to their privacy, and our products and policies demonstrate that commitment. We believe that success in online advertising and protecting our users' privacy are not mutually exclusive goals. We work hard to provide advertising in a way that is transparent to users, provides them with appropriate choices, and protects any personal information that we collect from inappropriate access by third parties.

In my testimony this morning, I would like to cover three key points:

First, I'll explain Google's main advertising products and the significant benefits that we at Google believe online advertising brings to advertisers, online publishers, and individual internet users.

Second, I'll discuss Google's approach to privacy, specific steps that we take to protect our users' privacy, and privacy issues involving our advertising business.

And finally, I'll explore ideas and make recommendations for how to better protect internet users' privacy both with respect to advertising as well as more generally as more and more information moves to the internet cloud.

THE BENEFITS OF ONLINE ADVERTISING

Google offers three main advertising products: AdWords, AdSense for Search, and AdSense for Content. Our AdWords product allows us to provide ads on Google.com in response to search queries entered by our users, as well as to provide ads on our AdSense for Content and AdSense for Search services. AdSense for Search allows us to provide ads in response to search queries entered by users of our partners' search engines, including AOL and Ask.com. AdSense for Content allows us to provide ads to visitors of our third-party publisher partners' websites. AdSense for Content ads are provided based on the content of the page that is being viewed by a user. The vast majority of the revenue that Google generates comes from these three products.

All three advertising products are primarily easy-to-create text ads, which is one of the many reasons that hundreds of thousands of small businesses advertise with us. We also provide the capability to show display ads – ads that incorporate graphics in addition to text – through AdSense for Content, and we plan to enhance our display ad serving capabilities with our recent acquisition of DoubleClick, a display ad serving technology company.

Advertisers, online publishers, and consumers all benefit from our advertising network. I'll start with consumers – our users – on whom our business depends.

In our experience, users value the advertisements that we deliver along with search results and other web content because the ads help connect them to the information, products, and services they seek. The ads we deliver to our users complement the natural search results that we provide because our users are often searching for products and services that our advertisers offer. Making this connection is critical, and we strive to deliver the ads that are the most relevant to our users, not just the ones that generate the most revenue for us. We do this through our innovative ad auction system, which gives weight to the relevancy – the usefulness – of the ad to our users based on their search queries or the content that they are viewing. And in our pay-per-click pricing model we only generate revenue when a user is interested enough to click on an ad.

The revenue that we generate from online advertising makes it possible for Google to offer dozens of free products to our users – everything from search and email to our word processing application, Google Docs. Each of these products underscores our commitment to improving our users' online experience. For example, Google Docs allows multiple users to edit a single document, presentation, or spreadsheet at the same time. And, despite the popularity of tools like Google Earth and YouTube, each of our products is free to individuals for personal use. Our online advertising business model subsidizes the creation, development, and ongoing improvements to and support for these and future products.

And our ads aren't always commercial. We run a program called Google Grants that provides free advertising to not-for-profit organizations engaged in areas such as science and technology, education, global public health, the environment, youth advocacy, and the arts. For example, we have provided Google Grants to non-profits such as Room to Read (www.roomtoread.org), which educates children in Vietnam, Nepal, India, and Cambodia, and CoachArt (www.coachart.org), which provides therapeutic art and athletic lessons to underprivileged children with life-threatening illnesses. Since April 2003, our grantees have collectively received almost $300 million in free advertising.

Our advertising network also enables small businesses to connect with consumers that they otherwise would not reach, and to do so affordably, efficiently, and effectively. The advertiser decides the maximum amount of money it wishes to spend on advertising and, as noted above, in the cost -per-click payment model the advertiser only pays Google when a user actually clicks on an ad.

Here are just two of many stories of small businesses succeeding thanks to Google advertising. Suzanne Golter owns the Happy Hound dog daycare (www.happyhound.com) in Oakland, California. She estimates that 90 percent of her business is generated through Google AdWords, which helps her bring in approximately 40 new clients per month. In Minneapolis, Minnesota, Kenny Kormendy, a then-struggling taxi driver built a site for out-of-state travelers called Gopher State Taxi (www.gopherstatetaxi.com) and utilized AdWords to compete online with bigger taxi companies. In under three years, Gopher State Taxi has grown to a network of over 36 cabs, and Mr. Kormendy credits AdWords with connecting nine out of ten customers that his company services.

Online advertising also promotes freer, more robust, and more diverse speech. It's no coincidence that blogs have proliferated over the past few years. Our AdSense product enables bloggers and other publishers to generate revenue from ads that we place on their web sites. Without online advertising, the individuals who run these sites would not be able to dedicate as much time and attention to their publications as they do today. In fact, we know that many website owners can afford to dedicate themselves to their sites full time because of online advertising.

AdSense revenues support hundreds of thousands of diverse websites, and a significant percentage of the revenue we earn from advertising ends up in the hands of the bloggers and web site operators who partner with us by featuring ads provided by Google. Last year we paid $4.5 billion in advertising revenue from our AdSense program to our publishing partners. In Nevada, Arizona, Florida, and Washington alone over 100,000 of our publishing partners collectively generated nearly $100 million from AdSense in 2007.

The vast majority of these AdSense partners are small businesses. For example, in Oregon, Hope Pryor, a grandmother of four, uses AdSense on her site – Cooksrecipes.com – to generate her primary source of income. And in Massachusetts, honey bee aficionado and retiree Albert Needham uses AdSense revenue generated from his Bees-online.com website to fund personal vacations. Similar small business success stories are found all across the United States.

It's no mistake that I've focused mainly on individual users, small publishers, and small advertisers. Google's business model has concentrated on what's known as the "long tail" of the internet – the millions of individuals and small businesses that cater to and need to connect with niche interests and markets. Google's advertising programs lower the barrier to entry for small publishers and advertisers alike, and connect them with users who are interested in what they have to say or sell. As our advertising business continues to grow and evolve, we will continue working hard to encourage the development of the long tail.

GOOGLE AND PRIVACY

We believe user trust is essential to building the best possible products. With every Google product, we work hard to earn and keep that trust with a long-standing commitment to protect the privacy of our users' personal information. We make privacy a priority because our business depends on it. In fact, if our users are uncomfortable with how we manage their personal information, they are only one click away from switching to a competitor's services.

Because user trust is so critical to us, we've ensured that privacy considerations are deeply embedded in our culture. Though I am Google's Senior Privacy Counsel, I am just one of many individuals at Google who work on privacy. For example, we have product counsels who work with engineers and product managers from the beginning of product development to ensure that our products protect our users' privacy. We also have product managers dedicated to privacy and other trust and safety issues. And we have a Privacy Council, which is comprised of a cross-functional group of Google employees that convenes on a regular basis to help Google address privacy issues.

Google's focus on user trust and privacy means that our product teams are thinking about user privacy by building privacy protections into our products from the ground up. For example, we have designed most of our products to allow people to use them anonymously, and to ensure that none of our products use any personally identifiable data unless that use is fully disclosed in our privacy policy.

We have also made sure that three design fundamentals – all of them rooted in fair information principles – are at the bedrock of our privacy products and practices:

- **Transparency:** We believe in being upfront with our users about what information we collect and how we use it so that they can make informed choices about their personal information. We have been an industry leader in finding new ways to educate users about privacy, such as through our Google Privacy Channel on YouTube (found at www.youtube.com/googleprivacy) where we feature privacy videos that explain our privacy policies, practices, and product features in simple, plain language.
- **Choice:** We strive to design our products in a way that gives users meaningful choices about how they use our services and what information they provide to us. Many of our products, including our Search service, do not require users to provide

any personally identifying information at all. When we do ask for personal information, we also endeavor to provide features that give users control over that information. For example, our Google Talk instant messaging service includes an "off the record " feature that prevents either party from storing the chat.

- **Security:** We take seriously the protection of data that our users entrust with us. Google employs some of the world's best engineers in software and network security and has teams dedicated to developing and implementing policies, practices and technologies to protect this information. More information about our approach to security can be found in a recent post at the Official Google Blog located at googleblog.blogspot.com/2008/03/how-google-keeps-your-information.html.

One of our newest products is Google Health, which enables individ uals to consolidate and store their medical records and personal health information online. Google Health demonstrates our commitment to all three design fundamentals. For example, wee have provided significant transparency about Google Health's privacy features through blog posts and the product's easy-to-understand privacy policy and frequently asked questions. In addition, Google Health provides users choice by empowering them with the decision of what information to import, share, and delete, and easy tools for accomplishing each.

The online advertising products that we offer today are also privacy-friendly because they are primarily contextual in nature. That is, we generally provide ads in response to what a user is searching for or viewing at the time, rather than based on who we believe the user may be or an extended history of the user's activities either online or off.

To respond to our users' desire for more relevant advertising, and to advertisers' desire to provide more relevant advertising to internet users, we are experimenting with some forms of online advertising that do involve more than the current search query to provide an ad. For example, we are currently experimenting in Google.com search with providing ads based on both the curr ent query and a previous search. A user who types "Italy vacation" into the Google search box, for instance, might see ads about Tuscany or affordable flights to Rome. If the user were to subsequently search for "weather," we might assume that there is a link between "Italy vacation" and "weather" and deliver ads regarding local weather conditions in Italy. However, Google does not build a profile of the user to serve these ads that is stored and used later to serve other ads to the user.

As we continue to incorporate DoubleClick into our business, our focus on display advertising – ads that feature images in addition to text – will increase across our advertising product offerings, as will our ability to provide metrics and an improved user experience to our AdSense network. We believe that expanding into display advertising products is one way that we can compete effectively in the highly competitive online advertising environment. This transition will not undermine Google's focus on privacy or our commitment to the fundamental principles of transparency, choice, and security. As we move to offer more display advertising and other advertising products, Google intends to continue to be a leader in offering products that protect and respect the privacy of our users.

GOOGLE'S EFFORTS TO CONTINUE INNOVATING IN PRIVACY

In our quickly evolving business environment, ensuring that we earn and keep our users' trust is an essential constant for building the best possible products. With every Google product, we work hard to earn and keep that trust with a long-standing commitment to protect the privacy of our users' personal information. As stated above, the bedrock of our privacy practices are three design fundamentals: transparency, choice, and security.

Another constant that we have found in our business is that innovation is a critical part of our approach to privacy. To best innovate in privacy, we welcome the feedback of privacy advocates, government experts, our users, and other stakeholders. This feedback, and our own internal discussions about how to protect privacy, has led us to several privacy innovations including our decision last year to anonymize our server logs after 18 months.

In the interest of continuing to protect individuals' privacy, we offer the following policy and technology recommendations – some of which can be accomplished by the private sector and some of which involve a government role – in the spirit of continuing the effort to innovate on consumer privacy. Our ideas and recommendations endorse a baseline and robust level of privacy protections for all individuals. On top of that baseline platform we believe that the private sector and government should cooperate to educate and inform consumers about privacy issues and to establish best practices that will help guide the development of the quickly evolving and innovative online advertising space. Finally, we believe that Google and others in the online advertising industry should work to provide tools to better protect individuals' privacy, and that government should encourage companies to experiment with new and innovative ways of protecting consumers' privacy.

Comprehensive Federal Privacy Law

Google supports the passage of a comprehensive federal privacy law that would accomplish several goals such as building consumer trust and protections; establishing a uniform framework for privacy, which would create consistent levels of privacy from one jurisdiction to another; and putting penalties in place to punish and dissuade bad actors. We believe that as information flows increase and more and more information is processed and stored in the internet cloud – on remote servers rather than on users' home computers Ð there is a greater need for uniform data safeguarding standards, data breach notification procedures, and stronger procedural protections relating to government and third party litigant access to individuals' information.

Behavioral Advertising Principles

We have participated actively in the Federal Trade Commission's efforts to develop privacy principles relating to online privacy and behavioral advertising. Our hope is that revised principles will be adopted widely by the online advertising industry and serve as a model for industry self-regulation in jurisdictions beyond the United States. In order for the principles to achieve such broad adoption, however, they need to be revised to ensure that they can be operationalized by industry and that they will give consumers appropriate transparency, choice, and security. In order for that to happen, the principles would, among other things, need to make a distinction between personally identifiable information (PII) and non-PII.

Consumer Education

Transparency is one of Google's bedrock design principles because we believe that informed and knowledgeable users are best able to protect their privacy. We believe that both the private sector and the government, including agencies like the FTC, can and should provide more information about what kinds of personal information are collected by companies, how such data is used, and what steps consumers can take to better protect their privacy.

At Google, for example, we take great pride in our effort to provide our users with a better understanding of how we collect, use, and protect their data through a series of short videos available at Google.com and on YouTube, as well as through blog posts. Too often, web site operators view their online privacy policy – which is typically impenetrable to the average user – as the beginning and end of their privacy obligations. Web companies that interact with individuals need to do more than simply provide and link to privacy policies; we need to offer consumer-friendly materials in different media to better help their users understand how their information is collected and used, and what choices they have to protect their privacy.

Transparency and Choice in Display Advertising

Google text ads are generally labeled "Ads by Google" or "Sponsored Links" and are accompanied by an explanation of what they are so that users understand that they are advertisements and that they have been provided by Google. We believe that this kind of notice and explanation should be adopted by industry and applied not only to text ads but also to display ads. We also believe that industry should continue working together to provide, for example, effective mechanisms that empower consumers with the ability to opt out of behaviorally targeted advertising.

Development of Technology to Empower Users

Products like Google Toolbar let a user choose to not have data collected, and that choice persists even if all cookies are cleared and until the user chooses to have data collected. Google also offers features like Web History, which allows users to view and search all search queries they have made on Google search while logged into Google. Web History also lets users delete and thus disassociate from their account information any searches that they conduct while they are logged in. Users can also pause Web History altogether if they do not want their searches to be associated with their account information – and this choice persists until users choose to resume Web History. We believe that more can be done by industry to ensure the persistence of users' choices, and we look forward to exploring such tools with industry and other stakeholders.

CONCLUSION

Chairman Inouye, Vice Chairman Stevens, and members of the Committee, thank you for the opportunity to testify today. I appreciate the opportunity to explain the benefits of our advertising business to consumers, advertisers, and publishers, and the chance to explain how Google protects our users' privacy.

I look forward to answering any questions you might have about our efforts, and Google looks forward to working with members of the Committee and others in the development of better privacy protections for internet users everywhere.

Thank you.

In: Electronic Breadcrumbs: Issues in Tracking Consumers
Editor: Dmitar N. Kovac
ISBN: 978-1-60741-600-5
© 2010 Nova Science Publishers, Inc.

Chapter 14

PRIVACY & ONLINE ADVERTISING HEARING- KELLY TESTIMONY

Chris Kelly

Thank you, Mr. Chairman, for the opportunity to address the Committee about the important privacy matters facing the online advertising industry.

I am Chris Kelly, the Chief Privacy Officer of Facebook, a social service on the internet that serves more than 80 million active users, roughly 30 million of whom are in the United States.

Facebook aims to create social value by empowering people to share their lives and experiences with the people they care about. From the founding of the company in a dorm room in 2004 to today, Facebook's privacy settings have given users control over who has access to their personal information by allowing them to choose the friends they accept and networks they join.

We are dedicated to developing advertising that is relevant and personal, and to transparency with our users about how we use their information in the advertising context. We are pleased to discuss both Facebook's general approach to privacy and how these principles have been implemented in advertising provided by Facebook.

With many mainstream media reports focusing on privacy concerns about "social networking sites," we first want to clarify how our site differs from most. Though we will not always address user concerns perfectly - no site can - Facebook is committed to empowering users to make their own choices about what information they share, and with whom they share it.

I. FACEBOOK AND PRIVACY

The statement that opens our privacy policy, a short plain-English introduction, is the best place to start this discussion. It reads:

We built Facebook to make it easy to share information with your friends and people around you. We understand you may not want everyone in the world to have the information you share on Facebook; that is why we give you control of your information. Our default privacy settings limit the information displayed in your profile to your networks and other reasonable community limitations that we tell you about.

Facebook follows two core principles:

You should have control over your personal information.
> Facebook helps you share information with your friends and people around you. You choose what information you put in your profile, including contact and personal information, pictures, interests and groups you join. And you control the users with whom you share that information through the privacy settings on the Privacy page.

You should have access to the information others want to share.
> There is an increasing amount of information available out there, and you may want to know what relates to you, your friends, and people around you. We want to help you easily get that information.

Sharing information should be easy. And we want to provide you with the privacy tools necessary to control how and with whom you share that information. If you have questions or ideas, please send them to privacy@facebook.com.

We implement these principles through our friend and network architectures, and through controls that are built into every one of our innovative products. Contrary to common public reports, full profile data on Facebook isn't even available to most users on Facebook, let alone all users of the Internet. Users have extensive and precise controls available to choose who sees what among their networks and friends, as well as tools that give them the choice to make a limited set of information available to search engines and other outside entities.

The "privacy" link that appears in the upper-right hand corner of every Facebook page allows users to make these choices whenever they are using the site, and everyday use of the site educates users as to the meanings of privacy controls. For instance, a user will see regularly that they have access to the profiles of their friends and those who share a network, but not to the profiles of those who are neither friends nor network members.

In February 2008, Facebook simplified and streamlined its presentation of privacy settings to users, adopting a common lock icon throughout the site to denote the presence of a user-configurable privacy setting. We also introduced the concept of "Friends Lists," which, when paired with privacy settings, allow users to easily configure subset of their confirmed friends who may see certain content. We are constantly looking for means to give users more effective control over their information and to improve communications with users and the general public about our privacy architecture so they can make their own choices about what they want to reveal.

For instance, we participated in the Federal Trade Commission's workshop on new advertising technologies, and have been working with government officials and non-governmental organizations throughout the globe. Facebook has also worked productively with state and federal officials, as well as law enforcement, to explain our longstanding strategy to make the Internet safer by promoting responsibility and identity online, and is currently participating in the state Attorneys General Internet Safety Technical Task Force.

II. PRIVACY AND ADVERTISING ON FACEBOOK

A. Personally Identifiable and Non-Personally Identifiable Information

It is important to stress here in the first instance that targeting of advertising generally benefits users. Receiving information that is likely to be relevant, whether paid for by an advertiser or not, leads to a better online experience. Facebook aims to be transparent with our users about the fact that advertising is an important source of our revenue and to explain to them fully the uses of their personal data they are authorizing by using Facebook. For instance, the following explanation of how we use information for advertising has been a prominent part of our privacy policy for nearly three years:

Facebook may use information in your profile without identifying you as an individual to third parties. We do this for purposes such as aggregating how many people in a network like a band or movie and personalizing advertisements and promotions so that we can provide you Facebook. We believe this benefits you. You can know more about the world around you and, where there are advertisements, they're more likely to be interesting to you. For example, if you put a favorite movie in your profile, we might serve you an advertisement highlighting a screening of a similar one in your town. But we don't tell the movie company who you are.

The critical distinction that we embrace in our policies and practices, and that we want users to understand, is between the use of personal information for advertisements in personally-identifiable form, and the use, dissemination, or sharing of information with advertisers in non-personally-identifiable form. Ad targeting that shares or sells personal information to advertisers (name, email, other contact oriented information) without user control is fundamentally different from targeting that only gives advertisers the ability to present their ads based on aggregate data. Most Facebook data is collected transparently in personally identifiable form — users know they are providing the data about themselves and are not forced to provide particular information.[1] Sharing information on the site is limited by user-established friend relationships and user-selected networks that determine who has access to that personal information. Users can see how their data is used given the reactions of their friends when they update their profiles, upload new photos or videos, or update their current status.

On Facebook, then, a feedback loop is established where people know what they are uploading and receive timely reactions from their friends, reinforcing the fact they have uploaded identifiable information. The privacy policy and the users' experiences inform them of how advertising on the service works -- advertising that enables us to provide the service for free to users is targeted to the expressed attributes of a profile and presented in the space on the page allocated for advertising, without granting an advertiser access to any individual user's profile.

Furthermore, advertising on Facebook is subject to guidelines designed to avoid deceptive practices, and with special restrictions and review with respect to any advertising targeted at minors.

I cannot stress strongly enough that Facebook does not authorize access by the Internet population at large, including advertisers, to the personally identifiable information that a user willingly uploads to Facebook. Facebook profiles have extensive user-configurable rules limiting access to information contained in them. Unless a user decides otherwise by willingly sharing information with an advertiser — for instance, through a contest -¬advertisers may only target advertisements against non-personally identifiable attributes about a user of Facebook derived from profile data.

We recognize that other Internet services may take a different approach to advertisers and the information available to them. Advertising products that sell personally identifiable information to advertisers without user permission, that rely on transforming non- personally identifiable information into personally identifiable information without robust notice and choice to users, or that rely on data collection that a user has scant notice of and no control over, raise fundamentally different privacy concerns. Facebook does not offer such products today and has no intention of doing so. Advertising products founded on the principles of transparency and user control, where data is collected directly from users in personally identifiable space and targeting is done based on aggregate or characteristic data in non-personally identifiable space, respect the principle that sits at the heart of privacy concerns.

B. History of Facebook Ads and Beacon

Perhaps because our site has developed so quickly, we have sometimes been inartful in communicating with our users and the general public about our advertising products. It therefore may be fruitful to provide a brief history of the current Facebook advertising offerings, including Facebook Ads and Social Ads, as well as the Beacon product that garnered significant public attention late last year.

In November 2007, Facebook introduced Facebook Ads, which consisted of both a basic self-service targeting infrastructure based on the non-personally identifiable use of keywords derived from profile data, and Social Ads, which allow for the paid promotion of certain interactions users take online to those users' friends in conjunction with an advertiser message. The basic targeting infrastructure of Facebook Ads is quite similar to many other Internet advertising systems, where media buyers and agencies can purchase guarantees that their advertisements will run to people who have certain characteristics, often expressed (as they are in Facebook Ads) in "keywords," or in demographic categories such as men between 29 and 34.

Social Ads are an innovation in that they allow advertisers to pay for promotion of certain interactions users take online to those users' friends. For example, if I become a supporter of a particular political figure on Facebook, their campaign could pay to promote that fact to more of my friends than would have been informed of it otherwise through the Facebook News Feed, and potentially pair a message from the campaign with it. It is notable first that only my action can trigger a Social Ad and that Social Ads are only presented to confirmed friends as opposed to the world at large; there will be no Social Ad generated noting my action to anyone but a confirmed friend. It is also notable that in this paid promotion context through Social Ads, an advertiser is not purchasing and does not have access to users' personal data — they are only told that a certain number of users have taken relevant actions and the number of ads generated by those actions.

We introduced at the same time as Facebook Ads a product called Beacon to allow users to bring actions they take on third-party sites into Facebook. Our introduction of this product with advertising technology led many to believe that Beacon was an ad product when it really was not. Participating third party sites do not pay Facebook to offer Beacon, nor must a third party site that wants to use Beacon purchase Facebook Ads. No Facebook user data is sold to or shared with these third party sites. In most cases, Beacon pertains to non-commercial actions like the playing of a game or the adding of a recipe to an online recipe box. In other cases, we and the participating third party sites experimented with capturing purchases for sharing within a user's Facebook friend network, obviously a more commercial enterprise. In both the non-commercial and commercial contexts, we discovered in the weeks after launch that users felt they did not have adequate control over the information and how it was being shared with their friends.

We quickly reached the conclusion that Beacon had inadequate built-in controls driving user complaints, helped along by an organized campaign by MoveOn.org to get us to alter the product. We made significant changes within weeks after its launch to make it a fully opt-in system. We remain convinced that the goal of helping users share information about their activities on the web with their friends is desirable and appreciated. Indeed, a number of services now exist which attempt to help users in this way. While Beacon was cast in the mainstream press as an advertising product, it operates fundamentally as a means to connect, with a user's permission and control, actions elsewhere on the Web with a user's Facebook friend network.

We are currently working on the next generation of Facebook's interactions with third party websites, called Facebook Connect, to empower users further to share content and actions with their friends using the Facebook infrastructure, and are focused on assuring that proper controls are built into this system.

III. FTC Principles on Behavioral Targeting

Finally, we would like to reinforce our earlier positive public comments about the Federal Trade Commission's leadership in addressing privacy concerns about how data is collected and shared online.

As explained above, Facebook Ads are materially different from behavioral targeting as it is usually discussed, but given our goals of transparency and user control, the important corollary of ensuring appropriate security and the goal of providing users notice and choice with respect to service changes, we applaud the FTC's desire to establish principles in the online advertising area. We believe the FTC should expand and enhance the discussion in the principles about the distinction between personally and non- personally identifiable information to clarify the need for different treatment of advertising based on those different types of information. We will continue our participation in discussion of the principles as they evolve.

Thank you again, Mr. Chairman, for the opportunity to share our views, and I am happy to answer any questions you may have.

END NOTES

1 Currently, only four pieces of data are required to establish and maintain a Facebook account — email address to provide a unique login identifier, birthdate to calculate age, name to provide a standard identifier (our Terms of Use require real name), and gender to promote the accuracy of grammar through the site infrastructure.

In: Electronic Breadcrumbs: Issues in Tracking Consumers   ISBN: 978-1-60741-600-5
Editor: Dmitar N. Kovac   © 2010 Nova Science Publishers, Inc.

Chapter 15

PRIVACY & ONLINE ADVERTISING HEARING- PARNES TESTIMONY

Lydia Parnes

I. INTRODUCTION

Chairman Inouye, Vice Chainnan Stevens, and Members of Committee, I am Lydia Parnes,[1] Director of the Bureau of Consumer Protection at the Federal Trade Commission (the "FTC" or "Commission"). I appreciate the opportunity to appear before you today to discuss the Commission's activities regarding online behavioral advertising, the practice of collecting information about an individual's online activities in order to serve advertisements that are tailored to that individual's interests. Over the past year or so, the Commission has undertaken a comprehensive effort to educate itself and the public about this practice and its implications for consumer privacy. This testimony will describe the Commission's efforts, which have included hosting a "Town Hall" meeting and issuing for public comment FTC staff's proposed online behavioral advertising principles.[2]

The Commission's examination of behavioral advertising has shown that the issues surrounding this practice are complex, that the business models are diverse and constantly evolving, and that behavioral advertising may provide benefits to consumers even as it raises concerns about consumer privacy. At this time, the Commission is cautiously optimistic that the privacy concerns raised by behavioral advertising can be addressed effectively by industry self- regulation.[3]

II. BEHAVIORAL ADVERTISING

Many businesses use online behavioral advertising in an attempt to increase the effectiveness of their advertising by targeting advertisements more closely to the interests of their audience. The practice generally involves the use of "cookies" to track consumers' activities online and associate those activities with a particular computer or device. In many cases, the information collected is not personally identifiable in the traditional sense — that is, the information does not include the consumer's name, physical address, or similar identifier that could be used to identify the consumer in the offline world. Many of the companies engaged in behavioral advertising are so-called "network advertisers," companies that serve advertisements across the Internet at websites that participate in their networks.[4]

An example of how behavioral advertising might work is as follows: a consumer visits a travel website and searches for airline flights to New York City. The consumer does not purchase any tickets, but later visits the website of a local newspaper to read about the Washington Nationals baseball team. While on the newspaper's website, the consumer receives an advertisement from an airline featuring flights to New York City.

In this simple example, the travel website where the consumer conducted his research might have an arrangement with a network advertiser to provide advertising to its visitors. The network advertiser places on the consumer's computer a cookie, which stores non-personally identifiable information such as the web pages the consumer has visited, the advertisements that the consumer has been shown, and how frequently each advertisement has been shown. Because the newspaper's website is also part of the advertising network, when the consumer visits the newspaper website, the network advertiser recognizes the cookie from the travel website as its own and identifies the consumer as likely having an interest in traveling to New York. It then serves the corresponding advertisement for airline flights to New York.

In a slightly more sophisticated example, the information about the content that the consumer had selected from the travel website could be combined with information about the consumer's activities on the newspaper's website. The advertisement served could then be tailored to the consumer's interest in, not just New York City, but also baseball (e.g., an advertisement referring to the New York Yankees).

As these examples illustrate, behavioral advertising may provide benefits to consumers in the form of advertising that is more relevant to their interests. Consumer research has shown that many online consumers value more personalized ads, which may facilitate shopping for the specific products that consumers want.[5] Further, by providing advertisements that are likely to be of interest to the consumer, behavioral advertising also may reduce the number of unwanted, and potentially unwelcome, advertisements consumers receive online

More broadly, the revenue model for the Internet is, to a large extent, advertising-based, and using behavioral techniques can increase the cost-effectiveness of online advertising. Thus, behavioral advertising may help subsidize and support a diverse range of free online content and services that otherwise might not be available or that consumers would otherwise have to pay for — content and services such as blogging, search engines, social networking, and instant access to newspapers and information from around the world.

At the same time, however, behavioral advertising raises consumer privacy concerns. As described below, many consumers express discomfort about the privacy implications of being tracked, as well as the specific harms that could result. In particular, without adequate safeguards in place, consumer tracking data may fall into the wrong hands or be used for unanticipated purposes.[6] These concerns are exacerbated when the tracking involves sensitive information about, for example, children, health, or a consumer's finances.

Recent high-profile incidents where tracking data has been released have magnified consumers' concerns. In August 2006, for example, an employee of internet service provider and web services company AOL made public the search records of approximately 658,000 customers.[7] The search records were not identified by name, and, in fact, the company had taken steps to anonymize the data. By combining the highly particularized and often personal searches, however, several newspapers, including the New York Times,[8] and consumer groups were able to identify some individual AOL users and their queries, challenging traditional notions about what data is or is not personally identifiable.

Another incident involved the social networking site Facebook. In November 2007, Facebook released a program called Beacon, which allowed users to share infolination about their online activities, such as the purchases they had made or the videos they had viewed. The Beacon service tracked the activities of logged-in users on websites that had partnered with Facebook. If a user did not opt out of this tracking, Facebook's partner sites would send to Facebook information about the user's purchases at the partner sites. Facebook then published this information on the user's profile page and sent it to the user's Facebook "friends."

The Beacon program raised significant concerns among Facebook users.[9] Approximately 30 groups formed on Facebook to protest Beacon, with one of the groups representing over 4,700 members,[10] and over 50,000 Facebook users signed a petition objecting to the new program.[11] Within a few weeks, Facebook changed its program by adding more user controls over what information is shared with "friends" and by improving notifications to users before sharing their information with others on Facebook.[12]

Surveys confirm that consumers are concerned about the privacy of their activities as they navigate online For example, in two recent surveys, a majority of consumers expressed some degree of discomfort with having information about their online activities collected and used to serve advertising.[13] Similarly, only 20 percent of consumers in a third survey stated that they would allow a marketer to share information about them in order to track their purchasing behaviors and to help predict future purchasing decisions.[14] Another survey found that 45 percent of consumers believe that online tracking should be banned, and another 47 percent would allow such tracking, but only with some form of consumer control.[15] These surveys underscore the importance of online privacy to consumers and highlight the fundamental importance of maintaining trust in the online marketplace.

III. FTC INITIATIVES CONCERNING CONSUMER PRIVACY AND BEHAVIORAL ADVERTISING

Since privacy first emerged as a significant consumer protection issue in the mid 1990s, it has been one of the Commission's highest priorities. The Commission has worked to address privacy issues through consumer and business education, law enforcement, and policy initiatives. For example, the FTC has promulgated and enforced the Do Not Call Rule to respond to consumer complaints about unsolicited and unwanted telemarketing;[16] has waged a multi-faceted war on identity theft;[17] has encouraged better data security practices by businesses through educational initiatives[18] and a robust enforcement program;[19] has brought numerous enforcement actions to reduce the incidence of spun and spyware;[20] and has held numerous workshops to examine emerging technologies and business practices, and the privacy and other issues they raise for consumers.[21] In early 2006, recognizing the ever-increasing importance of privacy to consumers and to a healthy marketplace, the Commission established the Division of Privacy and Identity Protection, a division devoted exclusively to privacy-related issues.

In developing and implementing its privacy program, the FTC has been mindful of the need for flexibility and balance — that is, the need to address consumer concerns and harms without stifling innovation or imposing needless costs on consumers and businesses.

A. 1999 Workshop on Online Profiling

The Commission first examined the issue of behavioral advertising in 1999, when it held a joint public workshop with the Department of Commerce on the practice — then called "online profiling." The workshop examined the practice of tracking consumers' activities online, as well as the role of self-regulation in this area.

In response to the concerns highlighted at the workshop, industry members formed the Network Advertising Initiative ("NAI"), a self-regulatory organization addressing behavioral advertising by network advertisers. Shortly thereafter, the NAI issued the NAI Self-Regulatory Principles ("NAI Principles") governing collection of information for online advertising by network advertisers.[22] In the early 2000s, however, with the "burst" of the dot coin bubble, many network advertisers — including most of the NAI membership — went out of business.

Emblematic of the highly dynamic nature of the online enviromnent, by the time the FTC held its public hearings on Protecting Consumers in the Next Tech-ade ("Tech-ade") only a few years later,[23] the issue of online tracking and advertising had reemerged. In the intervening years, behavioral advertising had become a highly successful business practice, and a number of Tech-ade participants raised concerns about its effects on consumer privacy.

B. The FTC Town Hall on Online Behavioral Advertising

Beginning in Fall 2006, the Commission staff held a series of meetings with numerous industry representatives, technology experts, consumer and privacy advocates, and academics to learn more about the practice of behavioral advertising. The purpose of these meetings was to explore further the issues raised at Tech-ade, learn about developments since the FTC's 1999 Workshop, and examine concerns about behavioral advertising that had been raised by privacy advocates and others.[24] Seeking a broader forum in which to examine and discuss these issues, and particularly the privacy issues raised by the practice, the FTC held a two-day Town Hall meeting on behavioral advertising in November 2007.

From the Town Hall, as well as the meetings preceding it, several key points emerged. First, as discussed above, online behavioral advertising may provide many valuable benefits to consumers in the form of free content, personalization that many consumers value, and a potential reduction in unwanted advertising. Second, the invisibility of the practice to consumers raises privacy concerns, as does the risk that data collected for behavioral advertising — including sensitive data about children, health, or finances — could be misused. Third, business and consumer groups alike expressed support for transparency and consumer control in the online marketplace.

Many participants at the Town Hall also criticized the self-regulatory efforts that had been implemented to date. In particular, these participants stated that the NAI Principles had not been sufficiently effective in addressing the privacy concerns raised by behavioral advertising because of the NAP s limited membership, the limited scope of the NAI Principles (which apply to network advertisers but not to other companies engaged in behavioral advertising), and the NAI Principles' lack of enforcement and cumbersome opt-out system.[25] Further, while other industry associations had promulgated online self-regulatory schemes to address privacy issues, these schemes had not generally focused on behavioral advertising.[26]

C. The FTC's Proposed Self-Regulatory Principles

In December 2007, in response to the issues discussed at the Town Hall and in public comments received in connection with that event, Commission staff issued and requested comment on a set of proposed principles titled, "Behavioral Advertising: Moving the Discussion Forward to Possible Self-Regulatory Principles" (the "Principles"). The proposed Principles address the central concerns about online behavioral advertising expressed by interested parties; they also build upon existing "best practices" in the area of privacy, as well as (in some cases) previous FTC guidance and/or law enforcement actions. At the same time, the Principles reflect FTC staffs recognition of the potential benefits provided by online behavioral advertising and the need to maintain vigorous competition in this area.

The purpose of the proposed Principles is to encourage more meaningful and enforceable self-regulation. At this time, the Commission believes that self-regulation may be the preferable approach for this dynamic marketplace because it affords the flexibility that is needed as business models continue to evolve.

In brief, the staff proposal identifies four governing principles for behavioral advertising.[27] The first is transparency and consumer control: companies that collect information for behavioral advertising should provide meaningful disclosures to consumers about the practices, as well as choice about whether their information is collected for this purpose.[28] The second principle is reasonable security: companies should provide reasonable security for behavioral data so that it does not fall into the wrong hands, and should retain data only as long as necessary to fulfill a legitimate business or law enforcement need.[29] The third principle governs material changes to privacy policies: before a company uses behavioral data in a manner that is materially different from promises made when the data was collected, it should obtain affirmative express consent from the consumer.[30] This principle ensures that consumers can rely on promises made about how their infoimation will be used, and can prevent contrary uses if they so choose. The fourth principle states that companies should obtain affirmative express consent before they use sensitive data — for example, data about children, health, or finances — for behavioral advertising.[31]

IV. NEXT STEPS

In response to the request for public comment, Commission staff received over 60 comments on the Principles, representing many thoughtful and constructive views from diverse business sectors, industry self-regulatory bodies, privacy advocates, technologists, academics, and consumers. The comment period for the Principles has closed, and Commission staff is carefully evaluating the comments received.

Included in the comments were a number of specific proposals for how self-regulation could be implemented, as well as reports regarding steps taken to address privacy concerns since the Town Hall. The FTC is encouraged by the efforts that have already been made by the NAT[32] and some other organizations and companies[33] and believes that the self-regulatory process that has been initiated is a promising one. Although there is more work to be done in this area, the Commission is cautiously optimistic that the privacy issues raised by online behavioral advertising can be effectively addressed through meaningful, enforceable self-regulation. The dynamic and diverse online environment demands workable and adaptable approaches to privacy that will be responsive to the evolving marketplace. Nevertheless, the Commission will continue to closely monitor the marketplace so that it can take appropriate action to protect consumers as the circumstances warrant.

V. CONCLUSION

The Commission appreciates this opportunity to discuss its work on behavioral advertising. The Commission is committed to addressing new and emerging privacy issues such as online behavioral advertising and looks forward to working further with the Committee on this important consumer issue.

END NOTES

[1] The views expressed in this statement represent the views of the Commission. My oral presentation and responses to any questions are my own, however, and do not necessarily reflect the views of the Commission or any individual Commissioner.

[2] *See* Federal Trade Commission, "Ehavioral Advertising: Tracking, Targeting, & Technology," *available at* http://www.ftc.gov/bcu/workshops/ehavioral/index.shtml.

[3] Although FTC staff has proposed self-regulation to address the general privacy concerns raised by behavioral advertising, the Commission will of course continue to bring enforcement actions to challenge law violations in appropriate cases.

[4] The advertisements are typically based upon data collected about a given consumer as he or she travels across the different websites in the advertising network. A website may belong to multiple networks.

[5] *See* Larry Ponemon, "FTC Presentation on Cookies and Consumer Permissions," presented at the FTC's Town Hall "Ehavioral Advertising: Tracking, Targeting, and Technology" (Nov. 1, 2007), at *7, available at* http://www.ftc.aov/bcp/workshops/ehavioral/presentations/31ponemon.pdf (survey found that 55 percent of respondents believed that an online ad that targeted their individual preferences or interests improved, to some degree, their online experience). *See also* TRUSTe/TNS Presentation, TRUSTe and TNS Global, "Consumer Attitudes about Behavioral Advertising" at 10 (March 28, 2008) (72 percent of respondents found online advertising annoying when it was not relevant to their interests or needs). *But see infra* note 13 and accompanying text.

[6] As a result of these concerns, a number of consumer groups and others have asked the Commission to take action in this area. *See, e.g.,* Center for Digital Democracy and U.S. Public Interest Research Group Complaint and Request for Inquiry and Injunctive Relief Concerning Unfair and Deceptive Online Marketing Practices (Nov. 1, 2006), *available at* http://www.democraticmedia.org/files/pdf/FTCadprivacy.pdf; Ari Schwartz and Alissa Cooper, Center for Democracy and Technology, "CDT Letter to Commissioner Rosch," (Jan. 19, 2007), *available at* http ://www. cdt.org/privacy/20070119rosch-b ehavioral-letter. pdf; Mindy B ockstein, "Letter to Chairman Majoras Re: DoubleClick, Inc. and Google, Inc. Merger," New York State Consumer Protection Board (May 1, 2007), *available at* http ://epic.org/privacy/ftc/t400gle/cpb .pdf.

[7] *See, e.g.,* Jeremy Kirk, "AOL Search Data Reportedly Released," Computerworld (Aug. 6, 2007), *available at* http ://computerworld. com/action/article. do ?c ornmand=viewArticleB asic&taxonomyName=priva cy&articleId=9002234&taxonomvId=84.

[8] *See* Michael Barbaro and Tom Zeller, "A Face Is Exposed for AOL Searcher No. 4417749," www.nytimes.com, Aug. 9, 2006, *available at* http://www.nvtimes.com/2006/08/09/technology/09aol.html.

[9] In one now-famous example, a man had bought a ring for his wife as a surprise; the surprise was ruined when his wife read about his purchase on the man's user profile page. *See, e.g.,* Ellen Nakashima, "Feeling Betrayed, Facebook Users Force Site to Honor Privacy," Washingtonpost.com, (Nov. 30, 2007), *available at* http://wvvw.washingtonpost.com/wp-dvn/content/article/2007/11/29/AR2007112902503 pf.html.

[10] *See* Facebook home page, http://www.facebook.com, viewed on March 21, 2008.

[11] MoveOn.org Civic Action^{TM} created an online petition for consumers to express their objection to Facebook's Beacon program. The petition stated, "Sites like Facebook must respect my privacy. They should not tell my friends what I buy on other sites — or let companies use my name to endorse their products — without my explicit permission. MoveOn.org Civic Action Petition, *available at http://ww w.civic.moveon.org/facebookprivacy/, viewed June 9, 2008.*

[12] *See* Reuters News, "Facebook Makes Tweak After Privacy Protest," RedHerring.com, Nov. 30, 2007, *available* at http://www.redherring.com/Home/23224.

[13] *See* Alan Westin, "Online Users, Behavioral Marketing and Privacy: Results of a National Harris/Westin Survey" (March 2008) (almost 60 percent of respondents were "not comfortable" to some degree with online behavioral marketing); TRUSTe/TNS Presentation, "Behavioral Advertising: Privacy, Consumer Attitudes and Best Practices," at 10 (April 23, 2008) (57 percent of respondents were not comfortable with advertisers using browsing history to serve ads, even if the information is not connected to personally identifiable information).

[14] *See* Ponemon Presentation, *supra* note 5, at 11.

[15] *See* George R Milne, "Information Exchange Expectations of Consumers, Marketing Managers and Direct Marketers," University of Massachusetts Amherst (presented on Nov. 1, 2007), *available at* http://www.ftc. ov/b cp/workshops/ehavioral/pres entations/3 gmilne pdf.

[16] Telemarketing Sales Rule: Final Rule, 16 C.F.R. Part 310 (2003), *available at http ://www.ftc.gov/os/2003/01/tsrfin.pdf.*

[17] *See, e.g.,* FTC ID theft website, *available at* www,ftc.aov/idtheft. In one recent effort, the FTC coordinated with the U.S. Postal Service to send a letter to every American household containing information about how to protect against identity theft. *See* Press Release, "Postmaster General Sends Advice to Prevent ID Theft," U.S. Postal Service (Feb. 19, 2008), *available at* http://www.usps.com/connnunications/newsroom/2008/pr08_014.htm.

[18] *See, e.g.,* Federal Trade Commission, "Protecting Personal Information: A Guide for Business," *available at* http://www.ftc.gov/infosecurity/; *see also* http://onguardonline gov/index.html.

[19] Since 2001, the Commission has obtained twenty consent orders against companies that allegedly failed to provide reasonable protections for sensitive consumer information. *See In the Matter of The TJX Companies,* FTC File No. 072-3055 (Mar. 27, 2008, settlement accepted for public comment); *In the Matter of Reed Elsevier Inc. and Seisint Inc.,* FTC File No. 052-3094 (Mar. 27, 2008, settlement accepted for public comment); *United States v. ValueClick, Inc.,* No. CV08-01711 (C.D. Cal. Mar. 13, 2008); *In the Matter of Goal Financial, LLC,* FTC Docket No. C-4216 (April 15, 2008); *In the Matter of Life is Good, Inc.,* FTC Docket No. C4218 (Apr. 18, 2008); *United States v. American United Mortgage,* No. CV07C 7064, (N.D. Ill. Dec. 18, 2007); *In the Matter of Guidance Software, Inc.,* FTC Docket No. C-4187 (Apr. 3, 2007); *In the Matter of CardSystems Solutions, Inc.,* FTC Docket No. C-4168 (Sept. 5, 2006); *In the Matter of Nations Title Agency, Inc.,* FTC Docket No. C-4161 (June 19, 2006); *In the Matter of DSW, Inc.,* FTC Docket No. C-4157 (Mar. 7, 2006); *United States v. ChoicePoint, Inc.,* No. 106-CV-0198 (N.D. Ga. Feb. 15, 2006); *In the Matter of Superior Mortgage Corp.,* FTC Docket No. C-4153 (Dec. 14, 2005); *In the Matter of BJ's Wholesale Club, Inc.,* FTC Docket No. C4148 (Sept. 20, 2005); *In the Matter of Nationwide Mortgage Group, Inc.,* FTC Docket No. 9319 (Apr. 12, 2005); *In the Matter of Petco Animal Supplies, Inc.,* FTC Docket No. C-4133 (Mar. 4, 2005); *In the Matter of Sunbelt Lending Services,* FTC Docket No. C-4129 (Jan. 3, 2005); *In the Matter of MTS Inc., d/b/a Tower Records/Books/Video,* FTC Docket No. C-4110 (May 28, 2004); *In the Matter of Guess?, Inc.,* FTC Docket No. C-4091 (July 30, 2003); *In the Matter of Microsoft Corp.,* FTC Docket No. C-4069 (Dec. 20, 2002); *In the Matter of Eli Lilly & Co.,* FTC Docket No. C-4047 (May 8, 2002).

[20] Since 2004, the Commission has initiated eleven spyware-related law enforcement actions. Detailed information regarding each of these law enforcement actions is available at http://www.ftc.aov/bcp/edu/microsites/spyware/law_enfor.htm. Since 1997, when the FTC brought its first enforcement action targeting unsolicited commercial email, or "spam," the FTC has brought 94 law enforcement actions. *See generally* Report on "Spain Summit: The Next Generation of Threats and Solutions" (Nov. 2007), *available at* http://www.ftc.gov/os/2007/12/071220spamsummitreport.pdf.

[21] *See* discussion *infra* pp. 9-12.

[22] Briefly, the NAI Principles set forth guidelines for online network advertisers and provide a means by which consumers can opt out of behavioral advertising at a centralized website. For more information on the FTC workshop and NAI, *see Online Profiling: A Report to Congress* (June 2000) at 22 and *Online Profiling A Report Congress Part 2 Recommendations (July 2000), available at* http://www.ftc.gov/os/2000/06/onlineprofilinueportjune2000.pdf and http://www.networkadvertising.org. As discussed further below, NAI recently proposed for public comment revised NAI Principles.

[23] The purpose of the Tech-ade hearings, held in November 2006, was to examine the technological and consumer protection developments anticipated over the next decade. *See generally* http://www.ftc. gov/bcp/workshops/techade/index.html.

[24] *See* CDD *et al.*, Complaint and Request for Inquiry and Injunctive Relief, *supra* note 6. Many of these concerns were amplified by the announcement of the proposed merger between Google and DoubleClick in April 2007. The Commission approved the merger on December 20, 2007, at the same time that it issued FTC staff's proposed self-regulatory guidelines. *See* "Staff Proposes Online Behavioral Advertising Policy Principles," Federal Trade Commission (Dec. 20, 2008), *available at http://www.ftc.,g,ov/opa/2007/12/principles.shtm.* The Principles are discussed *infra* at 13.

[25] According to critics, the NAI Principles' opt-out mechanism is difficult to locate and use because it is located on the NAI website, where consumers would be unlikely to find it. As noted above, in April of this year, the NAI issued a proposed revised set of self-regulatory principles designed to address criticisms of the original NAI Principles and to respond to the FTC staff's call for stronger self-regulation. The NAI has sought comment on its proposed revised principles, and comments were due June 12, 2008. *See* "Self-Regulatory Principles for Online Preference Marketing By Network Advertisers," Network Advertising Initiative (issued April 10, 2008), *available at* http://www.networkadvertisina.org/pdfs/NAI_principles.pdf.

[26] Since the Town Hall, some of these industry groups, as well as several online companies and privacy groups, have sought to address the concerns raised about behavioral advertising. *See, e.g.,* Interactive Advertising Bureau, "Privacy Principles," (adopted Feb. 24, 2008), *available at* http://www.iab .net/iabpro ducts and industry services/1421/1443/1464; Comment "Online Behavioral Advertising: Moving the Discussion Forward to Possible Self- Regulatory Principles," Microsoft Corp. (April 11, 2008), *available at* http://www.ftc.aov/os/comments/behavioraladprinciples/080411 microsoft.pdf; Comment "FTC Staff Proposed Online Behavioral Advertising Principles: Comments of AOL, LLC," AOL, LLC (April 11, 2008), *available at* http://www.ftc.gov/os/con nnents/behavioraladprinciples/080411aol.pdf; Ari Schwartz, Center for Democracy and Technology, *et al.*, "Consumer Rights and Protections in the Behavioral Advertising Sector," (Oct. 31, 2007) (proposing a "Do Not Track List" designed to increase consumers' control over tracking of their activities online), *available at* http://www.cdt.org/privacy/20071031consumerprotectionsbehavioral.pdf.

[27] Recent news reports have highlighted concerns about behavioral advertising involving Internet Service Providers ("ISPs"). The ISP-based model for delivering behaviorally-targeted advertising may raise heightened privacy concerns because it could involve the tracking of subscribers wherever they go online and the accumulation of vast stores of data about their online activities. Further, information about the subscriber's activities potentially could be combined with the personally identifiable information that ISPs possess about their subscribers. In issuing the proposed Principles for public comment, FTC staff intended the Principles to apply to ISPs.

[28] For more information and guidance on the use of disclosures in online advertising, see *Dot Com Disclosures, Information About Online Advertising*, http://www.ftc.2ov/bcp/conline/pubs/buspubs/dotcom/index.shtml (May 2000).

[29] The FTC has highlighted the need for reasonable security in numerous educational materials and enforcement actions to date. *See supra* notes 18-19.

[30] *See, e.g., Gateway Learning Corp.*, Docket No. C-4120 (Sept. 10, 2004), http://www.ftc.gov/opa/2004/07/2ateway.shtm (company made material changes to its privacy policy and allegedly applied such changes to data collected under the old policy; opt-in consent required for future such changes).

[31] Commission staff also sought comment on the potential uses of tracking data beyond behavioral advertising.

[32] Current NAI members include DoubleClick, Yahoo! Inc., TACODA, Inc., Acerno, AlmondNet, BlueLithium, Mindset Media, Revenue Science, Inc., 24/7 Real Media Inc., and Undertone Networks.

[33] *See supra* note 26. Although many organizations and consumer groups have undertaken efforts to address FTC staff's proposed Principles, a few organizations have expressed concern that implementing the Principles would be too costly and would undermine continued development of the online marketplace. FTC staff is evaluating all of these comments as it considers next steps in this area.

In: Electronic Breadcrumbs: Issues in Tracking Consumers
Editor: Dmitar N. Kovac

ISBN: 978-1-60741-600-5
© 2010 Nova Science Publishers, Inc.

Chapter 16

PRIVACY LAW AND ONLINE ADVERTISING: LEGAL ANALYSIS OF DATA GATHERING BY ONLINE ADVERTISERS SUCH AS DOUBLE CLICK AND NEBUAD

Kathleen Ann Ruane

SUMMARY

To produce revenue, websites have placed advertisements on their sites. Advertisers will pay a premium for greater assurance that the advertisement they are purchasing will be seen by users that are most likely to be interested in the product or service offered. As a result, technology has been developed which enables online advertisements to be targeted directly at individual users based on their web surfing activity. This practice is widely known as "behavioral" or "e-havioral" advertising.

This individual behavioral targeting has raised a number of privacy concerns. For instance, questions have been asked whether personally identifiable information is being collected; how the information collected is being protected; and whether current laws are being violated if data are being collected without the consent of the parties involved. It is often unclear whether current laws, such as the Electronic Communications Privacy Act and the Communications Act, apply to online advertising providers that are collecting data through click tracking, capturing search terms, and other methods. However, it is likely that in many cases these laws could be held to apply to such activities and that these methods of data collection would be forbidden unless consent is obtained from one of the parties to the communication. This report will examine the application of these statutes to online behavioral advertising in more detail.

There are no current federal regulations specific to online behavioral advertising. The Federal Trade Commission (FTC) has put forth a number of guiding principles intended to aid the industry in creating self-regulatory principles. The FTC maintains that self-regulation is preferable to government intervention in this case. Organizations such as the Network Advertising Initiative have created policies which many online advertising providers have pledged to follow that represent industry best practices for protecting the privacy of web users.

The 110th Congress has expressed interest in this issue. In July of 2008, both the Senate Committee on Commerce, Science, and Transportation and the House Energy and Commerce Committee held hearings to examine the data collection practices of NebuAd, an online advertising provider that collects data on web users by using "deep packet inspection." Representatives Markey and Stearn sent a letter to 33 companies (such as AT&T, Comcast, and Google) on August 1, 2008, requesting additional information about their usage of "deep packet inspection" to collect data on users of their services. The Senate Commerce Committee held another hearing addressing broadband providers and consumer privacy on September 25, 2008.

INTRODUCTION AND TECHNICAL BACKGROUND

Many website operators produce income by selling advertising space on their sites. Advertisers will pay a premium for ads that are more likely to reach their target demographic. In other media, such as broadcasting, advertisers engage in targeting by purchasing advertising time during programs that those who buy their products are most likely to watch. The Internet presented new challenges and opportunities for advertisers to reach their target audiences. Technology has been developed that allows advertisers to target advertising to individual web users. This is seen as an advantage for advertisers, because, rather than aiming their ads at groups of people who visit a particular site, their ads are aimed at the individual user. This maximizes the odds that the user who sees the ad will be interested in the product or service it touts. Targeting advertising to individuals involves gathering information about that individual's web surfing habits. The collection of this information has raised concerns among some over the privacy of web activity, particularly if the data collected are personally identifiable. Some have alleged that online advertisers are violating privacy laws by collecting these data.

In online advertising's simplest form, a commercial website rents out "space" on its site to another website which places a hot link banner advertisement in that space.[1] The banner ad, when clicked, sends the user directly to the advertiser's website. In this scenario, no matter who visits a particular website, that user will see the same advertisement, regardless of whether he/she may be interested in that product or service. However, many advertisers will pay a premium for the increased likelihood that users viewing their advertisement would be interested in the product or service offered. As a result, technology has developed to more accurately target online ads to the desired audience.

Online advertising providers, such as DoubleClick and NebuAd, have developed the ability to target ads to individual Internet users who would be most interested in seeing those ads. These techniques are known generally as "behaviorally targeted advertising." Behaviorally targeted advertising delivers ads that are geared toward specific Internet users by tracking certain, though not necessarily all, web activity of each user and inferring each user's interests based on that activity. Most online advertising providers monitor individual Internet users by placing a "persistent cookie" on that user's computer. "Cookies" are small text files that can store information. "Persistent cookies" reside on a hard drive indefinitely, unlike most "cookies" which expire when a browser window is closed. Generally, online advertisers give the "cookies" they place on user computers a unique alphanumeric code that identifies that user to the advertising company purportedly without revealing any personally identifiable information. "Cookies" may be placed on an individual's computer when an individual visits a website affiliated with the online advertisement supplier; however, the exact moment of "cookie" placement may be different when the relevant advertising partnership is between a user's Internet Service Provider (ISP) and an online advertising provider.

Once the cookie is in place, it gathers certain information related to that user's online activity on a continuous basis and relays that information to the online advertising provider. The advertising provider assembles that data into an individual profile that is then used to target advertising to that user's interests. This process is ongoing, but, in general, the user may opt out of continued monitoring at any point, assuming they are aware that it is occurring. In most types of behaviorally targeted advertising technology, the advertising firm gathers information about user activities on websites that are affiliated with the advertising firm. The behavioral advertiser DoubleClick, for instance, operates on this model. Information on individual users is transmitted to DoubleClick by DoubleClick's clients. In a newly emerging behavioral advertising model, the advertising provider is attempting to partner with the users' ISP. This partnership will presumably grant the advertising provider access to all web activity in which an ISP's subscribers engage. Both of these types of potential partnerships raise a number of questions regarding potential violations of existing privacy protections in federal law.

ELECTRONIC COMMUNICATIONS PRIVACY ACT

Concerns have been raised that online advertising providers, websites, and ISPs that agree to collect certain data generated by Internet traffic to behaviorally target advertising may be violating the Electronic Communications Privacy Act (ECPA)100 Stat. 1848, 18 U.S.C. 2510-2521.[2] ECPA is an amendment to Title III of the Omnibus Crime Control and Safe Streets Act of 1968, 87 Stat. 197, 18 U.S.C. 2510-2520 (1970 ed.), which prohibits the interception of electronic communications unless an exception to the general prohibition applies.[3] This section will discuss the potential application of ECPA to online advertising providers and the potential application of ECPA to ISPs.

The Online Advertising Provider

The first question that must be addressed is whether ECPA applies to the activities of online advertising providers. Online advertising providers are acquiring information such as the fact that a user clicked on a particular link (an action which is the equivalent of asking the site providing the link to send the user information), and they are acquiring that information while the communication is in transit.[4] Furthermore, these advertisers may acquire information, such as words entered into a search engine or answers to online forms, while it is in transit.[5] Under ECPA, it is illegal, with certain enumerated exceptions, for any person to "intentionally intercept, endeavor to intercept, or procure any other person to intercept or endeavor to intercept, any wire, oral or electronic communication."[6] It is important to lay out the statutory definitions of each of the key terms in order to assess whether the ECPA prohibition and/or any of its exceptions applies to activities conducted by online behavioral advertisers.

- "Intercept" means the aural or other acquisition of the contents of any wire, electronic, or oral communication through the use of any electronic, mechanical or other device.[7]
- "Contents" when used with respect to any wire, oral, or electronic communication includes any information concerning the substance, purport, or meaning of that communication.[8]
- "Electronic Communication" means any transfer of signs, signals, writing, images, sounds, data, or intelligence of any nature transmitted in whole or in part by a wire, radio, electromagnetic, photoelectronic, or photo optical system that affects interstate or foreign commerce.[9]

Because the advertisers record that a particular user requested information from a website by clicking on a particular link or sent information to a website via a search entry or other method, the advertisers appear to be "intercepting" the "contents" of those "electronic communications." Therefore, the interceptions are likely covered by ECPA.[10]

Merely determining that this type of data acquisition by online advertisers is an interception for the purposes of ECPA does not end the analysis. ECPA excepts certain communication interceptions from its prohibition. The exception to ECPA that would most likely apply to these types of interceptions is the exception that allows for interception of communications with the consent of one of the parties.[11] The question of when and how consent to the interception may be given is addressed below.

The Internet Service Provider

The second question to be addressed is whether ECPA applies to ISP providers that would allow online advertising providers to gather data from traffic over the ISP's network. ECPA prohibits any person or entity providing an electronic communications service from intentionally divulging the "contents of any communications ... while in transmission on that service to any person or entity other than an addressee or intended recipient of such communications or an agent of such addressee or intended recipient."[12] The same definitions outlined in the previous section apply here. This section seems to apply to ISPs that would agree to allow online advertising providers to acquire portions of the web traffic of ISP customers, because the ISP would be allowing the advertising providers to acquire the contents of communications while they are in transmission and neither the advertising provider nor the ISP would, in most cases, be the addressee or intended recipient of the communications.

Again, determining that the data collection is likely an interception for the purposes of ECPA does not end the analysis. An ECPA exception may apply. ISPs are allowed to intercept communications while in transit if such interception is part of "any activity which is a necessary incident to the rendition of [that service] or to the protection of the rights or property of the provider of that service."[13] It does not seem likely that this exception applies to ISPs when contracting with online advertising providers. Though the service for which they contract may help keep the websites of the advertising provider's clients free to the public by producing advertising revenue, the interception is not necessary to maintain an ISP's proper function or solvency and, therefore, likely is not necessary to the rendition of Internet access service.[14] ISPs also are allowed to divulge the contents of a communication in transit "with the lawful consent of the originator or any addressee or intended recipient of such communication."[15] If the ISPs obtain the consent of their customers to intercept some of their online activities, this exception to ECPA would seem to apply. Again, the questions of how and when consent may be obtained and what constitutes "lawful consent" arise and are addressed in the following section.

The Consent Exception to ECPA

As noted above, interception of electronic communications is not prohibited by ECPA if one of the parties to the communications has consented to the interception. Consent is not defined by ECPA; nor do precise instructions of how and when consent may be obtained under ECPA appear in regulation. Therefore, it has been left largely to the courts to determine when consent to intercept a communication otherwise covered by ECPA's prohibitions has been granted.[16] There have been few cases dealing with ECPA's application to online advertising providers and none examining ECPA's application to agreements between ISP providers and online advertising providers. As a result, many open-ended questions exist regarding how to obtain adequate consent. This section first will examine whether the consent exception to ECPA applies to data collection agreements between online advertising providers and website operators. It will then examine whether and how the consent exception applies to data collection agreements between ISPs and online advertising providers.

Data Collection Agreements Between Website Operators and Online Advertising Providers

Agreements for online advertising providers to monitor certain web traffic may be between the online advertising provider and the website operators seeking to have ads placed on their sites. The advertising providers receive information about user activity on participating websites and aggregate that data to better target ads. In litigation against the online advertising provider DoubleClick for violations of ECPA, the court examined whether websites were "users" of electronic communications services under ECPA.[17] ECPA defines a "user" as "any person or entity who (A) uses an electronic communication service; and (B) is duly authorized by the provider of such service to engage in such use."[18] The court reasoned that websites are "users" (and, therefore, "parties to the communications" at issue) because they actively respond to requests they receive over electronic communications services by deciding whether to send the requested document, breaking the document down into TCP/IP protocol, and sending the packets over the Internet.[19] Because websites are "users" of electronic communications, the court found that websites are also "parties to the communications" in dispute; therefore, website owners have the ability to consent to a communication's interception.[20]

The court also held that the website operators had consented, by virtue of their contract with DoubleClick, to allow the company to intercept certain traffic on their websites in order to target advertising to website visitors.[21] Consent for private interceptions of electronic communications cannot be granted if the purpose of the interception is the commission of criminal or tortuous conduct.[22] The court noted that the focus of the determination of criminal or tortious purpose under ECPA is "not upon whether the interception itself violated another law; it is upon whether the purpose for the interception—its intended use—was criminal or tortious."[23] Applying that standard, the court found that the plaintiffs had not alleged that DoubleClick's primary motivation for intercepting communications was to injure plaintiffs tortiously. In the court's view, even if DoubleClick's actions ultimately proved tortious or criminal, there was no evidence that DoubleClick was motivated by tortious intent. As a result, the court found that the consent exception to ECPA was satisfied.[24]

In a similar suit against online advertising provider Pharmatrak, the court outlined limitations to the consent exception regarding these types of agreements. In that case, Pharmatrak had contracted with certain drug companies to provide advertising on their websites. Included in the agreement was permission for the advertising provider to record certain web traffic that did not include personally identifiable information.[25] Perhaps inadvertently, the online advertising provider did collect a small amount of personally identifiable information though it had pledged not to do so. The advertiser argued that consent had been granted for such interception. The court disagreed. According to the court, it is for the party granting consent to define its scope, and the parties in this case had not consented to the collection of personally identifiable information.[26] In collecting personally identifiable information by intercepting data without the consent of one of the parties, the online advertiser potentially had violated ECPA, but may have lacked the requisite intent to be found liable under the statute.[27] The appeals court directed the trial court to conduct further investigation into the matter.

Given the conclusions in the above cases, it appears that online advertising providers, like DoubleClick, that partner to collect data from individual websites generally are not violating ECPA, because the websites are "parties to the communication" with the ability to consent to interception. Based on these cases, the advertising providers will not be seen as running afoul of ECPA so long as the data the advertising providers collect do not fall outside the scope of the data the advertising providers' clients have agreed to disclose.

Data Collection Agreements Between ISPs and Online Advertising Providers

On the other hand, when the partnership is between the ISP and the online advertising provider, neither of the parties to the agreement to intercept web traffic is a party to the communications that are being intercepted. Therefore, it would appear that consent for the interceptions must be obtained from individual customers of the ISPs. The questions, in these circumstances, are whether consent must be "affirmative," or if it can be "implied," and if consent must be "affirmative" what process must be used to obtain such consent from individual users.

"Affirmative" or "Implied" Consent

Consent to interceptions has been implied by the surrounding circumstances of communications. While consent may be implied, it may not be "casually inferred."[28] It seems unlikely, as a result, that merely by using an ISP's service, a customer of that service has implied her consent to the interception of her electronic communications by online advertising providers. If consent likely may not be implied simply from use of an ISP's service, then a form of affirmative consent from the ISP's customer would be necessary.

"Opt-in" v. "Opt-out" Consent

In other statutes requiring consent for certain types of disclosure, regulatory regimes have developed to define when and how affirmative consent should be obtained.[29] A similar debate is occurring now involving how ISPs should obtain consent from their customers to share data about their online activities with online advertising providers. The debate centers around whether ISPs and advertisers must obtain "opt-in" consent or if they may continue to obtain "opt-out" consent for these interceptions.

"Opt-in" consent is obtained when a party to the communication is notified that his or her ISP has agreed to allow an online advertiser to track that person's online activity in order to better target advertising to that person. The advertiser, however, may not begin to track that individual's web activity until the individual responds to the notification granting permission for such activity.[30] If the individual never responds, interception can never begin. "Opt-out" consent, by contrast, is obtained when a party to the communication is notified that his or her ISP has agreed to allow an online advertiser to track that person's online activity and the advertising provider will begin such tracking *unless* the individual notifies the ISP or the advertiser that he or she does not grant permission for such activity.[31] If the individual never responds, interception will begin. Currently, it appears that companies such as NebuAd are obtaining or planning to obtain "opt-out" consent for the information gathering they engage in with ISPs.[32] The present question is whether "optout" consent is sufficient to satisfy the ECPA consent requirement. This question has yet to be addressed by a federal court or clarified by legislation or regulation. However, as discussed below, if Section 631 of the Communications Act applies to this type of data collection, "opt-in" consent may already be required for cable companies acting as ISPs (though this may not be required of telco companies such as Verizon or AT&T that operate as ISPs).

SECTION 631 OF THE COMMUNICATIONS ACT

It is also possible that privacy provisions of the Communications Act apply to agreements between cable operators acting as ISPs and online advertising providers.[33] Section 631 of the Communications Act provides basic privacy protections for personally identifiable information gathered by cable operators.[34] Specifically, cable operators must provide notice to subscribers, informing them of the types of personally identifiable information the cable operator collects, how it is disclosed, how long it is kept, etc.[35] Cable operators are prohibited from collecting personally identifiable information over the cable system without a subscriber's prior written or electronic consent.[36] Cable operators are also forbidden to disclose personally identifiable information without prior written or electronic consent of subscribers and must take action to prevent unauthorized access to personally identifiable information by anyone other than the subscriber or cable operator.[37] NebuAd has argued that Section 631 does not apply to the activities of cable operators when cable operators are acting as cable modem service providers.[38]

Section 631 governs the protection of information about subscribers to "any cable service or other service" provided by a cable operator. "Other service" is defined as "any wire or radio communications service provided using any of the facilities of a cable operator that are used in the provision of cable service."[39] In its order classifying cable modem services as "information services," the FCC stated the belief that "cable modem service would be included in the category of 'other service' for the purposes of section 631."[40] Furthermore, in 1992, Congress added the term "other services" to Section 631 as part of the Cable Television and Consumer Protection and Competition Act.[41] The House Conference Report on the law clarified that provisions redefining the term "other services" were included in order "to ensure that new communications services provided by cable operators are covered by the privacy protections" of Section 631.[42]

Section 631 is judicially enforced, however, and it is for the courts to interpret the scope of its application absent more specific guidance from Congress.[43] It is unclear whether all of the provisions of Section 631 encompass Internet services. "Other services" have been interpreted by at least one district court to encompass Internet services.[44] On the other hand, in 2006, the Sixth Circuit Court of Appeals found that the plain language of Section 631(b) precluded its application to broadband Internet service.[45] Section 631(b) prohibits cable operators from using their cable systems to collect personally identifiable information without the consent of subscribers.[46] The court based its decision that Internet services were not covered by this prohibition on its interpretation of the definition of "cable systems."[47] The court found that the systems that deliver Internet services are not the systems that Section 631(b) addresses, and therefore, cable operators were not prohibited by Section 631(b) from collecting personally identifiable information over systems that delivered Internet access services. The Supreme Court has yet to rule on this issue.

Even if Section 631(b) does not prevent cable operators from collecting personally identifiable information over broadband Internet services, Section 631(c) may prohibit the disclosure of such information to third parties regardless of whether the information was collected over the cable system.[48] Section 631(c) of the Communications Act states that "a cable operator shall not disclose personally identifiable information concerning any subscriber without the prior written or electronic consent of the subscriber concerned and shall take such actions as are necessary to prevent unauthorized access to such information by a person other than the subscriber or cable operator."[49] If a cable operator, as an ISP, agrees to allow an online advertising provider to inspect traffic over its cable system and to acquire some of that information, it seems that the cable operator/ISP is disclosing information to the online advertising provider. Such disclosure would apparently be a violation of the Communications Act if (1) the information disclosed is personally identifiable information and (2) the cable operator/ISP is disclosing it without the prior written or electronic consent of the subscribers to whom the information pertains.

Whether online advertising providers are gathering personally identifiable information in order to provide their services is a matter of much debate. Section 631 does not define what personally identifiable information is; it defines what personally identifiable information is not. According to 631, Personally Identifiable Information (PII) does not include "any record of aggregate data which does not identify particular persons."[50] Online advertising providers claim that they do not collect any personally identifiable information.[51] Public interest groups and other commentators disagree, citing scenarios in which data which was not supposed to contain personally identifiable information was used to identify individuals.[52] Because Section 631 is judicially enforced, it is likely that whether online advertisers are acquiring personally identifiable information as opposed to aggregate data that do not identify particular persons will be a determination made by a federal trial court. To date, there have been no cases addressing this question.

Assuming even that online advertising providers are gathering personally identifiable information, cable operators are allowed to disclose personally identifiable information as long as they obtain the prior written or electronic consent of the relevant subscribers, essentially an "optin" standard.[53] In the event that online advertising companies are determined to be gathering personally identifiable information and that Section 631(c) applies to cable operators in their provision of cable modem services, cable operators would be required to obtain consent for such disclosure under an "opt-in" regime.

FEDERAL TRADE COMMISSION ONLINE ADVERTISING PRINCIPLES

The Federal Trade Commission (FTC) has held a number of hearings and town hall meetings to examine the privacy issues raised by online behavioral advertising.[54] The FTC continues to advocate for industry self-regulation in this area, but has put forth a number of principles intended to provide guidance. Some of the proposed principles include acquiring affirmative express consent to use sensitive data for behavioral advertising, implementing reasonable security for data collected, and limiting the time such data is retained.[55] The FTC has also suggested that every website where data are collected provide a "clear, concise, consumer-friendly, and prominent statement that (1) data about consumers' activities online is being collected at the site ... and (2) consumers can choose whether or not to have their information collected...."[56]

These principles were published on the FTC's website in December of 2007. The FTC also sought comments from the public on the principles. The comment period closed in April of 2008. The comments received were posted on the FTC's website in order to aid in the development of self-regulatory programs.[57] The FTC noted that, though the agency believed self-regulation remained the best course of action, it did not foreclose the use of the FTC's enforcement or regulatory authority, including its authority to challenge unfair or deceptive trade practices.

NETWORK ADVERTISING INITIATIVE STANDARDS

The Network Advertising Initiative (NAI) is an industry group composed of online advertising providers that has developed voluntary privacy, notice, and consent standards that are considered to represent industry best practices for the protection of data gathered for the purposes of behavioral advertising.[58] These standards do not have the force of law, but a number of online advertising providers have pledged to abide by them.

In December of 2008, the NAI released a new "Self-Regulatory Code of Conduct."[59] Under these standards, members of the NAI must post clear and conspicuous notice on their websites describing their data collection, transfer, and use practices. The Code instructs NAI members to require the sites with which they contract for behavioral advertising to post conspicuous notice of, among other things, the types of data collected by the company and how that data is used or transferred to third parties. Members also must contractually require any third parties to whom they provide personally identifiable information to comply with the Self-Regulatory Code of Conduct.

The Self-Regulatory Code creates three tiers of information that may be collected for behavioral advertising: non-personally identifiable information (Non-PII),[60] personally identifiable information (PII),[61] and Sensitive Consumer Information.[62] The code requires "opt-out" consent for the use of Non-PII. The prospective use of PII that is to be merged with Non-PII requires "opt-out" consent accompanied by a "robust notice"[63] that occurs prior to data collecion. The use of PII that is to be merged with previously collected Non-PII requires "opt-in" consent. The use of Sensitive Consumer Information always requires "opt-in" consent. Members must provide reasonable security for the data that they collect, and they may only retain the data collected "as long as necessary to fulfill a legitimate business need, or as required by law." Behavioral advertising that targets children under the age of thirteen (regardless of the type of information) is prohibited.

AUTHOR CONTACT INFORMATION

Kathleen Ann Ruane
Legislative Attorney
kruane@crs.loc.gov, 7-9135

END NOTES

[1] For a basic description of the technology involved in delivering behaviorally targeted advertising, please see the following source material: In re DoubleClick, Inc. Privacy Litigation, 154 F.Supp. 2d 497 (S.D.N.Y. 2001), In re Pharmatrak Privacy Litigation, 329 F.3d 9 (1st Cir. 2003), and Paul Lansing and Mark Halter, *Internet Advertising and Right to Privacy Issues*, 80 U. Det. Mercy L. Rev. 181 (2003). *See also,* Testimony of Mr. Robert R. Dykes, CEO of NebuAd Inc., *Privacy Implications of Online Advertising: Hearing Before the S. Comm. On Commerce, Science, and Transportation,* 110th Cong. (2008)(hereinafter NebuAd Testimony), available at http://commerce.senate.gov/public/_files/RobertDykesNebuAdOnlinePrivacyTestimony.pdf.

[2] Testimony of Ms. Leslie Harris, CEO of the Center for Democracy and Technology, *Privacy Implications of Online Advertising: Hearing Before the S. Comm. On Commerce, Science, and Transportation,* 110th Cong. (2008)(hereinafter CDT Testimony), available at
http://commerce.senate.gov/public/_files/LeslieHarrisCDTOnlinePrivacyTestimony.pdf.

[3] For a more detailed discussion of the history of ECPA, see CRS Report 98-326, *Privacy: An Overview of Federal Statutes Governing Wiretapping and Electronic Eavesdropping,* by Gina Marie Stevens and Charles Doyle.

[4] *See e.g.,* NebuAd Testimony at 3-4.

[5] *See id.*; In re DoubleClick, Inc. Privacy Litigation, 154 F.Supp. 2d 497 (S.D.N.Y. 2001).

[6] 18 U.S.C. §2511(1)(a).

[7] 18 U.S.C. §2510(4).

[8] 18 U.S.C. §2510(8).

[9] 18 U.S.C. §2510(12).

[10] It is worth noting that there has yet to be a court case to decide definitively that ECPA applies to this type of data collection. In the cases cited here, the online advertising providers made their cases by assuming, but not

conceding, that ECPA applied to the data collection. *See* In re Pharmatrk, Inc. Privacy Litigations, 329 F.3d 9 (1st Cir. 2003); In re DoubleClick, Inc. Privacy Litigation, 154 F.Supp. 2d 497 (S.D.N.Y. 2001).

[11] "It shall not be unlawful under this chapter for a person not acting under color of law to intercept a wire, oral, or electronic communication where such person is a party to the communication or where one of the parties to the communications has given prior consent to such interception unless such communication is intercepted for the purpose of committing any criminal or tortious act in violation of the Constitution or laws of the United States or any State." 18 U.S.C. §2511(2)(d).

[12] 18 U.S.C. §2511(3)(a).

[13] 18 U.S.C. §2511(2)(a)(i).

[14] *See, e.g.*, U.S. Census 2006 Annual Survey (Information Sector), *Internet Service Providers—Estimated Sources of Revenue and Expenses for Employer Firms: 2004 Through 2006* at 32, Table 3.4.1 (April 15, 2006) (indicating that internet access service are responsible for the greatest percentage of revenue earned by ISPs) available at http://www.census.gov/svsd/www/services/sas/sas_data/51/2006_NAICS51.pdf; Comcast Corporation, Quarterly Report (Form 10-Q) (June 30, 2008) (reporting that 95% of Comcast Corporation's consolidated revenue is derived from its cable operations, which includes the provision of high-speed internet services) available at http://sec.gov/Archives/edgar/data/1166691/000119312508161385/d10q.htm.

[15] 18 U.S.C. 2511(3)(b)(ii).

[16] *See e.g.*, United States v. Friedman, 300 F.3d 111, 122-23 (2d Cir. 2002)(inmate use of prison phone);United States v. Faulkner, 439 F.3d 1221, 1224 (10th Cir. 2006)(same); United States v. Hammond, 286 F.3d 189, 192 (4th Cir. 2002) (same); *United States v. Footman*, 215 F.3d 145, 154-55 (1st Cir. 2000) (same); Griggs-Ryan v. Smith, 904 F.2d 112, 116-17 (1st Cir. 1990) (use of landlady's phone); United States v. Rivera, 292 F. Supp. 2d 838, 843-45 (E.D. Va. 2003)(inmate use of prison phone monitored by private contractors). For a discussion of the consent exception to the Wiretap Act as it is applied in other contexts, see, CRS Report 98-326, *Privacy: An Overview of Federal Statutes Governing Wiretapping and Electronic Eavesdropping*, by Gina Marie Stevens and Charles Doyle.

[17] In re DoubleClick, Inc. Privacy Litigation, 154 F.Supp. 2d 497 (S.D.N.Y. 2001).

[18] 18 U.S.C. §2510(13).

[19] In re DoubleClick, Inc. Privacy Litigation, 154 F.Supp. 2d at 508-09.

[20] *Id.* at 514.

[21] *Id.* at 509-513.

[22] 18 U.S.C. §2511(2)(d).

[23] In re DoubleClick, Inc. Privacy Litigation, 154 F.Supp. 2d at 516 (quoting Sussman v. ABC, 196 F.3d 1200, 1202 (9th Cir. 1999)).

[24] *Id.* at 518-19.

[25] In re Pharmatrk, Inc. Privacy Litigations, 329 F.3d 9 (1st Cir. 2003).

[26] *Id.* at 20.

[27] *Id.* at 23.

[28] Williams v. Poulos, 11 F.3d 271, 281 (1st Cir. 1993)(finding that defendant corporation violated the Wiretap Act, because it did not have implied consent or a business necessity to place wiretaps).

[29] *See e.g.*, *In the Matter of Implementation of the Telecommunications Act of 1996; Telecommunications Carriers; Use of Customer Proprietary Network Information and Other Customer Information; IP-Enabled Services*, 22 FCC Rcd 6927 (2007)(outlining under what circumstances voice service providers must obtain "opt-in" v. "opt-out" consent in order to disclose Customer Proprietary Network Information(CPNI)). For a discussion of the FCC's CPNI disclosure regulations, see CRS Report RL34409, *Selected Laws Governing the Disclosure of Customer Phone Records by Telecommunications Carriers*, by Kathleen Ann Ruane.

[30] *See* The Network Advertising Initiative's Self-Regulatory Code of Conduct for Online Behavioral Advertising, Draft: For Public Comment, available at http://networkadvertising.org/networks/NAI_Principles_2008_Draft_for_Public.pdf (last visited July 28, 2008). *See also*, 47 C.F.R. §2003(k)(defining "opt-in" approval in the CPNI context).

[31] *See* The Network Advertising Initiative's Self-Regulatory Code of Conduct for Online Behavioral Advertising, Draft: For Public Comment, available at http://networkadvertising.org/networks/NAI_Principles_2008_Draft_for_Public.pdf (last visited July 28, 2008). *See also*, 47 C.F.R. §2003(l)(defining "optout" approval in the CPNI context).

[32] NebuAd Testimony at 4.

[33] Testimony of Ms. Leslie Harris, CEO of the Center for Democracy and Technology, *Privacy Implications of Online Advertising: Hearing Before the S. Comm. On Commerce, Science, and Transportation*, 110th Cong. (2008).

[34] Codified at 47 U.S.C. §551. It is important to note that those providing DSL Internet service over phone lines, such as Verizon or AT&T, would not be subject to the provisions of Section 631, because they are not cable operators. Testimony of Ms. Gigi B. Sohn, President, Public Knowledge, *Broadband Providers and Consumer Privacy: Hearing Before the S. Comm. On Commerce, Science, and Transportation*, 110th Cong. (2008)(hereinafter Public Knowledge Testimony), available at

          http://commerce.senate.gov/public/_files/SohnTestimony.pdf.

[35] 47 U.S.C. §551(a).

[36] 47 U.S.C. §551(b).

[37] 47 U.S.C. §551(c).

[38] Memorandum from NebuAd, Inc., Legal and Policy Issues Supporting NebuAd's Services at 6.

[39] 47 U.S.C. Sec. §551(a)(2)(B).

[40] *In the Matter of Inquiry Concerning High-Speed Access to the Internet Over Cable and Other Facilities; Internet Over Cable Declaratory Ruling; Appropriate Regulatory Treatment for Broadband Access to the Internet Over Cable Facilities,* 17 FCC Rcd at 4854, ¶ 112.

[41] Cable Television and Consumer Protection and Competition Act, P.L. 102-385.

[42] H.Rept. 102-862.

[43] *See* 47 U.S.C. 551(f).

[44] *See* Application of the United States of America for an Order Pursuant to 18 U.S.C. Sec. 2703(D), 157 F. Supp. 2d 286, 291 (SDNY 2001)(finding that the notice requirement for the disclosure of personally identifiable information under 47 U.S.C. §551 included Internet services, except under 47 U.S.C. §551(h), which was exempt specifically from the broad definition of "other services").

[45] Klimas v. Comcast Cable, Inc., 465 F.3d 271, 276 (6th Cir. 2006).

[46] 47 U.S.C. §551(b)(1).

[47] *Klimas,* 465 F.3d at 276.

[48] 47 U.S.C. §551(c)(1).

[49] 47 U.S.C. §551(c)(1). Cable operators, however, may collect such information without consent for the purposes of obtaining information necessary to provide cable services or other services provided to the subscriber or to detect unauthorized reception of cable communications. Cable operators may disclose personally identifiable information without consent when it is necessary to render cable services or other services provided by the cable operator to the subscriber, pursuant to a valid court order, and in other limited circumstances. 47 U.S.C. 551 (c)(2). These exemptions do not appear to apply in this case.

[50] 47 U.S.C. §551(a)(2)(A).

[51] *See, e.g.,* NebuAd Testimony.

[52] *See, e.g.,* CDT Testimony.

[53] 47 U.S.C. §551(c).

[54] FTC Staff Proposes Online Behavioral Advertising Privacy Principles, http://www.ftc.gov/opa/2007/12/principles.shtm (last visited October 1, 2008).

[55] Online Behavioral Advertising, Moving the Discussion Forward to Possible Self-Regulatory Principles, released December 20, 2007, available at http://www.ftc.gov/os/2007/12/P859900stmt.pdf (last visited September 23, 2008).

[56] *Id.*

[57] See FTC, # 228; Project No. P859900: Online Behavioral Advertising: Moving the Discussion Forward to Possible Self-Regulatory Principles (2008), http://www.ftc.gov/os/comments/behavioraladprinciples/index.shtm.

[58] Network Advertising Initiative, http://networkadvertising.org/index.asp.

[59] The Network Advertising Initiative's Self-Regulatory Code of Conduct, available athttp://www.networkadvertising.org/networks/2008%20NAI%20Principles_final%20for%20Website.pdf (last visited January 13, 2009).

[60] Non-PII is information that is not PII or Sensitive Consumer Information.

[61] "PII includes name, address, telephone number, email address, financial account number, government-issued identifier, and any other data used or intended to be used to identify contact or precisely locate a person." The Network Advertising Initiative's Self-Regulatory Code of Conduct, Section II, available at http://www.networkadvertising.org/networks/2008%20NAI%20Principles_final%20for%20Website.pdf (last visited January 13, 2009).

[62] "Sensitive Consumer Information includes: Social Security Number or other Government-issued identifier; insurance plan numbers, financial account numbers; information that describes the precise real-time geographic location of an individual derived through location-based services such as through GPS-enabled services; precise information about past, present, or potential future health or medical conditions or treatments, including genetic, genomic, and family medical history." It seems that some of the information included in the definition of PII is also included in the definition for Sensitive Consumer Information. The Code of Conduct indicates that the definition of Sensitive Consumer Information will be further developed in the coming implementation guidelines. The Network Advertising Initiative's Self-Regulatory Code of Conduct, Section II, available at http://www.networkadvertising.org/networks/2008%20NAI%20Principles_final%20for%20Website.pdf (last visited January 13, 2009).

[63] Robust Notice is defined by the Code of Conduct. "For the notice to be robust the consumer must be afforded clear and conspicuous notice about the scope of any non-PII to be merged with PII, and how the merged data would be used for [behavioral advertising]. Such notice must be provided immediately above or before the

mechanism used to authorize submission of any PII." The Network Advertising Initiative's Self-Regulatory Code of Conduct, Section II, available at http://www.networkadvertising.org/networks/2008%20NAI%20 Principles_final%20for%20Website.pdf (last visited January 13, 2009).

In: Electronic Breadcrumbs: Issues in Tracking Consumers   ISBN: 978-1-60741-600-5
Editor: Dmitar N. Kovac   © 2010 Nova Science Publishers, Inc.

Chapter 17

FTC STAFF REPORT: SELF-REGULATORY PRINCIPLES FOR ONLINE BEHAVIORAL ADVERTISING

Behavioral Advertising

EXECUTIVE SUMMARY

Since the emergence of "e-commerce" in the mid-1990s, the online marketplace has continued to expand and evolve, creating new business models that allow greater interactivity between consumers and online companies. This expanding marketplace has provided many benefits to consumers, including free access to rich sources of information and the convenience of shopping for goods and services from home. At the same time, the ease with which companies can collect and combine information from consumers online has raised questions and concerns about consumer privacy.

Starting in 1995, the Federal Trade Commission ("FTC" or "Commission") has sought to understand the online marketplace and the privacy issues it raises for consumers. The Commission has hosted numerous public workshops and has issued public reports focusing on online data collection practices, industry self-regulatory efforts, and technological developments affecting consumer privacy. As part of this effort, the Commission has examined online behavioral advertising – the practice of tracking an individual's online activities in order to deliver advertising tailored to the individual's interests. In November 2007, the FTC held a two- day "Town Hall," which brought together numerous interested parties to discuss online behavioral advertising in a public forum.

Participants at the Town Hall discussed the potential benefits of the practice to consumers, including the free online content that online advertising generally supports, the personalized advertising that many consumers may value, and a potential reduction in unwanted advertising. They also discussed the privacy concerns that the practice raises, including the invisibility of the data collection to consumers; the shortcomings of current disclosures about the practice; the potential to develop and store detailed profiles about consumers; and the risk that data collected for behavioral advertising – including sensitive data regarding health, finances, or children – could fall into the wrong hands or be used for unanticipated purposes. Following the Town Hall, FTC staff released for public comment a set of proposed principles (the "Principles") designed to serve as the basis for industry self-regulatory efforts to address privacy concerns in this area.

In drafting the Principles, FTC staff drew upon its ongoing examination of behavioral advertising, as well as the public discussion at the Town Hall. Staff also attempted to balance the potential benefits of behavioral advertising against the privacy concerns. Specifically, the Principles provide for transparency and consumer control and reasonable security for consumer data. They also call for companies to obtain affirmative express consent from consumers before they use data in a manner that is materially different than promised at the time of collection and before they collect and use "sensitive" consumer data for behavioral advertising. In addition to proposing the Principles, staff also requested information concerning the use of tracking data for purposes unrelated to behavioral advertising.

Staff received sixty-three comments on the Principles from eighty-seven stakeholders, including individual companies, business groups, academics, consumer and privacy advocates, and individual consumers. Many commenters addressed the Principles' scope, an issue that cuts across each of the individual principles. In particular, commenters discussed whether the Principles should apply to practices involving information that is not personally identifiable and whether they should apply to "first party" and "contextual" behavioral advertising models. As discussed further in this Report, staff believes that the Principles should apply to data that could reasonably be associated with a particular consumer or computer or other device, regardless of whether the data is "personally identifiable" in the traditional sense. Indeed, in the context of online behavioral advertising, rapidly changing technologies and other factors have made the line between personally identifiable and non-personally identifiable information increasingly unclear. Moreover, this approach is consistent with existing self-regulatory efforts in this area.

Staff agrees with some of the commenters, however, that the Principles' scope could be more narrowly focused in two important respects. First, it appears that "first party" behavioral advertising – behavioral advertising by and at a single website – is more likely to be consistent with consumer expectations, and less likely to lead to consumer harm, than other forms of behavioral advertising. Second, staff believes that contextual advertising – advertising based on a consumer's current visit to a single web page or a single search query that involves no retention of data about the consumer's online activities beyond that necessary for the immediate delivery of an ad or search result – is likely to be less invasive than other forms of behavioral advertising. Accordingly, staff believes that the Principles need not cover these practices. Staff notes, however, that some of the Principles are based on existing Commission law and policy. Therefore, regardless of the scope of the Principles, companies must still comply with existing legal obligations to provide reasonable security for consumer data. Further, companies must adhere to the promises they make regarding how they collect, use, store, and disclose data, and cannot make unilateral, "material changes" to such promises without consumers' consent.

In addition to addressing the Principles' overall scope, numerous commenters discussed the individual principles. In particular, commenters discussed whether and how to provide transparency and consumer choice for online behavioral advertising. They also raised issues related to the material change principle and questioned how to define "sensitive" data and the appropriate protections for such data. Relatively few of the commenters answered staff's request for additional information on other uses for tracking data. This Report discusses the main points addressed in the comments, provides further guidance regarding the scope and application of the Principles, and sets forth revised Principles. It also discusses recent initiatives by industry, consumer groups, and others to address the consumer privacy concerns raised by online behavioral advertising.

This Report constitutes the next step in an ongoing process to examine behavioral advertising that involves the FTC, industry, consumer and privacy organizations, and individual consumers. Although the comments have helped to frame the policy issues and inform public understanding of online behavioral advertising, the practices continue to evolve and significant work remains. Some companies and industry groups have begun to develop new privacy policies and self-regulatory approaches, but more needs to be done to educate consumers about online behavioral advertising and provide effective protections for consumers' privacy. Staff, therefore, will continue to examine this marketplace and take actions to protect consumers as appropriate.

I. INTRODUCTION

On December 20, 2007, Federal Trade Commission ("FTC" or "Commission") staff released for public comment a set of proposed self-regulatory principles related to online behavioral advertising – the practice of tracking an individual's online activities in order to deliver advertising tailored to the individual's interests.[1] Staff developed these principles (the "Principles") based on an ongoing examination of the consumer issues raised by behavioral advertising and the public discussion of these issues at the FTC's November 2007 "Ehavioral Advertising" Town Hall.[2] Staff's goals in releasing the Principles were to spur continuing public dialogue about the issues and to encourage industry to develop meaningful self-regulation in this area.

In developing the proposed Principles, staff attempted to balance the privacy concerns raised by online behavioral advertising against the potential benefits of the practice. Consumers have genuine and legitimate concerns about how their data is collected, stored, and used online. They may also benefit, however, from the free content that online advertising generally supports, as well as the personalization of advertising that many consumers appear to value. Thus, any self-regulatory program in this area should address practices that raise genuine privacy concerns without interfering with practices – or stifling innovation – where privacy concerns are minimal.

In response to the proposed Principles, staff received over sixty comments from various stakeholders, including industry, privacy advocates, technologists, consumers, academics, and state and foreign governmental entities. The comments have helped to further staff's understanding of the complex and rapidly evolving online behavioral advertising marketplace. At the same time, the comments raised additional issues and questions for consideration, and many of them called upon Commission staff to provide more guidance. This Report summarizes and responds to the main issues raised in the comments. In addition, the Report provides guidance on the Principles and sets forth revised principles consistent with this guidance.

II. BACKGROUND

A. What is Online Behavioral Advertising?

Online behavioral advertising involves the tracking of consumers' online activities in order to deliver tailored advertising. The practice, which is typically invisible to consumers, allows businesses to align their ads more closely to the inferred interests of their audience. In many cases, the information collected is not personally identifiable in the traditional sense – that is, the information does not include the consumer's name, physical address, or similar identifier that could be used to identify the consumer in the offline world. Instead, businesses generally use "cookies"[3] to track consumers' activities and associate those activities with a particular computer or device.[4] Many of the companies engaged in behavioral advertising are so-called "network advertisers," companies that select and deliver advertisements across the Internet at websites that participate in their networks.[5]

An example of how behavioral advertising might work is as follows: a consumer visits a travel website and searches for airline flights to New York City. The consumer does not purchase any tickets, but later visits the website of a local newspaper to read about the Washington Nationals baseball team. While on the newspaper's website, the consumer receives an advertisement from an airline featuring flights from Washington D.C. to New York City.

In this simple example, the travel website where the consumer conducted his research might have an arrangement with a network advertiser to provide advertising to its visitors. The network advertiser places on the consumer's computer a cookie, which is tied to non-personally identifiable information such as the web pages the consumer has visited, the advertisements that the consumer has been shown, and how frequently each advertisement has been shown. Because the newspaper's website is also part of the advertising network, when the consumer visits the newspaper website the network advertiser's cookie identifies the consumer as a visitor to the travel website who likely has an interest in traveling to New York. It then serves the corresponding advertisement for airline flights to New York.

In a slightly more sophisticated example, the information about the consumer's activities on the travel website could be combined with information about the content that the consumer viewed on the newspaper's website. The advertisement served could then be tailored to the consumer's interest in, not just New York City, but also baseball (*e.g.*, an advertisement referring to the New York Yankees).

B. The FTC's Examination of Online Behavioral Advertising

The Federal Trade Commission's involvement with online privacy issues, including behavioral advertising, dates back to the emergence of "e-commerce."[6] Since that time, the Commission has sought to understand the marketplace, to evaluate the costs and benefits of various practices affecting consumers, and to stop unfair or deceptive practices. At the same time, given the dynamic nature of this marketplace and the technologies that make it possible, the Commission has consistently sought to avoid stifling innovation so that responsible business practices could develop and flourish. The Commission has engaged in a continuous dialogue with members of industry, consumer and privacy advocates, technology experts, consumers, and other interested parties. Starting in 1995, the Commission has conducted a series of public workshops and has issued reports focusing on online data collection practices, industry's self- regulatory efforts, and technological efforts to enhance consumer privacy.[7] In addition to these policy initiatives, the Commission and its staff have conducted investigations and brought law enforcement actions challenging such practices as deceptive privacy claims and improper disclosure of consumer data.[8]

1. Online Profiling Workshop

As a part of these efforts, in November 1999 the FTC and the Department of Commerce jointly sponsored a public workshop to examine the privacy implications of "online profiling" – essentially, an early form of online behavioral advertising.[9] Based upon the workshop, the FTC prepared two reports to Congress. The first, *Online Profiling: A Report to Congress* (June 2000) ("June 2000 Report"), described how online profiling operates and addressed the concerns that many of the workshop participants raised about the collection of detailed consumer data and the practice's lack of transparency.[10] The June 2000 Report also described online profiling's potential benefits to consumers, as well as to businesses. These benefits included delivering more relevant ads to consumers, subsidizing free online content, and allowing businesses to market more precisely and spend their advertising dollars more effectively.

The Commission's second report, *Online Profiling: A Report to Congress Part 2 Recommendations* (July 2000) ("July 2000 Report"),[11] supplemented the first report by addressing self-regulatory principles developed by the Network Advertising Initiative ("NAI"). NAI, an organization consisting of online network advertisers, had developed these principles ("NAI Principles") in response to concerns raised at the 1999 workshop and submitted them to the FTC and the Department of Commerce for consideration. In the July 2000 Report, the Commission commended the NAI companies' efforts in developing principles that included various protections to govern the collection and use of consumer data online.[12] Nevertheless, while acknowledging that "self-regulation is an important and powerful mechanism for protecting consumers," a majority of the Commission recommended that Congress enact "backstop legislation" to address online profiling.[13]

Ultimately, Congress did not enact legislation to address online profiling. In the meantime, with the "burst" of the dot-com bubble, the number of network advertisers declined dramatically such that by the early 2000s, many had gone out of business.[14]

2. Tech-Ade Hearings and the Ehavioral Advertising Town Hall

By the middle of the decade, the online advertising market, including the behavioral advertising market, had regained its footing. Indeed, online advertising spending grew dramatically between 2002 and 2006, with estimated sales rising from $6 billion to over $16.6 billion.[15] These changes in the marketplace, and the growing practice of behavioral advertising, were a featured topic at the FTC's November 2006 "Tech-ade" hearings,[16] which examined the consumer protection challenges anticipated over the next ten years. Participants at the hearings described how technological advances had allowed for greater and more efficient use of online profiling (now called "behavioral" advertising, targeting, or marketing) and brought renewed attention to the practice.[17]

In the months after the Tech-ade hearings, staff launched an effort to learn more about online behavioral advertising. At the same time, several organizations petitioned the Commission to reexamine the privacy issues raised by the practice.[18] Further, the announcement of the proposed merger between Google, Inc. ("Google") and DoubleClick, Inc. in April 2007 raised concerns about the combination of large databases of consumer information and the potential development of detailed consumer profiles.[19] Commission staff met with dozens of industry representatives, technology experts, consumer and privacy advocates, and academics. These meetings aided staff's understanding of the changes to the industry since the 1999 workshop and allowed staff to identify key questions and issues for further discussion.

In November 2007, the FTC held its "Ehavioral Advertising Town Hall," a two-day public meeting that brought together various interested parties to discuss the privacy issues surrounding online behavioral advertising.[20] Based on the discussion, several core principles emerged. First, as discussed above, online behavioral advertising[21] may provide valuable benefits to consumers in the form of free content, personalization that many consumers appear to value, and a potential reduction in unwanted advertising. Second, the invisibility of the practice to consumers raises privacy concerns, as does the risk that data collected for behavioral advertising – including sensitive data about children, health, or finances – could be misused. Third, business and consumer groups alike expressed support for transparency and consumer control in the online marketplace.[22]

A number of Town Hall participants also criticized existing self-regulatory efforts. Specifically, these participants stated that the NAI Principles had not been effective to address the privacy concerns that online behavioral advertising raises. They argued that the NAI Principles were too limited because they applied only to network advertisers and not to other business models. Other critics cited the purported lack of enforcement of the NAI Principles and its cumbersome and inaccessible opt-out system.[23] Further, while various industry associations discussed their online self-regulatory schemes to address privacy issues, these schemes did not generally focus on behavioral advertising.[24]

C. Staff's Proposed Self-Regulatory Principles

In response to the issues raised at the Town Hall, and to continue the dialogue with interested parties, in December 2007 Commission staff released the proposed self-regulatory Principles for public comment. Staff supported self-regulation because it provides the necessary flexibility to address evolving online business models. At the same time, however, staff recognized that existing self-regulatory efforts had not provided comprehensive and accessible protections to consumers. Accordingly, in issuing the proposed Principles, staff intended to guide industry in developing more meaningful and effective self-regulatory models than had been developed to date.

The proposed Principles include four governing concepts. The first is transparency and control: companies that collect information for behavioral advertising should provide meaningful disclosures to consumers about the practice and choice about whether to allow the practice. The second principle proposes reasonable security and limited data retention: companies should provide reasonable data security measures so that behavioral data does not fall into the wrong hands, and should retain data only as long as necessary for legitimate business or law enforcement needs. The third principle governs material changes to privacy policies: before a company uses behavioral data in a manner that is materially different from promises made when the company collected the data, it should obtain affirmative express consent from the consumer.[25] The fourth principle states that companies should obtain affirmative express consent before they use sensitive data – for example, data about children, health, or finances – for behavioral advertising.[26] Finally, staff's proposal requested additional information regarding the potential uses of tracking data other than for behavioral advertising, including whether such secondary uses raise concerns and merit heightened protection.

D. Recent Initiatives to Address Privacy Concerns

Following the Town Hall and the release of the Principles, various individual companies, industry organizations, and privacy groups have taken steps to address some of the concerns and issues raised by online behavioral advertising. For example, a number of companies have developed new policies and procedures to inform consumers about online tracking and provide additional protections and controls over the practice.[27] In particular, both Google and Yahoo! Inc. ("Yahoo!") have announced new tools that will allow consumers to opt out of receiving targeted online advertisements.[28] Microsoft Corporation has announced that the new version of its Internet browser will include a tool that, when enabled by a user, will not save browsing and searching history, cookies, form data, or passwords, and will automatically clear the browser cache at the end of each session.[29] Other steps include educational programs to inform consumers about online tracking[30] and new policies to reduce the length of time companies store personal data collected about online searches.[31]

In December 2008, in response to the criticism of the NAI Principles at the Town Hall and the FTC's call for stronger self-regulation, the NAI issued revised principles ("NAI 2008 Principles").[32] Although NAI has strengthened certain aspects of its self-regulatory regime – most notably by dramatically increasing its membership – staff believes that NAI could do more to ensure the transparency of online behavioral advertising to consumers. Staff also notes that certain elements of NAI's revised approach have yet to be clarified through implementation guidelines, which NAI plans to issue in 2009.[33] More recently, a joint industry task force including marketing and industry trade associations, as well as the Council of Better Business Bureaus, announced a cooperative effort to develop self-regulatory principles to address privacy concerns related to online behavioral advertising.[34]

Several other organizations have also developed materials to assist online businesses in identifying and addressing privacy concerns raised by online behavioral advertising. For example, the Future of Privacy Forum – an advocacy group of privacy scholars, lawyers, and corporate officials – has launched an initiative to develop new ways to provide consumers with control over the use of their personal information for online behavioral advertising.[35] The Center for Democracy and Technology ("CDT") also recently released an assessment tool, developed in conjunction with internet companies and public interest advocates, to help online companies evaluate the consumer privacy implications of their online behavioral advertising practices and to create appropriate, meaningful privacy protections.[36] Finally, TRUSTe, a privacy seal organization, has issued a white paper reviewing the current online behavioral advertising environment and providing a checklist to assist online companies to address issues raised by online behavioral advertising, especially those concerning transparency.[37]

Congress has also expressed concern about the privacy issues raised by online behavioral advertising. On July 9, 2008, the Senate Committee on Commerce, Science, and Transportation ("Senate Committee") held a hearing entitled "Privacy Implications of Online Advertising," which examined the online advertising industry and the impact of these practices on consumers' privacy.[38] Witnesses from the FTC,[39] consumer groups, and industry discussed both the methods of online behavioral advertising employed by industry and the government's role in protecting consumer privacy. The Senate Committee held a follow-up hearing on September 25, 2008, which focused on behavioral advertising in conjunction with Internet Service Providers ("ISPs").[40] Testifying at the second hearing, corporate officers representing Verizon Communications, Inc., AT&T Services, Inc., and Time Warner Cable expressed support for self- regulation by the various entities engaged in online behavioral advertising practices. Specifically, these representatives called for a requirement that companies obtain opt-in consent from consumers before collecting online information for behavioral advertising purposes.

The House Committee on Energy and Commerce ("House Committee"), and its Subcommittee on Telecommunications and the Internet ("Telecommunications Subcommittee"), also have been active in this area, focusing in particular on ISP-related practices. On July 17, 2008, the Telecommunications Subcommittee held a hearing entitled "What Your Broadband Provider Knows About Your Web Use: Deep Packet Inspection and Communications Laws and Policies" that included testimony from industry, experts, and consumer groups.[41] Thereafter, on August 1, 2008, four members of the House Committee issued letters to thirty-four companies seeking information on their practices with respect to behavioral advertising.[42] The companies' responses are available online.[43]

These developments suggest that there is continuing public interest in the issues that behavioral advertising raises and increasing engagement by industry members in developing solutions.

III. SUMMARY OF THE COMMENTS RECEIVED AND STAFF'S ANALYSIS

In response to the proposed Principles, FTC staff received sixty-three comments from interested parties; because some of the comments represent the views of multiple parties, a total number of approximately eighty-seven stakeholders participated in the comment process. FTC staff greatly appreciates the substantial work of the parties that submitted comments. The comments have helped to clarify the differing perspectives regarding how best to address the privacy issues that online behavioral advertising raises.

As a threshold matter, some commenters stated that FTC staff's call for self-regulation is unnecessary and that the Principles could interfere with a developing and rapidly changing marketplace.[44] Others concluded that the Principles do not go far enough and that sweeping legislation is necessary. Between these positions, a majority of the commenters expressed support for some form of self-regulation. Most commenters also identified certain aspects of the Principles that, in their view, raise important issues, merit more guidance, or should be changed.

Set forth below is a summary of the comments arranged by topic. This summary highlights and discusses the main points and positions represented by the comments as a whole. Also included are FTC staff's responses to these main points, along with additional guidance regarding the Principles. The key theme underlying this guidance is the need to balance the potential benefits of the various practices covered by the Principles against the privacy concerns the practices raise. Among other things, staff considered consumer expectations regarding the practices; the extent to which the practices are transparent; the potential for consumer harm; and the need to maintain vigorous competition in the online marketplace and avoid stifling innovation.

In providing this guidance, staff notes that nothing in the discussion is intended to preclude or discourage the implementation of responsible or "best" practices outside of the Principles. Staff also notes that some of the Principles closely parallel FTC law and policy, which continue to apply regardless of the scope or coverage of the Principles. For example, depending upon on the circumstances, a company whose practices fall outside the Principles may still be required to implement reasonable measures to address any privacy or security risks to consumers' information.[45] Similarly, regardless of the Principles, companies may not unilaterally alter their policies and use previously collected data in a manner that materially differs from the terms under which the data was originally collected.[46] Companies should also be mindful of the federal and state laws that may apply to their operations.

Finally, staff notes that the FTC's work in this area, including its commitment to engage the public on these issues, will continue beyond this Report. Although the comments provided considerable information about the various business models and policy issues surrounding behavioral advertising, staff has ongoing questions about the precise operation of this marketplace, particularly as it continues to develop and evolve. In addition, much remains to be learned about consumers' awareness, attitudes, and understanding of the practices. Staff therefore will continue to examine the issues as the market develops and will propose additional actions as needed. Staff also intends, where appropriate, to initiate investigations of possible unfair or deceptive acts or practices in this area that would potentially violate Section 5 of the FTC Act.

A. The Principles' Scope

As proposed, the Principles apply broadly to companies engaged in online behavioral advertising, defined as tracking consumers' online activities in order to deliver advertising that is targeted to the individual consumers' interests. Numerous commenters addressed the Principles' scope – specifically, the Principles' applicability to different types of data and different advertising practices. These commenters emphasized three significant issues: the applicability of the Principles not only to the collection and use of personally identifiable information ("PII"), but also of non-personally identifiable information ("non-PII");[47] the applicability to "first party," or "intra-site," collection and use of data; and the applicability to online contextual advertising.

1. Applicability to Non-PII

A number of commenters, representing industry groups and individual companies, stated that because the Principles' definition of online behavioral advertising fails to distinguish between PII and non-PII, the Principles apply too broadly. Claiming that there is little or no privacy interest in non-PII and a limited potential for harm, these commenters argued that the FTC should exclude such data from the Principles. The commenters also maintained that application of the Principles to non-PII would impose significant costs on business and could interfere with companies' ability to provide free online content to consumers.

Similarly, some commenters noted that non-PII has traditionally fallen outside the bounds of U.S. privacy laws and self-regulatory programs and that the Principles' inclusion of such data marks a departure from the Commission's current approach to privacy issues. Not all industry comments supported a bright line distinction between PII and non-PII, however. For instance, an individual company and a seal organization recommended that the Principles recognize a third category of data – *i.e.*, data that falls in between PII and non-PII. Another individual company noted that even information that is not considered personally identifying can raise privacy concerns.

In contrast to the majority of industry comments, a number of consumer and privacy groups expressed support for applying the Principles to data typically considered to be non-PII. Specifically, these commenters would apply the Principles to such data as Internet Protocol (IP) addresses,[48] cookie data, and other information that the commenters stated could allow a set of behaviors or actions to be associated with a particular individual or computer user, even if that individual is never identified by name.

Staff believes that, in the context of online behavioral advertising, the traditional notion of what constitutes PII versus non-PII is becoming less and less meaningful and should not, by itself, determine the protections provided for consumer data. Indeed, in this context, the Commission and other stakeholders have long recognized that both PII and non-PII raise privacy issues,[49] a view that has gained even more currency in recent years for a number of reasons. First, depending on the way information is collected and stored, it may be possible to link or merge non-PII with PII. For example, a website might collect anonymous tracking data and then link that data with PII (*e.g.*, name, address) that the consumer provided when registering at the site. Second, with the development of new and more sophisticated technologies, it likely will become easier to identify an individual consumer based on information traditionally considered to be non-PII. For instance, although industry has traditionally considered most IP addresses to be non-PII, it soon may be possible to link more IP addresses to specific individuals.[50]

Third, even where certain items of information are anonymous by themselves, they can become identifiable when combined and linked by a common identifier. For example, a consumer's Internet activity might reveal the restaurants in the neighborhood where she eats, the stores at which she shops, the property values of houses recently sold on her block, and the medical conditions and prescription drugs she is researching; when combined, such information would constitute a highly detailed and sensitive profile that is potentially traceable to the consumer. The storage of such data also creates the risk that it could fall into the wrong hands or be used later in combination with even richer, more sensitive, data.[51]

Fourth, in some circumstances, such as when more than one individual in a household shares or has access to a single computer, the distinction between PII and non-PII may have no bearing on the privacy risks at issue. For example, one user may visit a website to find information about a highly personal or sensitive topic, such as the user's health issues or sexual preference. In such circumstances, the delivery of advertising associated with that user's searches to the shared computer, even if the advertising does not identify the user, could reveal private information to another user of the same computer.

Finally, available evidence shows that consumers are concerned about the collection of their data online, regardless of whether the information is characterized as PII or non-PII. Recent survey data suggests that significant percentages of consumers are uncomfortable with having their online activities tracked for purposes of delivering advertisements, even where the data collected is not personally identifiable.[52] Further, many consumers reacted strongly to the AOL incident, described above, in which AOL made public purportedly anonymous data about its subscribers' online activities. Upon learning that the data had been posted online, these consumers expressed surprise and concern that the company stored data about their online activities – and stored it in a way that allowed the data to be associated, at least in some cases, with particular individuals.[53]

In staff's view, the best approach is to include within the Principles' scope any data collected for online behavioral advertising that reasonably could be associated with a particular consumer or with a particular computer or device. Whether information "reasonably could be associated" with a particular consumer or device will depend on the factual circumstances and available technologies, but would include, for example: clickstream data that, through reasonable efforts, could be combined with the consumer's website registration information; individual pieces of anonymous data combined into a profile sufficiently detailed that it could become identified with a particular person; and behavioral profiles that, while not associated with a particular consumer, are stored and used to deliver personalized advertising and content to a particular device.[54] Such an approach will ensure protections for consumer data that raises a consumer privacy interest without imposing undue costs where data is truly anonymous and privacy concerns are minimal. As noted above, this is also consistent with NAI's approach, the predominant industry self-regulatory model, which has mandated protections for both PII and non-PII since 2000.

2. Applicability to "First Party" Online Behavioral Advertising

The Principles' applicability to "first party," or "intra-site," online behavioral advertising also generated numerous comments, primarily from industry groups and individual companies. Most of these commenters objected to the Principles' application to behavioral advertising by, and at, a single website. Instead, they urged the Commission to limit the Principles to practices that involve the tracking of consumers' activities across different websites. These commenters argued that "first party" collection and use of consumer information is transparent and consistent with consumer expectations. Additionally, the commenters described a variety of services and operations, valued by consumers, that require "first party" data collection and use. These include product recommendations, tailored content, shopping cart services, website design and optimization, fraud detection, and security.

Some commenters, including an individual company and a seal organization, recognized that the tracking of consumers across multiple sites raises increased concern, but did not support excluding "first party" practices from self-regulation entirely. Other commenters, including an individual company and several consumer groups, generally supported the Principles' application to "first party" behavioral advertising.

After considering the comments, staff agrees that "first party" behavioral advertising practices are more likely to be consistent with consumer expectations, and less likely to lead to consumer harm, than practices involving the sharing of data with third parties or across multiple websites. For example, under the "first party" model, a consumer visiting an online retailer's website may receive a recommendation for a product based upon the consumer's prior purchases or browsing activities at that site (*e.g.*, "based on your interest in travel, you might enjoy the following books"). In such case, the tracking of the consumer's online activities in order to deliver a recommendation or advertisement tailored to the consumer's inferred interests involves a single website where the consumer has previously purchased or looked at items. Staff believes that, given the direct relationship between the consumer and the website, the consumer is likely to understand why he has received the targeted recommendation or advertisement and indeed may expect it. The direct relationship also puts the consumer in a better position to raise any concerns he has about the collection and use of his data, exercise any choices offered by the website, or avoid the practice altogether by taking his business elsewhere. By contrast, when behavioral advertising involves the sharing of data with ad networks or other third parties, the consumer may not understand why he has received ads from unknown marketers based on his activities at an assortment of previously visited websites. Moreover, he may not know whom to contact to register his concerns or how to avoid the practice.

In addition, staff agrees that "first party" collection and use of consumer data may be necessary for a variety of consumer benefits and services. These include not only personalized content and other elements of the interactive online experience that consumers may value, but also important internal functions such as security measures, fraud prevention, and legal compliance.[55]

Finally, maintaining data for internal use only also limits the risk that the data will fall into the wrong hands. For that reason, privacy schemes in varied contexts have distinguished between a site's internal use of data and the sharing of data with third parties, imposing stronger privacy protections for the latter.[56] Staff believes that the same distinction holds true here.

Based on these considerations, staff agrees that it is not necessary to include "first party" behavioral advertising practices within the scope of the Principles.[57] If a website collects and then sells or shares data with third parties for purposes of behavioral advertising,[58] or participates in a network that collects data at the site for purposes of behavioral advertising, however, such practices would remain within the scope of the Principles.[59]

3. Applicability to Contextual Advertising

Numerous commenters, representing both industry and consumer groups, recommended that the Commission revise the Principles' behavioral advertising definition to expressly exclude contextual advertising. These commenters explained that online contextual advertising differs from behaviorally targeted advertising because it is based only on the content of a particular website or search query, rather than on information about the consumer collected over time. For example, where a consumer is shown an advertisement for tennis rackets solely because he is visiting a tennis-focused website or has used a search engine to find stores that sell tennis rackets, the advertisement is contextual.

The commenters described contextual advertising as transparent and consistent with consumers' expectations, similar to the "first party" practices discussed above. They also stated that, rather than being surprised by the practice, consumers expect and want to receive an ad for a product or service when visiting a website that is related to that product or service. Additionally, a number of commenters noted that contextual advertising creates fewer risks to privacy because the practice does not rely on the collection of detailed information about the consumer's actions over time. One group of consumer and privacy advocates also stated that excluding contextual advertising from the Principles may provide companies with an incentive to store less data about consumers.

In general, the comments described online contextual advertising as the delivery of ads based upon a consumer's current visit to a single web page or a single search query, without the collection and retention of data about the consumer's online activities over time. Based on this description, staff agrees that contextual advertising provides greater transparency than other forms of behavioral advertising, is more likely to be consistent with consumer expectations, and presents minimal privacy intrusion when weighed against the potential benefits to consumers. As discussed above, these benefits may include free content – made possible by the revenue from the sale of the advertisements – and receipt of contextually relevant ads that consumers may value. Staff consequently does not believe that it is necessary for the Principles to cover this form of online advertising.[60] It should be stressed that, based on the comments and other considerations, staff has defined contextual advertising narrowly. Where a practice involves the collection and retention of consumer data for future purposes beyond the immediate delivery of an ad or search result, the practice does not constitute contextual advertising.

B. Transparency and Consumer Control

Numerous commenters – including individual consumers, industry representatives, and consumer and privacy advocates – discussed the first proposed principle, which calls for greater transparency and consumer control of online behavioral advertising practices. Specifically, FTC staff proposed that websites where data is collected for behavioral advertising should provide prominent notice to consumers about such practices and should also offer consumers the ability to choose whether to allow such collection and use. In discussing this principle, commenters focused primarily on two issues: whether to provide choice for the collection and use of non-PII, and how best to provide disclosures about the practices.

1. Choice for Non-PII

The commenters generally agreed that companies should notify consumers when they are collecting information about consumers' online activities for behavioral advertising. Indeed, several commenters noted that existing self-regulatory regimes currently require such notice.[61] Some industry trade groups and an individual company, however, stated that the first principle goes too far in proposing *choice* for the collection of non-PII. In general, these commenters made the same arguments with respect to choice for non-PII that are discussed above with respect to the overall scope of the Principles: that choice for non-PII is inconsistent with existing self-regulatory privacy schemes and laws; that there is a reduced privacy interest in, and risk of harm from, non-PII; and that choice will interfere with the free content and other benefits that online behavioral advertising offers. Some commenters also noted that consumers already have the ability to choose not to conduct business with websites that collect their data. These commenters suggested that consumers do not own the data that websites collect about them, and that there is no precedent for giving consumers the ability to dictate the terms upon which they use a website.[62]

In contrast, various consumer and privacy interest groups, as well as a number of individual consumers, supported the concept of choice for the collection and use of non-PII for behavioral advertising and several asserted that the principle should go even further. Some of these commenters called for an *opt-in* choice[63] before data is collected and recommended that consumers receive clear notice about the purpose for which their data is collected. A coalition of consumer groups described the principle as inadequate and recommended the "Do Not Track" registry to allow consumers to limit online tracking.[64] Individual consumers also submitted comments expressing support for notice and the ability to control whether to allow collection of information about their online activities. One consumer stated that companies should be required to obtain permission to collect data regardless of how they use it.

For the reasons discussed above with respect to the Principles' overall scope, FTC staff believes that companies should provide consumer choice for the collection of data for online behavioral advertising if the data reasonably could be associated with a particular consumer or with a particular computer or device. As noted, the line separating PII and non-PII has become increasingly indistinct, and the predominant industry self-regulatory program has already adopted an approach that protects both types of information. Available research also suggests that consumers are concerned about their data collected online, regardless of whether it is characterized as PII or non-PII. Finally, because staff has clarified that the Principles do not cover "first party" and "contextual" advertising, the costs of providing choice should be significantly less than stated in some comments.

2. Providing Effective Notice and Choice

Many commenters also addressed the issue of *how* businesses engaged in behavioral advertising should notify and offer choice to consumers concerning the collection and use of their data. Several companies stated that the appropriate location for any disclosure regarding online behavioral advertising is the website's privacy policy, and suggested that additional or alternative mechanisms for such disclosures could confuse consumers or encumber online functions. These commenters argued that consumers expect to find information on data practices in privacy policies and that this existing framework effectively informs consumers. Other companies and some privacy advocates highlighted the need for additional disclosure mechanisms beyond the privacy policy and suggested various options, such as: (i) providing "just-in-time" notice at the point at which a consumer's action triggers data collection; (ii) placing a text prompt next to, or imbedded in, the advertisement; and (iii) placing a prominent disclosure on the website that links to the relevant area within the site's privacy policy for a more detailed description.

A number of consumer and privacy groups' comments focused on the content of the disclosures and suggested that, in order for notice and consent to be effective, websites should not only disclose that information is collected, but should also specify the type of information collected, its uses, how long it will be retained, and with whom it will be shared. Other commenters – including an individual consumer and an online advertising company – suggested that the use of standard or uniform disclosures would make disclosures more effective and would increase consumers' understanding of data collection practices. A group of privacy and consumer advocates recommended that, where a consumer opts out of behavioral advertising, companies should honor that choice until the consumer decides to opt in and should not attempt to circumvent the consumer's choice through technological means. These commenters also called on companies to allow consumers to view and change their choices at any time.

Another comment, filed by two academics, discussed the inherent problem with using cookies both to track consumers' online activities[65] and to record consumers' choice of whether to allow such tracking. These commenters noted that where consumers take steps to control the privacy of their online activities, through the use of anti-spyware software or by deleting cookies from their computer browsers, the consumers may unintentionally also block or delete the cookies that record their behavioral advertising preference. The commenters suggested possible solutions to this problem, including the development of standards for distinguishing between opt-out cookies and other types of cookies and modifying browser settings to give consumers greater control over their cookies.

Several companies also requested guidance regarding the form and content of notice in different contexts – such as on mobile devices, on "Web 2.0," and through ISPs – and questioned whether a uniform or standard approach can be created. For example, commenters raised questions regarding the mechanics of providing notice and choice in the Web 2.0 world, where a consumer may use several different third-party applications on a single, unrelated host web page. Some commenters raised issues regarding appropriate notice in the mobile context. Others stated that, as proposed, the transparency and control principle would exclude certain business models, including where an ISP collects, or allows a third party to collect, consumers' online data.[66] With respect to ISP-based behavioral advertising, these commenters recommended that the principle permit notice through direct communication from the ISP to its subscribers rather than on a website.

The differing perspectives on how best to provide consumers with effective notice and choice highlight the complexities surrounding this issue. Staff recognizes that it is now customary to include most privacy disclosures in a website's privacy policy. Unfortunately, as noted by many of the commenters and by many participants at the FTC's November 2007 Town Hall, privacy policies have become long and difficult to understand, and may not be an effective way to communicate information to consumers.[67] Staff therefore encourages companies to design innovative ways – outside of the privacy policy – to provide behavioral advertising disclosures and choice options to consumers.

A number of the commenters' recommendations appear promising. For example, a disclosure (*e.g.*, "why did I get this ad?") that is located in close proximity to an advertisement and links to the pertinent section of a privacy policy explaining how data is collected for purposes of delivering targeted advertising, could be an effective way to communicate with consumers. Indeed, such a disclosure is likely to be far more effective than a discussion (even a clear one) that is buried within a company's privacy policy. Further, as described above, some businesses have already begun to experiment with designing other creative and effective disclosure mechanisms. Staff encourages these efforts and notes that they may be most effective if combined with consumer education programs that explain not only what information is collected from consumers and how it is used, but also the tradeoffs involved – that is, what consumers obtain in exchange for allowing the collection and use of their personal information.

With respect to the concern about using cookies to allow consumers to exercise their control over whether to allow behavioral advertising, staff encourages interested parties to examine this issue and explore potential standards and other tools to assist consumers. Moreover, as to some commenters' call for guidance on the mechanics of disclosures outside the website context, staff notes that different business models may require different types of disclosures and different methods for providing consumer choice. Staff therefore calls upon industry to develop self-regulatory regimes for these business models that effectively implement the transparency and consumer control principle. Regardless of the particular business model involved, the disclosures should clearly and prominently inform consumers about the practice and provide them with meaningful, accessible choice.

Finally, staff notes that research suggests that it is important to test proposed disclosures to ensure that they serve their intended purpose.[68] Staff therefore encourages stakeholders to conduct empirical research to explore the effects of possible disclosures on consumer understanding in this area.

C. Reasonable Security and Limited Data Retention for Consumer Data

Commenters also discussed the second proposed principle, which calls upon companies to provide reasonable security for, and limited retention of, consumer data collected for behavioral advertising purposes.

A number of companies generally supported this principle as drafted. Echoing the arguments raised about the Principles' applicability to non-PII, other companies, as well as industry groups, recommended that the Commission limit the application of this principle to PII. These commenters also called for more flexibility in applying this principle, and stated that data retention should not constitute a separate, stand-alone principle; instead, according to these commenters, data retention should be viewed as one possible component of an effective security program. Several industry commenters suggested that the principle should allow companies to consider various factors in evaluating appropriate data retention periods, and should refrain from imposing a uniform requirement.

Although the consumer groups generally supported this principle as proposed, some argued that the FTC should strengthen certain aspects of the principle. Individual consumers and one privacy group suggested that the principle is too vague and should provide more detailed and precise security standards. Two privacy groups stated that companies should retain data only as long as needed to fulfill the identified use for which the company collected the data. Other proposals included a requirement that companies anonymize all retained data, a requirement that data be retained for no longer than six months, and a suggestion that the FTC hold a workshop to explore issues related to the appropriate data retention standard.

For the reasons addressed above, staff believes the Principles should apply to all data collected and used for behavioral advertising that reasonably could be associated with a particular consumer or with a particular computer or device. Staff recognizes, however, that there is a range of sensitivities within this class of data, with the most sensitive data warranting the greatest protection. Accordingly, as proposed, the data security principle stated that, consistent with existing data security laws and the FTC's many data security enforcement actions,[69] the "protections should be based on the sensitivity of the data [and] the nature of a company's business operations, the types of risks a company faces, and the reasonable protections available to a company." Staff believes that this scalable standard addresses the commenters' concerns while also ensuring appropriate protections for consumer data. Staff therefore retains this language in the Principles without change.

Staff agrees with many of the commenters, however, that data retention is one component in the reasonable security calculus, rather than a separate, stand-alone principle, and has clarified the principle to reflect this position. The intent behind the principle remains unchanged, however: companies should retain data only as long as is necessary to fulfill a legitimate business or law enforcement need. As noted above, over the past year some companies have changed their data retention policies to reduce substantially the length of time they maintain information about consumers' online activities. Staff commends such efforts.

D. Affirmative Express Consent for Material Retroactive Changes to Privacy Promises

Many commenters discussed the material change principle, which calls upon companies to obtain affirmative express consent before they use data in a manner that is materially different from the promises the company made at the time of collection. A number of industry commenters objected to this principle as proposed. These commenters called for more flexibility so that companies, in determining the type of notice and choice to offer consumers, can take into account the type of data affected and its sensitivity. The commenters argued that requiring notice and opt-in choice for material changes with respect to all types of data is not only unnecessary, but also is technologically unworkable, and could cause consumer confusion and inconvenience. Additionally, several of these commenters stated that, as proposed, this principle goes beyond FTC case law and existing self-regulatory regimes and statutes. Other commenters expressed concern that this principle will be applied to prospective changes to companies' practices and noted that such changes should, at most, require opt-out consent.

By contrast, consumer and privacy groups, as well as an individual consumer, expressed strong support for this principle as proposed. One consumer organization acknowledged that a business may have legitimate reasons for altering its privacy promises and stated that the principle strikes the proper balance between consumers' interests in reliable promises and industry's need for flexibility. This commenter expressed concern, however, about the use of "pre-checked" boxes and similar mechanisms to obtain opt-in consent, and noted that such mechanisms might not reflect consumers' actual intent.[70]

It is fundamental FTC law and policy that companies must deliver on promises they make to consumers about how their information is collected, used, and shared.[71] An important corollary is that a company cannot use data in a manner that is materially different from promises the company made when it collected the data without first obtaining the consumer's consent.[72] Otherwise, the promise has no meaning. Staff recognizes, however, that a business may have a legitimate need to change its privacy policy from time to time, especially in the dynamic online marketplace. In addition, minor changes to a company's data practices may be immaterial to consumers and may not warrant the costs and burdens of obtaining consumers' consent.

For these reasons, the material change principle is limited to changes that are both *material*[73] and *retroactive*. Depending upon a company's initial privacy promises, a material change could include, for example: (i) using data for different purposes than described at the time of collection, or (ii) sharing data with third parties, contrary to promises made at the time of collection. A retroactive change is a change in a company's policies or practices that a company applies to previously collected data. This would include, for example, the situation where a company makes a material change to its privacy policy and then uses previously collected data in a manner consistent with the new policy, but not the old one. A retroactive change does not include the circumstance where a company changes its privacy policy and then proceeds to collect and use *new* data under the new policy. Staff agrees that the latter type of change – which would constitute a *prospective* change – may not raise the same concerns as a retroactive change, and may therefore call for a more flexible approach.[74]

Staff has revised the material change principle to make clear that it applies to retroactive changes only.

E. Affirmative Express Consent to (or Prohibition Against) Use of Sensitive Data

The fourth principle states that companies should only collect sensitive data for behavioral advertising after they obtain affirmative express consent from the consumer to receive the advertising. Many of the commenters who discussed this principle raised the issue of how to define the types of information that should be considered sensitive. Some commenters also questioned whether affirmative express consent is the appropriate standard or whether behavioral advertising based on sensitive data should be prohibited altogether.

Various commenters discussed the lack of agreement regarding the definition of "sensitive," and noted that whether specific information is considered sensitive can depend upon the context and the individual consumer's perspective. Other comments – including those filed on behalf of scientific and medical organizations, industry groups, and privacy and consumer advocates – listed specific categories of information that should be considered sensitive. According to these commenters, the categories include information about children and adolescents, medical information, financial information and account numbers, Social Security numbers, sexual orientation information, government-issued identifiers, and precise geographic location.[75]

Despite the lack of agreement on the definition of "sensitive data," there appears to be consensus that such data merits some form of heightened protection. Different commenters, however, provided differing views on the necessary level of protection. Several individual companies and industry groups objected to an opt-in approach. These commenters stated that opt-in consent for the collection of sensitive data for online behavioral advertising is too burdensome and is unnecessary in light of existing regulatory regimes.[76] Others stated that the uncertainty over how to classify sensitive data makes an opt-in approach difficult to implement and enforce.

Another group of commenters, including business and consumer groups, supported an affirmative express consent standard for certain sensitive data. They reasoned that such a standard strikes the correct balance and would allow those consumers who value advertising based on sensitive information to receive it.

A third group of commenters, including individual consumers, businesses, consumer groups, and a state government agency, supported a ban on behavioral advertising based on sensitive data. These commenters cited the risk of harm from sensitive data falling into the wrong hands. Other commenters recommended banning the use of specific types of sensitive data, such as information about children. Finally, a number of commenters called for additional examination of the issue, including discussion about how to define what constitutes sensitive data.

Given the heightened privacy concerns and the potential for significant consumer harm from the misuse of sensitive data, staff continues to believe that affirmative express consent is warranted.[77] Indeed, this protection is particularly important in the context of online behavioral advertising, where data collection is typically invisible to consumers who may believe that they are searching anonymously for information about medications, diseases, sexual orientation, or other highly sensitive topics. Moreover, contrary to the suggestions in the comments, existing statutory regimes do not address most types of online behavioral advertising or the privacy concerns that such advertising raises.

With respect to defining what constitutes sensitive data, staff agrees with the commenters that such a task is complex and may often depend on the context. Although financial data, data about children, health information, precise geographic location information, and Social Security numbers are the clearest examples, staff encourages industry, consumer and privacy advocates, and other stakeholders to develop more specific standards to address this issue. Staff also encourages stakeholders to consider whether there may be certain categories of data that are so sensitive that they should never be used for behavioral advertising.

F. Secondary Uses

Relatively few commenters responded to the Principles' call for information regarding the use of tracking data for purposes other than behavioral advertising. Most of the industry commenters that did address this question focused on such internal uses as website design and optimization, content customization, research and development, fraud detection, and security. For the reasons discussed above, staff believes that such "first party" or "intra-site" uses are unlikely to raise privacy concerns warranting the protections of the Principles. Other businesses and some consumer groups cited potential harmful secondary uses, including selling personally identifiable behavioral data, linking click stream data to PII from other sources, or using behavioral data to make credit or insurance decisions. These commenters noted, however, that such uses do not appear to be well-documented. Some commenters recommended that the FTC seek more information regarding secondary uses, including the extent to which the collection of data by third-party applications operating on a host website constitutes secondary use.

Given the dearth of responses to staff's request for specific information, it is unclear whether companies currently use tracking data for non-behavioral advertising purposes other than the internal operations identified above.[78] Staff therefore does not propose to address this issue in the Principles at this time. Staff agrees with some of the commenters, however, that the issue of secondary use merits additional consideration and dialogue. Therefore, as staff continues its work on behavioral advertising, it will seek more information on this issue and consider further revisions to the Principles as needed.

IV. REVISED PRINCIPLES

Based upon the staff's analysis of the comments discussing the Principles as initially proposed, and taking into account the key themes enumerated above, staff has revised the Principles. For purposes of clarification, the new language is set forth below in bold and italics. As noted above, these Principles are guidelines for self-regulation and do not affect the obligation of any company (whether or not covered by the Principles) to comply with all applicable federal and state laws.

A. Definition

For purposes of the Principles, online behavioral advertising means the tracking of a consumer's online activities *over time* – including the searches the consumer has conducted, the web pages visited, and the content viewed – in order to deliver advertising targeted to the individual consumer's interests. *This definition is not intended to include "first party" advertising, where no data is shared with third parties, or contextual advertising, where an ad is based on a single visit to a web page or single search query.*

B. Principles

1. Transparency and Consumer Control

Every website where data is collected for behavioral advertising should provide a clear, concise, consumer-friendly, and prominent statement that (1) data about consumers' activities online is being collected at the site for use in providing advertising about products and services tailored to individual consumers' interests, and (2) consumers can choose whether or not to have their information collected for such purpose. The website should also provide consumers with a clear, easy-to-use, and accessible method for exercising this option. *Where the data collection occurs outside the traditional website context, companies should develop alternative methods of disclosure and consumer choice that meet the standards described above (i.e., clear, prominent, easy-to-use, etc.)*

2. Reasonable Security, and Limited Data Retention, for Consumer Data

Any company that collects and/or stores consumer data for behavioral advertising should provide reasonable security for that data. Consistent with data security laws and the FTC's data security enforcement actions, such protections should be based on the sensitivity of the data, the nature of a company's business operations, the types of risks a company faces, and the reasonable protections available to a company. *Companies should also retain data only as long as is necessary to fulfill a legitimate business or law enforcement need.*

3. Affirmative Express Consent for Material Changes to Existing Privacy Promises

As the FTC has made clear in its enforcement and outreach efforts, a company must keep any promises that it makes with respect to how it will handle or protect consumer data, even if it decides to change its policies at a later date. Therefore, before a company can use *previously collected* data in a manner materially different from promises the company made when it collected the data, it should obtain affirmative express consent from affected consumers. This principle would apply in a corporate merger situation to the extent that the merger creates material changes in the way the companies collect, use, and share data.

4. *Affirmative Express Consent to (or Prohibition Against) Using Sensitive Data for Behavioral Advertising*

Companies should collect sensitive data for behavioral advertising only after they obtain affirmative express consent from the consumer to receive such advertising.

V. CONCLUSION

The revised Principles set forth in this Report constitute the next step in an ongoing process, and staff intends to continue the dialogue with all stakeholders in the behavioral advertising arena. Staff is encouraged by recent steps by certain industry members, but believes that significant work remains. Staff calls upon industry to redouble its efforts in developing self- regulatory programs, and also to ensure that any such programs include meaningful enforcement mechanisms. Self-regulation can work only if concerned industry members actively monitor compliance and ensure that violations have consequences.

Looking forward, the Commission will continue to monitor the marketplace closely so that it can take appropriate action to protect consumers. During the next year, Commission staff will evaluate the development of self-regulatory programs and the extent to which they serve the essential goals set out in the Principles; conduct investigations, where appropriate, of practices in the industry to determine if they violate Section 5 of the FTC Act or other laws; meet with companies, consumer groups, trade associations, and other stakeholders to keep pace with changes; and look for opportunities to use the Commission's research tools to study developments in this area.

The Commission is committed to protecting consumers' privacy and will continue to address the issues raised by online behavioral advertising.

END NOTES

[1] FTC Staff, *Online Behavioral Advertising: Moving the Discussion Forward to Possible Self-Regulatory Principles* (Dec. 20, 2007), *available at* http://www.ftc.gov/os/2007/12/P859900stmt.pdf.

[2] FTC Town Hall, *Ehavioral Advertising: Tracking, Targeting, & Technology* (Nov. 1-2, 2007), *available at* http://www.ftc.gov/bcp/workshops/ehavioral/index.shtml.

[3] A cookie is a small text file that a website's server places on a computer's web browser. The cookie transmits information back to the website's server about the browsing activities of the computer user on the site. This includes information such as pages and content viewed, the time and duration of visits, search queries entered into search engines, and whether a computer user clicked on an advertisement. Cookies also can be used to maintain data related to a particular individual, including passwords or items in an online shopping cart. In some contexts, such as where a number of separate websites participate in a network, cookies can be used to track a computer user across different sites. In addition to cookies, there are other devices for tracking online activities, including "web bugs," "web beacons," and "Flash cookies."

[4] As discussed below, however, it may be possible to link or merge the collected information with personally identifiable information – for example, name, address, and other information provided by a consumer when the consumer registers at a website.

[5] Ads from network advertisers are usually delivered based upon data collected about a given consumer as he or she travels across the different websites in the advertising network. An individual network may include hundreds or thousands of different, unrelated websites and an individual website may belong to multiple networks.

[6] See, e.g., FTC Report, *Privacy Online: Fair Information Practices in the Electronic Marketplace 3-6* (May 2000), *available at* http://www.ftc.gov/reports/privacy2000/privacy2000.pdf. This report described the Commission's involvement in online privacy issues and recommended that Congress enact online privacy legislation based upon "fair information practice" principles for consumer- oriented commercial websites.

[7] *See, e.g.,* FTC Town Hall, *Beyond Voice: Mapping the Mobile Marketplace* (May 6-7, 2008), *available at* http://www.ftc.gov/bcp/workshops/mobilemarket/index.shtml; *FTC Workshop, Protecting Personal Information: Best Practices for Business* (Apr. 15, 2008, Aug. 13, 2008, and Nov. 13, 2008), *available at* http://www.ftc.gov/bcp/workshops/infosecurity/index.shtml; *FTC Workshop, Security in Numbers: SSNs and ID Theft* (Dec. 10-11, 2007), *available at* http://www.ftc.gov/bcp/workshops/ssn/index.shtml; *FTC Staff Report, Spam Summit: The Next Generation of Threats and Solutions* (Nov. 2007), *available at* http://www.ftc.gov/os/2007/12/071220spamsummitreport.pdf; *FTC Summit, Spam Summit: The Next Generation of Threats and Solutions* (July 11-12, 2007), *available at* http://www.ftc.gov/bcp/workshops/spamsummit/index.shtml; *FTC Staff Report, Radio Frequency IDentification: Applications and Implications for Consumers* (Mar. 2005), *available at* http://www.ftc.gov/os/2005/03/050308rfidrpt.pdf; *FTC Workshop, Radio Frequency IDentification: Applications and Implications for Consumers* (June 21, 2004), *available at* http://www.ftc.gov/bcp/workshops/rfid/index.shtm; *FTC Workshop, Monitoring Software on Your PC: Spyware, Adware and Other Software* (Apr. 19, 2004), *available at* http://www.ftc.gov/bcp/workshops/spyware/index.shtm; *FTC Forum, Spam Forum* (Apr. 30- May 2, 2003), *available at* http://www.ftc.gov/bcp/workshops/spam/index.shtml; *FTC Workshop, Consumer Information Security Workshop* (May 20-21, 2002), *available at* http://www.ftc.gov/bcp/workshops/security/index.shtml; *FTC Report, The Mobile Wireless Web, Data Services and Beyond: Emerging Technologies and Consumer Issues* (Feb. 2002), *available at* http://www.ftc.gov/bcp/reports/wirelesssummary.pdf; *FTC Workshop, The Information Marketplace: Merging and Exchanging Consumer Data* (Mar. 2001), *available at* http://www.ftc.gov/bcp/workshops/infomktplace/index.shtml; FTC Workshop, *The Mobile Wireless Web, Data Services and Beyond: Emerging Technologies and Consumer Issues* (Dec. 11-12, 2000), *available at* http://www.ftc.gov/bcp/workshops/wireless/index.shtml; *FTC Report, Consumer Protection in the Global Electronic Marketplace: Looking Ahead* (Sept. 2000), *available at* http://www.ftc.gov/bcp/icpw/lookingahead/electronicmkpl.pdf; *FTC Workshop, U.S. Perspectives on Consumer Protection in the Global Electronic Marketplace* (June 1999), *available at* http://www.ftc.gov/bcp/icpw/lookingahead/global.shtm; *FTC Staff Report, Public Workshop on Consumer Privacy on the Global Information Infrastructure* (Dec. 1996), *available at* http://www.ftc.gov/reports/privacy/privacy.pdf; FTC Workshop, *Consumer Privacy on the Global Information Infrastructure* (June 1996), *available at* http://www.ftc.gov/bcp/privacy/wkshp96/privacy.shtm.

[8] Since 2001, the Commission has brought twenty-three actions against companies that allegedly failed to provide reasonable protections for sensitive consumer information in both online and offline settings. *See FTC v. Navone*, No. 2:08-CV-01 842 (D. Nev. filed Dec. 30, 2008); *United States v. ValueClick, Inc.*, No. 2:08-C V-0171 1 (C.D. Cal. Mar. 13, 2008); *United States v. American United Mortgage*, No. 1:07-CV-07064 (N.D. Ill. Dec. 18, 2007*); United States v. ChoicePoint, Inc.*, No. 1 :06-CV-0198 (N.D. Ga. Feb. 15, 2006); *In the Matter of Genica Corp.*, FTC Matter No. 082-3133 (Feb. 5, 2009) (proposed consent agreement); *In the Matter of Premier Capital Lending, Inc.*, FTC Docket No. C-4241 (Dec. 10, 2008); *In the Matter of The TJX Cos.*, FTC Docket No. C-4227 (July 29, 2008); *In the Matter of Reed Elsevier Inc.*, FTC Docket No. C-4226 (July 29, 2008); *In the Matter of Life is good, Inc.*, FTC Docket No. C-42 18 (Apr. 16, 2008); In the Matter of Goal Fin., LLC, FTC Docket No. C-4216 (Apr. 9, 2008); *In the Matter of Guidance Software, Inc.*, FTC Docket No. C-4187 (Mar. 30, 2007); *In the Matter of CardSystems Solutions, Inc.*, FTC Docket No. C-4168 (Sept. 5, 2006); In the Matter of Nations Title Agency, Inc., FTC Docket No. C-4161 (June 19, 2006); *In the Matter of DSW, Inc.*, FTC Docket No. C-4157 (Mar. 7, 2006); *In the Matter of Superior Mortgage Corp.*, FTC Docket No. C-4153 (Dec. 14, 2005); *In the Matter of BJ's Wholesale Club, Inc.*, FTC Docket No. C-4148 (Sept. 20, 2005); *In the Matter of Nationwide Mortgage Group, Inc.*, FTC Docket No. 9319 (Apr. 12, 2005); In the Matter of Petco Animal Supplies, Inc., FTC Docket No. C-4133 (Mar. 4, 2005); *In the Matter of Sunbelt Lending Servs., Inc.*, FTC Docket No. C-4129 (Jan. 3, 2005); *In the Matter of MTS Inc., d/b/a Tower Records/Books/Video*, FTC Docket No. C-4110 (May 28, 2004); *In the Matter of Guess?*, Inc., FTC Docket No. C-4091 (July 30, 2003); *In the Matter of Microsoft Corp.*, FTC Docket No. C-4069 (Dec. 20, 2002); *In the Matter of Eli Lilly & Co.*, FTC Docket No. C-4047 (May 8, 2002).

[9] FTC and Department of Commerce Workshop, *Online Profiling Public Workshop* (Nov. 8, 1999), *available at* http://www.ftc.gov/bcp/workshops/profiling/index.shtm.

[10] June 2000 Report, available at http://www.ftc.gov/os/2000/06/onlineprofilingreportjune2000.pdf. The June 2000 Report stated that "[m]any commenters at the Workshop objected to networks' hidden monitoring of consumers and collection of extensive personal data without consumers' knowledge or consent; they also

noted that network advertisers offer consumers few, if any, choices about the use and dissemination of their individual information obtained in this manner." *Id.* at 10.

[11] July 2000 Report, *available at* http://www.ftc.gov/os/2000/07/onlineprofiling.pdf.

[12] Issued in 2000, the NAI Principles required network advertisers to notify consumers about profiling activities on host websites and to give consumers the ability to choose not to participate in profiling. The NAI Principles applied to both personally identifiable and non- personally identifiable consumer data. Where a member collected personally identifiable information, it had to provide notice and opt-out choice at the time and place of collection. For non-personally identifiable information, notice could appear in the publisher website's privacy policy with a link to the NAI website, where a consumer could opt out. The NAI Principles also imposed certain restrictions on the merger of personally identifiable information with non- personally identifiable information. As discussed in more detail below, NAI recently released revised principles.

[13] See July 2000 Report, *supra* note 11, at 10-11.

[14] *See, e.g.,* George Raine, *Dot-com Ads Make a Comeback*, S.F. CHRON., Apr. 10, 2005, *available at* http://www.sfgate.com/cgi-bin/article.cgi?f=/c/a/2005/04/10/BUG1GC5M4I1.DTL   (discussing   negative impact of dot-com implosion on online advertising generally).

[15] *Id. See also* Ryan Blitstein, *Microsoft, Google, Yahoo in Online Ad War*, SAN JOSE MERCURY NEWS, May 19, 2007.

[16] The complete transcripts of the hearings, entitled *Protecting Consumers in the Next Tech-Ade*, are *available at* http://www.ftc.gov/bcp/workshops/techade/transcripts.html.

[17] *See* Transcript of Hearing Record at 46-107, *Protecting Consumers in the Next Techade* (Nov. 7, 2006), *available at* http://www.ftc.gov/bcp/workshops/techade/pdfs/transcript 061107.pdf (panel discussion entitled "Marketing and Advertising in the Next Tech-ade").

[18] *See, e.g.,* Letter from Ari Schwartz, Executive Director, and Alissa Cooper, Policy Analyst, Center for Democracy and Technology ("CDT"), to J. Thomas Rosch, Commissioner, FTC (Jan. 19, 2007), *available at* http://www.cdt.org/privacy/20070119rosch-behavioral-letter.pdf; Center for Digital Democracy ("CDD") and U.S. Public Interest Research Group, Complaint and Request for Inquiry and Injunctive Relief Concerning Unfair   and   Deceptive   Online   Marketing   Practices   (Nov.   1,   2006),   *available   at* http://www.democraticmedia.org/files/pdf/FTCadprivacy.pdf.

[19] *See* Letter from Jeffrey Chester, Executive Director, CDD, to Deborah Platt Majoras, Chairman, FTC et al. (Dec. 10, 2007), *available at* http://www.democraticmedia.org/files/FTCletter121007.pdf; Letter from Mindy Bockstein, Executive Director, New York State Consumer Protection Board, to Deborah Platt Majoras, Chairman, FTC, Re: DoubleClick   Inc.   and   Google,   Inc.   Merger   (May   1,   2007),   *available   at* *http://epic.org/privacy/ftc/google/cpb.pdf.* The Commission approved the merger on December 20, 2007, at the same time that it issued the Principles. *See Statement of Federal Trade Commission Concerning Google/DoubleClick,*   FTC   File   No.   071-0170   (Dec.   20,   2007),   *available   at* http://www.ftc.gov/os/caselist/0710170/071220statement.pdf.

[20] The complete transcripts of the Town Hall entitled *Ehavioral Advertising: Tracking, Targeting & Technology* are available at http://www.ftc.gov/bcp/workshops/ehavioral/71101wor.pdf and http://www.ftc.gov/bcp/workshops/ehavioral/71102wor.pdf.

[21] To facilitate a comprehensive discussion of the issues at the Ehavioral Advertising Town Hall, the FTC applied a broad definition of online behavioral advertising – namely, the collection of information about a consumer's online activities in order to deliver advertising targeted to the individual consumer's interests. This definition was meant to encompass the various tracking activities engaged in by diverse companies across the web. *See* Transcript of Town Hall Record at 8, *Ehavioral Advertising: Tracking, Targeting & Technology* (Nov. 1, 2007), *available at* http://www.ftc.gov/bcp/workshops/ehavioral/71101wor.pdf (introductory remarks of Lydia B. Parnes, Director, FTC Bureau of Consumer Protection) [hereinafter "Nov. 1 Transcript"]. FTC staff used a similar definition in its proposed Principles.

[22] Many similar issues arose during the FTC Town Hall held in May 2008 on the mobile commerce marketplace. There, participants discussed consumers' ability to control mobile marketing applications, the challenges of effective disclosures given the size limitations in the mobile context, marketing to sensitive groups, and the developments of the next generation of mobile-based products and services. *See generally* FTC Town Hall, *Beyond   Voice: Mapping   the   Mobile   Marketplace*   (May   6-7,   2008),   *available   at* http://www.ftc.gov/bcp/workshops/mobilemarket/index.shtml.

[23] *See, e.g.,* Transcript of Town Hall Record at 144-149, *Ehavioral Advertising: Tracking, Targeting & Technology (Nov. 2, 2007), available at* http://www.ftc.gov/bcp/workshops/ehavioral/71102wor.pdf (statements of Pam Dixon, Executive Director, World Privacy Forum) [hereinafter "Nov. 2 Transcript"].

[24] *Id.* at 135-143, 155-159. As an alternative to the existing self-regulatory models, and in an effort to increase consumers' control over the tracking of their online activities, a coalition of privacy groups proposed the development of a "Do Not Track List." *See* Ari Schwartz, CDT, et al., *Consumer Rights and Protections in the Behavioral   Advertising   Sector,   available   at   http://www.cdt.org/privacy/20071031*

consumerprotectionsbehavioral.pdf (Oct. 31, 2007) (the proposed "Do Not Track List" is modeled after the FTC's national "Do Not Call" registry and would require online advertisers using a persistent identifier to provide to the FTC the domain names of the servers or other devices placing the identifier).

[25] *See, e.g., In the Matter of Gateway Learning Corp.,* FTC Docket No. C-4120 (Sept. 10, 2004), *available at* http://www.ftc.gov/os/caselist/0423047/040917comp0423047.pdf (alleging that the company made material changes to its privacy policy and applied such changes to data collected under the old policy). The FTC's order requires Gateway to obtain opt-in consent for such changes in the future.

[26] Staff recommended that companies obtain consumers' affirmative express consent for material, retroactive changes and for the use of sensitive data because of the increased privacy concerns raised by the collection and use of such data.

[27] FTC staff encourages continued stakeholder efforts to address the privacy concerns raised by behavioral advertising, but does not endorse any of the specific approaches described herein.

[28] *See* Press Release, Yahoo!, *Yahoo! Announces New Privacy Choice for Consumers* (Aug. 8, 2008), *available at* http://yhoo.client.shareholder.com/press/releasedetail.cfm?ReleaseID=327212; Posting of Rajas Moonka, Senior Business Product Manager, Google, to http://googleblog.blogspot.com/2008/08/new-enhancements-on-google-content.html (Aug. 7, 2008, 5:01 EST).

[29] *See* Gregg Keizer, *Microsoft Adds Privacy Tools to IE8,* COMPUTERWORLD.COM, Aug. 25, 2008, http://www.computerworld.com/action/article.do?command=viewArticleBasic&articleId=91134 19. As noted above, a coalition of privacy groups also has proposed and continues to support development of a "Do Not Track List" designed to increase consumer control over the tracking of their online activities. See Schwartz et al., supra note 24.

[30] *See* AOL, Privacy Gourmet Page, http://corp.aol.com/o/mr-penguin/ (last visited Jan. 9, 2009); YouTube, Google Search Privacy Playlist, http://www.youtube.com/view play list?p=ECB20E29232BCBBA (last visited Jan. 9, 2009).

[31] *See* Posting of Kim Hart, washingtonpost.com, to http://voices.washingtonpost.com/posttech/2008/12/yahoo changes data-retentionp.html?nav= rss _blog (Dec. 17, 2008, 13:50 EST) (stating that Yahoo! agreed to shorten online behavioral data retention periods from thirteen to three months); Posting of Stacey Higginbotham, GigaOM, to http://gigaom.com/2008/09/09/in-online-privacy-fight-google-blinks/ (Sept. 9, 2008, 7:47 PT) (stating that Google agreed to reduce storage of search engine inquiries from eighteen to nine months); *see also Microsoft to Cut Search Engine Data Retention to Six Months if Others Follow,* 7 PRIVACY & SEC. LAW REP. 1767 (2008) (stating that Microsoft announced it would reduce search engine data retention to six months in the European Union if all search companies agreed to do the same).

[32] *See* NAI, *2008 NAI Principles Code of Conduct* (Dec. 16, 2008), *available at* http://www.networkadvertising.org/networks/2008%20NAI%20Principles final%20for%20Web site.pdf [hereinafter "NAI 2008 Principles"]. In advance of issuing the NAI 2008 Principles, NAI issued proposed principles for public comment in April 2008. See *NAI, Draft 2008 NAI Principles* (Apr. 10, 2008), *available at* http://www.networkadvertising.org/networks/NAI Principles 2008 Draft for Public.pdf. In some respects, NAI's proposed principles contained stronger protections than those announced in December. For example, NAI's original proposal prohibited the use of certain categories of sensitive information, including information about children, for behavioral advertising. As finalized, the NAI 2008 Principles would allow use of these categories of information so long as consumers (or parents, in the case of children) provide their consent.

[33] The NAI 2008 Principles expand the security and access requirements to cover data used for behavioral advertising, as well as data used for practices such as tracking the number of ads served at a particular website. They also restrict NAI members' use of behavioral advertising data to marketing purposes and require that members retain such data only as long as needed for legitimate business purposes or as required by law. FTC staff commends NAI's attempts to strengthen its principles through these and other steps. At the same time, staff notes that there are areas where NAI may continue to improve. For example, staff notes that the NAI 2008 Principles' approach to providing notice and choice generally mirrors NAI's previous approach – i.e., members may continue to provide notice to consumers through website privacy policies. For the reasons discussed below, staff encourages companies engaged in online behavioral advertising to develop mechanisms that allow for prominent disclosure outside companies' existing privacy policies. Moreover, because the revisions tie some obligations to certain language (e.g., "directly engaging" in behavioral advertising) that will be defined through future implementation guidelines, the impact of these obligations is currently unclear. Similarly, because NAI plans to issue further guidance regarding the policies and procedures governing its compliance reviews, questions remain as to whether these reviews, and any penalties that are ultimately imposed, will be adequate to ensure compliance.

[34] The initiative includes the American Association of Advertising Agencies, the Association of National Advertisers, the Direct Marketing Association, and the Interactive Advertising Bureau ("IAB"). See K.C. Jones, *Agencies to Self-Regulate Online Behavioral Ads,* INFORMATIONWEEK, Jan. 13, 2009, http://www.informationweek.com/news/showArticle.jhtml?articleID=212900156. The IAB, an organization of companies engaged in online advertising, previously issued a set of privacy principles recommending that its

member companies notify consumers about data collection practices and provide choice when appropriate. IAB, *Privacy Principles* (Feb. 24, 2008), *available at* http://www.iab.net/iab products and industry services/1421/1443/1464.

[35] *See* Kim Hart, *A New Voice in Online Privacy*, WASH. POST, Nov. 17, 2008, at A06, *available at* http://www.washingtonpost.com/wp-dyn/content/article/2008/11/16/AR2008111601624.html?nav=hcmoduletmv.

[36] *See* CDT, *Threshold Analysis for Online Advertising Practices* (Jan. 2009), *available at* http://www.cdt.org/privacy/20090128threshold.pdf.

[37] *See* TRUSTe, *Online Behavioral Advertising: A Checklist of Practices that Impact Consumer Trust, available at* http://www.truste.com/about/online behavioral advertising.php (last visited Feb. 3, 2009).

[38] *Privacy Implications of Online Advertising: Hearing Before the S. Comm. on Commerce, Sci. & Transp., 110th Cong.* (2008), *available at* http://commerce.senate.gov/public/index.cfm?FuseAction=Hearings.Hearing&HearingID=e46b 0d9f-562e-41 a6-b460-a7 14bf3701 7.

[39] *See id.* (statement of Lydia Parnes, Director of the FTC Bureau of Consumer Protection).

[40] *Broadband Providers and Consumer Privacy: Hearing Before the S. Comm. on Commerce, Sci. & Transp., 110th Cong.* (2008), *available at* http://commerce.senate.gov/public/index.cfm?FuseAction=Hearings.Hearing&Hearing ID=778 594fe-a171-4906-a585-15f19e2d602a. In the ISP-based behavioral advertising model, a consumer's online activities are collected directly from the consumer's ISP, rather than from the individual websites the consumer visits. This model, which is also often referred to as "deep packet inspection," could potentially allow targeting of ads based on substantially all of the websites a consumer visits, rather than simply a consumer's visits to, and activities within, a given network of websites. *See* Peter Whoriskey, *Every Click You Make*, WASH. POST, Apr. 4, 2008, *available at* http://www.washingtonpost.com/wp-dyn/content/article/2008/04/03/AR2008040304052.html.

[41] *What Your Broadband Provider Knows About Your Web Use: Deep Packet Inspection and Communications Laws and Policies: Hearing Before the H. Subcomm. on Telecomm. & the Internet*, 110th Cong. (2008), *available at* http://energycommerce.house.gov/cmtemtgs/110-ti-hrg.071708.DeepPacket.shtml.

[42] Letter from John D. Dingell, Chairman of the H. Comm. on Energy & Commerce, et al., to William Bresnan, Chairman & C.E.O. of Bresnan Communications, et al. (Aug. 1, 2008), *available at* http://energycommerce.house.gov/Press 110/11 0-ltr.080 1 08.AOL-TILetters.pdf.

[43] H. Comm. on Energy & Commerce, Responses to Aug. 1, 2008 Letter to Network Operators Regarding Data Collection Practices, *available at* http://energycommerce.house.gov/Press110/080108.ResponsesDataCollectionLetter.shtml (last visited Jan. 9, 2009). In light of concerns expressed by Congress and others, at least one high profile company suspended its plans to engage in ISP-based behavioral advertising. See Ellen Nakashima, *NebuAd Halts Plans For Web Tracking*, WASH. POST, Sept. 4, 2008, *available at* http://www.washingtonpost.com/wp-dyn/content/article/2008/09/03/AR2008090303566.html.

[44] One trade association comment also suggested that self-regulation at the behest of a governmental entity such as the FTC cannot truly be self-regulatory. In addition, a newspaper association stated that applying the Principles to a newspaper's advertising-supported website would violate the First Amendment because it could affect the selection of content that is presented to the reader. In response, staff notes that the Commission has often called for, studied the effectiveness of, and made suggestions for improving self-regulatory schemes, and that such efforts do not implicate the First Amendment. *See, e.g.*, FTC Report, *Marketing Violent Entertainment to Children: A Fifth Follow-Up Review of Industry Practices in the Motion Picture, Music Recording & Electronic Game Industries* 33 (Apr. 2007), *available at* http://www.ftc.gov/reports/violence/070412MarketingViolentEChildren.pdf; FTC Report, *Self- Regulation in the Alcohol Industry* 25 (June 2008), *available at* http://www.ftc.gov/os/2008/06/080626alcoholreport.pdf.

[45] *See supra* note 8 (citing FTC settlements requiring companies to implement reasonable information security programs to protect sensitive personal information).

[46] *See In the Matter of Gateway Learning Corp.*, FTC Docket No. C-4120 (Sept. 10, 2004), *available at* http://www.ftc.gov/os/caselist/0423047/040917comp0423047.pdf.

[47] Traditionally, PII has been defined as information that can be linked to a specific individual including, but not limited to, name, postal address, email address, Social Security number, or driver's license number. Non-PII includes anonymous data that, without more, cannot identify a specific person. *See, e.g.*, June 2000 Report, *supra* note 10, at 4 & n.14.

[48] An IP address is a numerical identifier assigned to a computer or device that connects to the Internet.

[49] *See, e.g.*, July 2000 Report, *supra* note 11, at 11 n.33 (majority of the Commission recommended online privacy legislation applicable to both PII and non-PII); NAI 2008 Principles, *supra* note 32, at 3, 7-8 (since 2000, Principles have provided protections for PII and non-PII); Dingell et al., *supra* note 42 (seeking information

from 34 companies on all aspects of their online behavioral advertising practices, regardless of whether the practices implicated PII or non-PII).

[50] In recent years, portable devices with multiple built-in functionalities tied to individual consumers have proliferated. These include devices such as "smart" mobile phones that allow Internet access and email, as well as BlackBerrys and other similar tools. The explosion in the number of devices in use world-wide is rapidly exhausting the available IP addresses required for online connectivity. In order to accommodate this growing demand, the market is undergoing a transition to a new generation of IP addresses – "IPv6." IPv6 will dramatically increase the number of unique IP addresses. While improving connectivity, IPv6 will rely more heavily on static IP addresses, which can link an individual IP address to a particular device that is associated with a specific individual.

[51] This hypothetical is supported by the 2006 incident in which AOL made public some 20 million search queries conducted by thousands of subscribers over a three-month period. After replacing subscriber names or user IDs with identification numbers in order to protect the searchers' anonymity, AOL posted the data for research purposes. The data, which was posted for about a week, connected the "anonymized" AOL member with his or her search queries, the number of websites identified by AOL's search engine as responsive to the search queries, and the responsive website the individual chose to visit. Using this information, the media was able to identify, with little additional investigation, at least one individual subscriber and "bloggers" and other Internet users claimed to be able to identify others. *See, e.g.*, Michael Barbaro & Tom Zeller, Jr., *A Face Is Exposed for AOL Searcher No. 4417749*, N.Y. TIMES, Aug. 9, 2006, *available at*
http://www.nytimes.com/2006/08/09/technology/09aol.html?   r=1   &scp=1   &sq=aol%20queries&
st=cse&oref=slogin; Ellen Nakashima, *AOL Takes Down Site With Users' Search Data*, WASH. POST, Aug. 8, 2006, *available at*
http://www.washingtonpost.com/wp-dyn/content/article/2006/08/07/AR2006080701150.html.

[52] *See, e.g.,* Press Release, Consumers Union, *Consumer Reports Poll: Americans Extremely Concerned About Internet Privacy* (Sept. 25, 2008), *available at* http://www.consumersunion.org/pub/core telecom and utilities/0061 89 .html
(over half of respondents uncomfortable with internet companies using their browsing histories to send relevant ads or third parties collecting information about their online behavior); Press Release, Harris Interactive Inc., *Majority Uncomfortable with Websites Customizing Content Based Visitors Personal Profiles* (Apr. 10, 2008), *available at* http://www.harrisinteractive.com/harris poll/index.asp?PID=894 (59% of survey respondents were "not comfortable" with online behavioral advertising; however, after being shown model privacy policies, 55% said they would be more comfortable); Press Release, TRUSTe, *TRUSTe Report Reveals Consumer Awareness and Attitudes About Behavioral Targeting* (Mar. 26, 2008), *available at* http://www.truste.org/about/press_release/03_26_08.php (57% of survey respondents "not comfortable" with advertisers using browsing history to serve relevant ads, even when information cannot be tied to their names or other personal information); George Milne, "Information Exchange Expectations of Consumers, Marketing Managers, and Direct Marketers" at 3, *Ehavioral Advertising: Tracking, Targeting & Technology* (Nov. 1, 2007), *available at* http://www.ftc.gov/bcp/workshops/ehavioral/presentations/3gmilne.pdf (45% of respondents think online tracking should not be permitted; 47% would permit tracking with opt- in or opt-out rights); see also Larry Ponemon, "FTC Presentation on Cookies and Consumer Permissions" at 11, *Ehavioral Advertising: Tracking, Targeting & Technology* (Nov. 1, 2007), *available at* http://www.ftc.gov/bcp/workshops/ehavioral/presentations/3lponemon.pdf (only 20% of respondents would voluntarily permit marketers to share buying behavior with third parties to project future buying decisions).

[53] *See, e.g., AOL is Sued Over Privacy Breach*, L.A. TIMES, Sept. 26, 2006, at C2, available at http://articles.latimes.com/2006/sep/26/business/fi-aol26; Barbaro & Zeller, Jr., supra note 51; Michael Arrington, *AOL Proudly Releases Massive Amounts of Private Data*, TechCrunch, Aug. 6, 2006, http://www.techcrunch.com/2006/08/06/aol-proudly-releasesmassive-amounts-of-user-search-data/all-comments/. The AOL incident highlights the difficulties in making data truly anonymous. Simply eliminating name, contact information, or other traditional PII may not be sufficient. For example, a study conducted in 2000 used U.S. Census summary data to find that 87% of the U.S. population could likely be uniquely identified based only on three pieces of data: a 5-digit zip code; gender; and date of birth. Latanya Sweeney, Abstract, *Uniqueness of Simple Demographics in the U.S. Population* (Carnegie Mellon U., Laboratory for Int'l Data Privacy 2000), *available at* http://privacy.cs.cmu.edu/dataprivacy/papers/LIDAP-WP4abstract.html; see also Bruce Schneier, *Why "Anonymous" Data Sometimes Isn't*, WIRED, Dec. 13, 2007, available at http://www.wired.com/politics/security/commentary/securitymatters/2007/12/securitymatters   12   13 (describing University of Texas experiments with de-anonymized Netflix data); Latanya Sweeney, *Comments to the Department of Health and Human Services on "Standards of Privacy of Individually Identifiable Health Information"* (Apr. 26, 2002), *available at*
http://privacy.cs.cmu.edu/dataprivacy/HIPAA/HIPAAcomments.pdf (describing experiments on a state's anonymized cancer registry).

[54] As discussed below, staff has limited the scope of the Principles in several ways that also limit their application to data traditionally considered to be non-PII. *See* discussion *infra* Parts III.A.2 and 3.

[55] Staff notes that to the extent that these functions do not involve the tracking of consumers' online activities in order to deliver advertising based on those activities, they do not constitute online behavioral advertising and thus already fall outside the Principles' scope.

[56] For instance, the Children's Online Privacy Protection Rule ("COPPA Rule") recognizes that sharing of children's personal information with third parties raises more concern than use of the information simply for internal purposes. For this reason the COPPA Rule requires that website operators obtain the highest level of verifiable parental consent where such information is shared and, where possible, that the website enable parents to choose whether to allow sharing. *See* 16 C.F.R. § 312.4 (2006); Children's Online Privacy Protection Rule, 64 Fed. Reg. 59,888, 59,899 (Nov. 3, 1999), *available at* http://www.ftc.gov/os/1999/10/64fr59888.pdf. *See also* Direct Marketing Assocation ("DMA"), *Direct Marketing Association's Online Marketing Guidelines and Do the Right Thing Commentary* (Jan. 2002), *available at* http://www.the-dma.org/guidelines/onlineguidelines.shtml (recommending choice when data is shared with third parties).

[57] Staff notes that some of the principles are based on existing Commission case law and policy. As such, a company engaged in first party practices may still be required to provide reasonable security for the consumer data it collects and maintains. Additionally, depending upon the specific circumstances, a company may be precluded from using previously collected data in a way that conflicts with the privacy promises in effect at the time the company collected the data.

[58] To the extent that websites share data with third-party service providers in order to deliver ads or perform some of the internal functions described above, such sharing will still be considered "first party" use, provided there is no further use of the data by the service provider.

[59] Several commenters argue that data collection and use within a family of websites – *e.g.*, sites under common ownership or control – should be considered "first party" for purposes of the Principles. The commenters stated that consumers will save costs due to partnering arrangements, that consumers expect and want the additional marketing opportunities created through data sharing among affiliated websites, and that the Gramm-Leach-Bliley Act (the "GLB Act") allows financial institutions to share data with affiliates.
Staff believes that whether data sharing among affiliated companies should be considered "first party," and thus outside the scope of the Principles, should turn on whether the relationship among the sites – and the possibility that they may share data – is sufficiently transparent and consistent with reasonable consumer expectations. For instance, although one might expect that Citibank and Citifinancial are closely linked entities, the link between affiliates Smith Barney and Citibank is likely to be much less obvious. Such a determination will depend upon the particular circumstances. Staff also notes that the GLB Act does not, in fact, address affiliate sharing among financial institutions; rather, the Fair Credit Reporting Act governs affiliate sharing and allows consumers to opt out of sharing certain data with affiliates. *See* 15 U.S.C. §§ 1681a(d)(2)(A), 1681s-3 (2003).

[60] As discussed with respect to first party practices, companies engaged in online contextual advertising may still be subject to laws and policies that impose obligations outside of the Principles. *See supra* note 57.

[61] These commenters cited self-regulatory regimes such as DMA's "Online Marketing Guidelines," IAB's "Interactive Advertising Privacy Principles," and the NAI Principles.

[62] Some commenters also state that encouraging companies to provide choice for the mere *collection* of data is inconsistent with existing legal and self-regulatory regimes, which focus on choice in connection with particular *uses* of data. In fact, the Principles focus on the collection of data *for behavioral advertising*, which presumes both collection and use (or at least intended use) for that purpose. Further, the central goal of the Principles is to minimize potential misuses of data, including uses of data that could cause harm or are contrary to consumer expectations. Nevertheless, because many of the privacy concerns raised about behavioral advertising relate directly to information *collection* – including the invisibility of the practice and the risk that sensitive data, once collected, could fall into the wrong hands – staff believes that it is important to protect the data at the time of collection.

[63] The proposed Principles do not specify whether this choice would be opt-in or opt-out choice – just that it be clear, easy-to-use, and accessible to consumers. As discussed below, however, the Principles do specify affirmative express consent (opt-in) for uses of data that raise heightened privacy concerns – specifically, material changes affecting the use of previously collected data and the use of sensitive consumer data.

[64] *See supra* note 24.

[65] *See supra* note 3.

[66] Specifically, one commenter noted that, where data about a consumer's online activities is collected through the ISP rather than from individual websites that the consumer visits (*see* discussion *supra* note 40), the company collecting the data does not have a direct relationship with the web sites. Therefore, the company is not in a position to require the sites to provide consumers with notice and choice about data collection and use for behavioral advertising. Consequently, this commenter suggested that the Principles should contemplate notice and choice mechanisms outside the website context.

[67] *See, e.g.*, Jon Leibowitz, Commissioner, FTC, Remarks at the FTC Town Hall Meeting on "Ehavioral Advertising: Tracking, Targeting, & Technology" at 4-5 (Nov. 1, 2007), *available at* http://www.ftc.gov/speeches/leibowitz/071031ehavior.pdf;
Nov. 1 Transcript, *supra* note 21, at 200-253 (Session 5: Roundtable Discussions of Data Collection, Use and Protection); Nov. 2 Transcript, *supra* note 23, at 9-94 (Session 6: Disclosures to Consumers).

[68] See, e.g., FTC Bureau of Economics Staff Report, *Improving Consumer Mortgage Disclosures: An Empirical Assessment of Current and Prototype Disclosure Forms* (June 2007), *available at* http://www.ftc.gov/os/2007/06/P025505MortgageDisclosureReport.pdf; Kleimann Comm. Group, Inc., Evolution of a Prototype Financial Privacy Notice: A Report on the Form Development Project (Feb. 28, 2006), available at http://www.ftc.gov/privacy/privacyinitiatives/ftcfinalreport060228.pdf.

[69] *See, e.g.*, Standards for Safeguarding Customer Information, 16 C.F.R. Part 314 (2002). Information about the FTC's data security program and enforcement actions can be found at http://www.ftc.gov/privacy/.

[70] Staff agrees that pre-checked boxes and choice mechanisms that are buried within a lengthy privacy policy or a uniform licensing agreement are insufficient to express a consumer's "affirmative express consent." *See, e.g.*, Deborah Platt Majoras, Chairman, FTC, Remarks at the Anti-Spyware Coalition at 7 (Feb. 9, 2006), *available at* http://www.ftc.gov/speeches/majoras/060209cdtspyware.pdf ("[B]urying critical information in the End User License Agreement ("EULA") does not satisfy the requirement for clear and conspicuous disclosure. Buried disclosures do not work."); FTC Publication, *Dot Com Disclosures: Information About Online Advertising* at 5 (May 2000), *available at* http://www.ftc.gov/bcp/edu/pubs/business/ecommerce/bus41.pdf ("Making [a] disclosure available . . . so that consumers who are looking for the information *might* find it doesn't meet the clear and conspicuous standard . . . . [D]isclosures must be communicated effectively so that consumers are likely to notice and understand them.") (emphasis in original); *see also* FTC Policy Statement on Deception at Part III, appended to *In the Matter of Cliffdale Assocs., Inc.*, 103 F.T.C. 110, 174 (1984), *available at* http://www.ftc.gov/bcp/policystmt/ad-decept.htm (fine print disclosures not adequate to cure deception).

[71] *See, e.g., FTC v. Toysmart.com, LLC*, No. 00-1 1341-RGS (D. Mass. filed July 10, 2000) (alleging that company violated privacy promises); *In the Matter of Life is good, Inc.*, FTC Docket No. C-42 18 (Apr. 16, 2008) (alleging that company violated promises about the security provided for customer data); *In the Matter of Petco Animal Supplies, Inc.*, FTC Docket No. C-4133 (Mar. 4, 2005) (same); *In the Matter of MTS Inc., d/b/a Tower Records/Books/Video*, FTC Docket No. C-41 10 (May 28, 2004) (same); *In the Matter of Educ. Research Ctr. of Am.*, FTC Docket No. C-4079 (May 6, 2003) (alleging that company violated privacy promises); *In the Matter of Microsoft Corp.*, FTC Docket No. C-4069 (Dec. 20, 2002) (alleging that company violated privacy and security promises).

[72] *See, e.g., In the Matter of Gateway Learning Corp.*, FTC Docket No. C-4120 (Sept. 10, 2004); *see also In the Matter of Orkin Exterminating Co.*, 108 F.T.C. 263 (1986).

[73] Under Commission law and policy, the term "material" refers to whether a practice, or information about a practice, is likely to affect a consumer's conduct or decisions with regard to a product or service. *See* FTC Policy Statement on Deception, *supra* note 70, at Part IV. Similarly, a "material change" refers to a change in a company's practices that, if known to the consumer, would likely affect the consumer's conduct or decisions with respect to the company's products or services.

[74] Many companies provide some form of prominent notice and opt-out choice for prospective changes – by sending an email notice to their customers, for example, or providing a prominent notice on the landing page of their website. Depending on the circumstances, such an approach may be sufficient. Of course, in deciding how to address prospective material changes, companies must consider such factors as: what claims were made in the original privacy policy, the sensitivity of the information at issue, and the need to ensure that any repeat visitors to a website are sufficiently alerted to the change.

[75] The sensitivity of precise geographic location information was also discussed at a panel on mobile "location-based services" during the FTC's 2008 Town Hall on mobile marketing. *See* Transcript of Town Hall Record, *Beyond Voice: Mapping the Mobile Marketplace* (May 6, 2008) (Session 4, "Location-Based Services"), *available at* http://htc-0 1.media.globix.net/COMP008760MOD 1/ftc web/transcripts/050608 sess4.pdf.

[76] These commenters specifically cited the COPPA Rule (children's information), the Health Insurance Portability and Accountability Act ("HIPAA") (health information), and the GLB Act (financial information).

[77] As discussed previously, *supra* note 70, pre-checked boxes or disclosures that are buried in a privacy policy or a uniform licensing agreement are unlikely to be sufficiently prominent to obtain a consumer's "affirmative express consent."

[78] Where companies are using tracking data for non-behavioral advertising purposes, such uses may involve sharing the data with third parties. If so, the notice and choice that a company provides concerning such sharing may address at least some of the concerns raised about secondary uses. A secondary use may also constitute a retroactive "material change" to a company's existing privacy policy, in which case consumers could choose whether to provide affirmative express consent to the change

CHAPTER SOURCES

The following chapters have been previously published

Chapter 1 – This is an edited, reformatted and augmented version of remarks delivered as Testimony before the U. S. Senate Committee on Commerce, Science and Transportation Hearing on "Broadband Providers and Consumer Privacy" September 25, 2008 by Dorothy Attwood, Senior Vice President, Public Policy & Chief Privacy Officer, AT & T Inc.

Chapter 2 - This is an edited, reformatted and augmented version of remarks delivered as Testimony before the U.S. Senate Committee on Commerce, Science & Transportation Hearing on "Broadband Providers and Consumer Privacy," September 25, 2008, Gigi B. Sohn President, Public Knowledge.

Chapter 3 - This is an edited, reformatted and augmented version of remarks delivered as Statement before the U.S. Senate Committee on Commerce, Science and Transportation Hearing on "Broadband Providers and Consumer Privacy," September 25, 2008, Peter Stern, Executive Vice President, Chief Strategy Officer of Time Warner Cable.

Chapter 4 - This is an edited, reformatted and augmented version of remarks delivered as Testimony before the U. S. Senate Committee on Commerce, Science and Transportation on "Broadband Providers and Consumer Privacy, September 25, 2008, Thomas J. Tauke, Verizon Executive Vice President.

Chapter 5 - This is an edited, reformatted and augmented version of remarks delivered as a Concurring Statement regarding Staff Report, "Self-Regulatory Principles for Online Behavioral Advertising" on November 24, 2008. Pamela Jones Harbour, Commissioner, Federal Trade Commission.

Chapter 6 - This is an edited, reformatted and augmented version of remarks from "So Private, So Public: Individuals, the Internet & The Paradox of Behavioral Marketing", delivered as Testimony before the FTC Town Hall Meeting on "Behavioral Advertising: Tracking, Targeting & Technology" on November 1, 2007, Jon Leibowitz, FTC Commissioner.

Chapter 7 - This is an edited, reformatted and augmented version of remarks delivered as a Concurring Statement from an FTC Staff Report: "Self-Regulatory Principles for Online "Behavioral Advertising," February 2009, Jon Leibowitz, FTC Commissioner.

Chapter 8 - This is an edited, reformatted and augmented version of remarks delivered as Testimony from "Online Behavioral Advertising Moving the Discussion Forward to Possible Self-Regulatory Principles," November 1 and 2, 2007, Building on Tech-ade hearings.

Chapter 9 - This is an edited, reformatted and augmented version of remarks delivered as Testimony before the Committee on Commerce, U.S. Senate "Privacy Implications of Online Advertising", Wednesday, July 9, 2008, Wayne Crews, Vice President for Policy/Director of Technology Studies. Competitive Enterprise Institute

Chapter 10 – This is an edited, reformatted and augmented version of remarks delivered as Testimony before the Senate Committee on Commerce, Science & Transportation, "Privacy Implications of Online Advertising, July 9, 2008, Bob Dykes, CEO Nebaud, Inc.

Chapter 11 – This is an edited, reformatted and augmented version of remarks delivered as Testimony before the Senate Committee on Commerce, Science & Transportation, "Privacy Implications of Online Advertising", July 9, 2008, Leslie Harris, President/CEO, Center for Democracy & Technology

Chapter 12 – This is an edited, reformatted and augmented version of remarks delivered as Statement before the Senate Committee on Commerce, Science & Transportation, "Privacy Implications of Online Advertising", July 9, 2008, Michael D. Hintze Associated General Counsel Microsoft Corporation.

Chapter 13 – This is an edited, reformatted and augmented version of remarks delivered as Testimony before the Senate Committee on Commerce, Science & Transportation, "Privacy Implications of Online Advertising", July 9, 2008, Jane Horvath, Senior Privacy Counsel, Google, Inc.

Chapter 14 – This is an edited, reformatted and augmented version of remarks delivered as Testimony before the Senate Committee on Commerce, Science & Transportation, "Privacy Implications of Online Advertising", July 9, 2008, Chris Kelly, Chief Privacy Officer, Facebook.

Chapter 15 – This is an edited, reformatted and augmented version of remarks delivered as a Prepared Statement of the Federal Trade Commission on "Behavioral Advertising" before the Senate Committee on Commerce, Science & Transportation, June 18, 2008, Lydia Parnes, Director Bureau Consumer Protection at the Federal Trade Commission.

Chapter 16 – This is an edited, reformatted and augmented version of a Congressional Research Service publication, Report RL34693, updated January 16, 2009. "Privacy Law and Online Advertising: Legal Analysis of Data Gathering by Online Advertisers such as Double Click and NebuAd". Kathleen Ann Ruane, Legislative Attorney. Report RL34693, January 16, 2009.

Chapter 17 – This is an edited, reformatted and augmented version of a FTC Staff Report, Self Regulatory Principles for Online Behavioral Advertising. Behavioral Advertising, Tracking, Targeting, and Technology, February 2009.

INDEX

C

D

E

H

I

J

L

M

N

O

T

U

V

W